Inclusive Education

Studies in Inclusive Education

VOLUME 45

The titles published in this series are listed at *brill.com/stie*

Inclusive Education

Global Issues and Controversies

Edited by

Christopher Boyle, Joanna Anderson, Angela Page and Sofia Mavropoulou

Foreword by Adrian Ashman

BRILL
SENSE

LEIDEN | BOSTON

Cover illustration: *Friend* by Emma Cleine

All chapters in this book have undergone peer review.

Library of Congress Cataloging-in-Publication Data

Names: Boyle, Christopher (Christopher M.), 1972- editor. | Anderson, Joanna, editor. | Page, Angela, editor. | Mavropoulou, Sofia, editor.
Title: Inclusive education : global issues and controversies / Edited by Christopher Boyle, Joanna Anderson, Angela Page and Sofia Mavropoulou.
Description: Leiden ; Boston : Brill | Sense, [2020] | Series: Studies in inclusive education, 2542-9825 ; Volume 45 | Includes bibliographical references and index.
Identifiers: LCCN 2020012957 (print) | LCCN 2020012958 (ebook) | ISBN 9789004431164 (hardback) | ISBN 9789004431157 (paperback) | ISBN 9789004431171 (ebook)
Subjects: LCSH: Inclusive education. | Education--Aims and objectives. | School environment.
Classification: LCC LC1200 .I5183 2020 (print) | LCC LC1200 (ebook) | DDC 371.9/046--dc23
LC record available at https://lccn.loc.gov/2020012957
LC ebook record available at https://lccn.loc.gov/2020012958

Typeface for the Latin, Greek, and Cyrillic scripts: "Brill". See and download: brill.com/brill-typeface.

ISSN 2542-9825
ISBN 978-90-04-43115-7 (paperback)
ISBN 978-90-04-43116-4 (hardback)
ISBN 978-90-04-43117-1 (e-book)

This book is printed on acid-free paper and produced in a sustainable manner.

Education is the most powerful weapon you can use to change the world.

NELSON MANDELA

∴

Contents

Foreword

For all of my 40-year career as an academic I have been devoted to research; to discovering and promoting ways of educating young – and not-so-young – students in the most effective and efficient ways possible. One of my intellectual foci since the late 1980s has been inclusion. Of course, it wasn't always called that. Over several decades there has emerged a vast professional literature dealing first with mainstreaming, then integration, then inclusion with the latter morphing into a contemporary set of concepts having essentially the same logic, orientation, and practical application. These include universal design for learning, differentiation, responsive teaching, and most recently, personalised learning.

There are substantial literature collections relating to the philosophy, the moral imperatives and associated values of providing an education that addresses and satisfies the learning needs of all students. In parallel with these is a robust collection of commentaries on policy and practice. Despite the almost universal acceptance of inclusion as a fundamental tenet of education at all levels, the number of empirical studies about the success of inclusive practices, relative to the vastness of the overall body of literature, is quite small. Few studies have reported significant academic gains achieved by including students with special learning needs into regular/mainstream classes, and many that do are largely anecdotal in nature and emphasise the social benefits of inclusive classrooms.

Many of the commentaries report positive changes in attitude toward included children as a result of their contact with other students who provide exemplary behaviour models. And while there are many optimistic conclusions about inclusive classrooms there are also reports of far fewer encouraging outcomes. These typically involve students with emotional and behaviour disorders and those with intellectual disability.

A recent search through the literature has not convinced me that much has changed. While the volume of literature has continued to expand, a prominent theme remains: the assertion that education policy and school and teaching practices must ensure that all students have access to a curriculum and to teaching and learning opportunities that will address their individual learning needs. There appears to be no argument with this statement.

There is research on inclusive education that provides evidence of successful teaching and learning programs and practices. These include Response to Intervention (RTI), cooperative/collaborative and peer-mediated learning, and a collection of specific literacy and numeracy interventions. However, the introduction and use of these empirically validated approaches is considerably less universal than the acceptance of inclusion.

This brings me to the present volume. It is not a comprehensive review of successful teaching and learning systems. It is also not a compendium of theories, models, processes, approaches, or tips and tricks for teachers. Instead, the authors invite the reader to reconsider first principles, that is, what is good education and how are the concepts of social justice, advantage, and equality best addressed when considering inclusion. It is argued that education is often considered within the context of social justice and the implication that a primary role of education systems and schools is to fulfil the role as an agent of social justice through quality teaching and learning experiences. But how is this achieved? What are the building blocks?

The authors argue that school system administrators and school leaders need a clear vision in terms of the purpose and objectives of school education and how they can be realised. There is often a reliance on the purported wisdom contained in the special education and inclusion literature and the limitations to which I have alluded to above, rather than framing educational experiences in the context of empirically validated approaches that accommodate students' strengths and differences. This is somewhat surprising as the provision of the most beneficial teaching and learning experiences is the essential premise upon which inclusive education is based.

When I talk to practising teachers, they invariably talk about the challenges of being a teacher. That they are subject to a plethora of often conflicting pressures that affect the extent to which they address the purpose of their employment, that is, teaching students. These pressures include but are not limited to political agendas relating to students' learning outcomes, funding issues, curriculum imperatives, parental perceptions and expectations, workplace and industrial issues, community attitudes, students' learning preferences, school location, teachers' perception of their roles and responsibilities, and teacher training agendas and program outcomes. From a teacher educator's perspective, the impact of this constellation of factors that affect student learning outcomes might seem (and possibly is) beyond local control.

For some years, I have argued for a change in the way in which teacher education is delivered. To me, it seems as though we have been tinkering with an old and very ineffective model, adjusting the teacher education curriculum and learning experiences to accommodate national, regional, and state/provincial political agendas. At the same time teachers are required to cover curriculum areas that are far removed from the basics. This produces knee-jerk reactions at all levels that focus on the minutiae of issues rather than addressing the inherent flaws within school and tertiary education domains and without addressing the heterogeneity of students' capabilities, needs, and interests. As Kauffman and his colleagues put it in the opening of Chapter 5, "Many of us have experienced becoming our own worst enemies". I completely accept that throwing out the old model and constructing a new one from first principles would be hard, but it would seem to be the only way of eliminating the regular political pressures that blame the education system, teachers, parents, and students for the failure to attain the gold standards of student performance and full inclusion.

When it comes to the realities of inclusion, Kaufman et al. draw attention to economic realities that must inevitably affect students' education, the complex realities of disability and impairment, and the dangers of oversimplification of teaching based on the belief that full inclusion will solve all educational problems, and those who hold alternative views are misinformed or simply wrong. I am strongly drawn to their final sentence, "We would rather be guided by science and reason than by romanticism or 'pure' but crude ideology". Hurrah!

The importance of research and science is addressed in Elliott's chapter dealing with dyslexia, arguing that many teacher practitioners do not base their practices on empirically validated research. He emphasises, for example, the conflicting views concerning dyslexia held by the scientific community and practising professionals and advocates. He argues that, in regard to dyslexia, there is only one intervention approach that currently has sufficient scientific support, that is, systematic phonics-based instruction. He warns, however, that using this approach will not necessarily solve all reading difficulties. He advocates the RTI approach, saying that where it operates effectively, all struggling readers are identified, have their reading needs assessed, and where appropriate, receive a scientifically validated intervention. Parallel concerns to those Elliott has raised are likely to be found in most, if not all, curriculum areas.

The challenge for both education practitioners and researchers alike is establishing the academic and social advantages of inclusive practices, and, in some cases, even evidence of the existence of inclusion itself. And while the present volume does not provide a comprehensive review of the research, it urges us to take a step away from the classroom, outside the administrators' offices or meeting rooms, and a good distance from the legislature and reconsider exactly what we are trying to address, why, and what the significant blockages are that have led to a situation in which good intentions and ideals fail to achieve the results we want. We need to see more published work that demonstrates the presence of inclusive practices and the benefits of inclusion for all students, including those with the most demanding needs.

Reading the chapters in this book has caused me to stop and think about what has been achieved over the past 50 years. I suggest that we have spent considerable time and energy debating the philosophy and principles that might underlie inclusion but far less time and energy determining what has not been achieved. Inclusion is a magnificent ideal and it will remain only that until we identify and implement educational programs, strategies, and practices that stand up to the rigour of scientific scrutiny.

Adrian Ashman
Professor Emeritus, School of Education
The University of Queensland
Australia

Preface

This book is about the contemporary issues and challenges surrounding the complexities of inclusive education. As education is a reflection on society's philosophies, beliefs and values, educational norms shift to the tide of a political agenda. Sitting within the context of the broader education system, inclusive education moves with, and sometimes against, current policies and opinions. In this way, inclusive education may be conceptualised as being pulled along behind the 'big brother' of mainstream education, receiving at times great popularity and at others, falls into relative obscurity. It might be considered that such positioning has not served inclusive education advocates well. To be mentioned in passing, or to be allocated the status of 'little brother', presents a challenge for advocates to disrupt the fundamentals of the construction of a flawed 20th century education system.

While critiques of the 20th century education system are many and varied, changes to the existing school system have been highlighted by a move away from the Industrial Age and an emphasis on education as a producer of citizens for the workforce. Despite moving into an era of the rapid adoption of technology, fuelled by a knowledge economy that values critical thinking and problem solving, traditional forms of educational delivery are yet to be transformed. While 21st century learning is supposed to revolutionise the educational delivery, time will tell. What is also yet to be realised is the place for students with additional learning needs in a system that once again, aims to prepare students in a market economy that they might not be able to participate in. In short, the Information Age values different skills than those considered important in the past; however, the political agenda remains the same. What skills in young people might have been valuable to consider if the agenda was to focus on more than just to make students active and engaged productive citizens? Inclusive educators and advocates are again charged with the task of confronting the educational status quo. While we remain in a society that pushes inclusive education to the periphery, we must continue to endorse the foundations of an inclusive culture which values diversity and difference.

In this book, we challenge some of the directions that inclusive education has taken. It grew out of the contradictions and frustrations that have stymied the progress of inclusivity. In writing the book we have therefore continued to provoke debate around inclusive education as it sits within the context of its current paradigm, as well as to interrogate the issues that may be ultimately counterproductive. We begin the book in Part 1 by lessons emerging about the values, philosophies and debates that face inclusive education in relation to a 'good education' in particular. In Part 2, we address the issues and controversies surrounding the lack of progress towards inclusivity and ask, "why are we not more inclusive?" Finally, in Part 3 we explore some of the existing strategies and approaches that occur to enhance inclusive practices and discuss the possibilities for the future of inclusive education. The editors hope that this book will be of interest to an international readership wishing to engage with a critical, yet inherently progressive, view of inclusion from the perspective of many international scholars in inclusive and special education.

The book is designed to be read in a systematic order but can be read just as easily as standalone chapters in no particular order. The editors hope that you will be, in equal measure, as engaged, informed, confused, and excited as we were whilst producing this ground-breaking volume.

Acknowledgements

We, as editors, would like to thank the esteemed group of academics and researchers who have contributed to this publication. Without their commitment to work with us on this project, we would not have been able to put together such a strong edited volume.

We would also like to acknowledge the excellent support provided to us by Brill | Sense, most notably Evelien van der Veer and Jolanda Karada. They really do make publishing with them a pleasure. Professor Roger Slee is the series editor, and we are very grateful to have been invited to be part of an engaging and informative set of books.

Figures and Tables

Figures

Tables

Notes on Contributors

Kelly-Ann Allen
(Ph.D.) is an educational and developmental psychologist, senior lecturer at the Faculty of Education, Monash University and senior honorary fellow of the University of Melbourne with more than ten years' experience as a school psychologist. Kelly-Ann is also a fellow of the College of Educational and Developmental Psychologists, Treasurer of the National committee and acting Editor of the *Educational Developmental Psychologist.*

Dimitris Anastasiou
(Ph.D.) is Associate Professor of Special Education at Southern Illinois University, Carbondale. Topics of his many publications include disability rights, educational policy, comparative education, and interventions in reading and writing.

Joanna Anderson
is a Ph.D. research student in the Graduate School of Education at the University of Exeter in the UK. Her main research interests are inclusive education and the contexts within which it exists, and school leadership and inclusive education. Joanna works as a Head of Special Education within a large primary school, and as a lecturer in inclusive education in the School of Education at the University of New England, Australia.

Adrian Ashman
(Ph.D.) is Emeritus Professor at The University of Queensland, Australia. He has an extensive research and publication record in educational psychology and inclusive education accumulated over four decades. He has doctoral qualifications from Canadian and Australian universities.

Jeanmarie Badar
(Ph.D.) (special education, University of Virginia) was a special education teacher for 25 years and has been an assistant professor of special education at James Madison University, Harrisonburg, Virginia. She is interested primarily in emotional and behavioral disorders and effective instruction.

Christopher Boyle
(Ph.D.) is based in the Graduate School of Education, University of Exeter, UK. He is a Fellow of the British Psychological Society and an Associate Professor of Educational Psychology and Inclusion. He has been an education and

psychology practitioner for over 20 years. He is an internationally recognised and respected academic and author on the subjects of inclusive education, and psychology.

Jonathan M. Campbell
(Ph.D.) is a licensed psychologist and Professor, Department of Psychology, Western Carolina University. Dr. Campbell has worked in the field of neurodevelopmental disabilities for 20 years. He was a LEND trainee at the Boling Center for Developmental Disabilities at the University of Tennessee Health Sciences Center during his doctoral training. He completed pre-doctoral and postdoctoral training at the Yale Child Study Center in New Haven, CT. Dr. Campbell's research focuses on identifying and modifying attitudes of typically developing peers towards students with autism spectrum disorder.

Heather Craig
is currently a student at Monash University, enrolled in the MPhil program in the School of Public Health and Preventive Medicine. With a particular interest in Positive Psychology, Heather is currently completing research into the association between optimism and health outcomes in elderly Australians.

Leire Darretxe
(Ph.D.) joined the University of the Basque country in 2005. Her research interests are in the area of social and educational inclusion. Dr. Darretxe has participated in several funded projects (e.g. Erasmus+). She has conducted research with university colleagues across Spain and the UK.

Julian Elliott
(Ph.D.) is Principal of Collingwood College, and Professor of Educational Psychology, Durham University. Initially, a teacher, he subsequently practised as an educational psychologist, and a university lecturer. He is a Fellow of the Academy of Social Sciences, a Chartered Psychologist, and a Fellow of the British Psychological Society.

Zuriñe Gaintza
(Ph.D.) is a lecturer in pedagogy at the University of the Basque Country. After eight years working as a primary school teacher, Dr. Gaintza did her Ph.D. in the area of pedagogy. Currently, she lectures and researches in the area of educating children, who have rare diseases, in mainstream education. Her experience in different school settings ensures that she has a wide knowledge of the educational reality of the Basque country.

Betty A. Hallenbeck
(Ph.D.) (special education, University of Virginia) teaches at York Community College in Wells, Maine. She was previously an assistant professor of special education at Utah State University, Logan. Her primary interests are emotional and behavioral disorders and parents of children with special needs.

Divya Jindal-Snape
(Ph.D.) is a Professor of Education, Inclusion and Life Transitions in the School of Education and Social Work at the University of Dundee, UK. She is also the Director of Transformative Change: Educational and Life Transitions (TCELT) Research Centre.

Marguerite Jones
(Ph.D.) is a lecturer and researcher at the University of New England. Her research areas include innovations to pre-service teacher professional experience, teacher mentoring, and the politics of casual teaching, gifted education, and higher education. She liaises with professionals across Australia to enhance leader and teacher practice.

James M. Kauffman
(Ed.D.) is Professor Emeritus of Education at the University of Virginia. He has published widely about special education. His publications include books, chapters, and articles about emotional and behavioral disorders, learning disabilities, special education policy, and the history of special education.

George Koutsouris
(Ph.D.) is a Lecturer in Special Educational Needs and Inclusive Education in the University of Exeter. Between 2015–2017, George was the research officer of the Nuffield Foundation-funded trial of the Integrated Group Reading (IGR) programme. He has published in the area of inclusive education, lesson study and early reading.

Fraser Lauchlan
(Ph.D.) is a registered educational psychologist. He works as a trainer and consultant in the UK (doi.fraserlauchlan.com). He is also an Honorary Lecturer at the universities of Strathclyde and Manchester. His main research interests are the cognitive benefits of bilingualism and the use of dynamic assessment by educational psychologists.

Gerry Mac Ruairc
(Ph.D.) is the Professor of Education and Head of the School of Education at the National University of Ireland, Galway. Gerry was a teacher, School Inspector and Associate Professor in the School of Education in University College Dublin (UCD). He has published widely in the areas of leadership for inclusive schooling, language and social class, and literacy as well as in the areas of leadership and school improvement for equity and social justice. He has a strong track record in the area of funded research and leadership development work, including projects funded by Atlantic Philanthropies, the World Bank and the European Commission.

Sofia Mavropoulou
(Ph.D.) is Senior Lecturer of Inclusive Education at Queensland University of Technology in Australia. She has extensive experience as a lecturer in autism education in universities in Greece, Cyprus and Australia. Her research, being conducted in Greece and Australia, is focused on educational strategies for students with autism in inclusive contexts, and social inequalities and families raising children with autism.

Daniel Mays
(Dr. phil.) is Professor of Special Education with a focus on emotional and social development at the University of Siegen, Germany. His main research areas are the socio-emotional development of children and adolescents; permeability of the school system/transition research and multiprofessional cooperation in school.

Brahm Norwich
(Ph.D.) is Professor of Educational Psychology and Special Educational Needs, Graduate School of Education, University of Exeter. He was previously Professor of Special Needs Education, Institute of Education, University of London. He is interested in theoretical issues about the nature of special needs and inclusive education, having published books and papers on these and many other areas.

Angela Page
(Ed.D.) has worked as an Inclusive Education advisor to schools and governments in New Zealand and the Pacific region. Dr. Page currently lectures in inclusive education and classroom management at the University of Newcastle, Australia. She has a particular interest in inclusive and special education practices within new or emerging contexts.

Kirsten S. Railey
(M.S., BCBA) is a doctoral student in the School Psychology program at the University of Kentucky. She is currently completing her pre-doctoral internship through Emory University Department of Pediatrics' Marcus Autism Center in Atlanta, Georgia. Kirsten's research interests focus on interactions between first responders and individuals with Autism Spectrum Disorder (ASD) as well as peer education on behalf of students with ASD.

Federico R. Waitoller
(Ph.D.) is an Associate Professor at the Department of Special Education at the University of Illinois at Chicago. His research focuses on urban inclusive education and racial inequities for students with disabilities. His research agenda has two strands: teacher education for inclusive education and market-driven policies in education.

CHAPTER 1

Inclusive Education: An Enigma of 'Wicked' Proportions

Joanna Anderson, Christopher Boyle, Angela Page and Sofia Mavropoulou

1 Introduction

Inclusive education: a seemingly simple term that belies the issues and controversies that have ensued over the decades since its entrance into educational vernacular in the last decades of the 20th century. This came almost 25 years ago when the Salamanca Statement lay at the feet of nations globally – a Framework for Action to promote the notion that all students should access an inclusive education within their local schools, regardless of ability (UNESCO, 1994). Ainscow and César (2006) declared this as being 'the most significant document that has ever appeared in the field of special education' (p. 231), given it received approval from the more than 90 nations who were part of its inception. Since the release of this statement, the construct of inclusive education has broadened to being about the education of all students, no matter sexual orientation, social status, ethnicity, religion or perceived ability/disability (Boyle & Sharma, 2015). Despite the hard work and attempted reform by advocates of inclusive education, in 25 years the construct has not been successfully or consistently implemented as the way of educating all children and young people across the globe (Boyle & Anderson, 2019). Regardless of this, advocacy for inclusive education remains strong in some quarters (Boyle & Anderson, 2019). Reasons for this are varied, but many pertain in some way to the notion that education provides so much more than just academic achievement (Armstrong, 2018). It is also widely accepted that the process of education contributes to the psychological, social/emotional, and behavioural development of the children and young people in its provision (Armstrong, Elliot, Hallett, & Hallett, 2015; Oldfield, Humphrey, & Hebron, 2015). This is even more important for students who are considered to sit on the margins of the community, as it is this democratic access to schooling that provides these students with what it is they need to be successful within their local and wider communities; an important discussion to be having at a time when school populations globally are becoming increasingly diverse (Schwab, Sharma, & Loreman, 2018).

 | DOI: 10.1163/9789004431171_001

Given the perceived benefits of inclusive education for everyone, from the students once placed into segregated settings (Schwab, Sharma, & Loreman, 2018), to the other students (Allan, 2009), teachers (Yada, Tolvanen, & Savolainen, 2018) and the wider school community (Osiname, 2018), the question must be asked – why are we not yet there? Topping's (2012) notion that inclusive education should be viewed as a journey, not a destination, could go some way to explaining why we are not 'there', as perhaps there is no destination to arrive at. However what is indisputable is that many of the world's nations have stagnated in their progress towards the provision of a fully inclusive education system (Boyle & Anderson, 2019), and in some systems (such as in Australia and the UK), marginalised or students with more complex educational needs are once again being separated or segregated from their peers, and rates of educational exclusion are increasing (Anderson & Boyle, 2019; Norwich & Black, 2015). Furthermore, for nations such as Italy, who espouse a fully inclusive system, cracks are beginning to appear and the once highly regarded system is facing its own challenges (Lauchlan & Fadda, 2012). Again, the discussion comes back to that persistent question. Why? Why has the implementation of inclusive education been racked with so many challenges, paradoxes, and ambiguities?

2 Challenges, Paradoxes, and Ambiguities: A Brief Exploration

Armstrong (2017), in his series looking at 'wicked problems' in education, chose the fields of special and inclusive education as his first topic of discussion. This was not coincidental. The term 'wicked problem', a term coined by Rittel and Webber (1973) to describe highly complex issues that do not present any obvious solutions, sits aptly in any discussion about inclusive education, for all of the reasons scrutinised within the pages of this book. However before delving into the issues presented by the contributing authors, it is worth exploring, in a more general way, some of the complex issues inclusive education raises, to understand just how 'wicked' the problems of its implementation are.

One of the biggest challenges has been the inability to define what inclusive education actually is. This ambiguity, according to Connolley and Hausstätter (2009), has led to confusion and angst amongst those trying to plan for its implementation. Two obvious difficulties arise from this. Firstly, there is no clear understanding of what inclusive education should look like, and therefore no consistent idea of what needs to be done to achieve it. This has led to things happening under the guise of inclusive education that are, in fact, exclusive (Slee, 2018). With no clear working definition, questions around what constitutes (or not) inclusive practice are contentious. Secondly, without an unambiguous understanding or set of criteria to define what inclusive education is, measuring its success has been problematic (Loreman, 2014), and yet this is something deemed necessary within the current era of educational reform that relies on 'evidence based' approaches (Muller, 2018). What should be measured and how? Who should be measured and how? What is certain is that the current reliance by systems on data collected from high stakes testing does not provide what is needed to gauge the success (or not) of inclusive education. Researchers, policy makers and those working within the field have bandied about different ideas, however without a definitive understanding of what inclusive education is and what is actually being measured, this has proven to be a challenge that has yet to be overcome.

Another of the challenges facing inclusive education is a paradoxical one. Inclusive education is an egalitarian ideal that has sitting at its core the concepts of equity and social justice (UNICEF, 2013), yet the global political zeitgeist, which dictates the direction of all educational reform, is one that upholds and adheres to neo-liberal principles (Denniss, 2018). Choice, accountability, and standardisation are all terms that are now commonplace in discussions about educational reform, even though they sit somewhat counter intuitively to the values of equity and social justice. These neo-liberal principles presume an equal starting place, where everyone has the same access to educational opportunities and outcomes, and responsibility for success is placed upon the individuals involved (see Mounk, 2018 for a discussion on individual responsibility). Reality however provides a very different story. Inequality has always existed and it is a growing phenomenon (Niesche & Keddie, 2016), with renowned English businessman Tim Smit describing it (along with poverty) as one of the 'greatest issues of the day' (2016, p. 163). While here is not the place for a detailed discussion about global inequality, it follows that the children and young people who access education are not doing it from an equal starting point. Therefore, a system built around this premise is going to face difficulties when considering its success (or not) through an equity and social justice, or inclusive education, lens. In this sense, education systems can be viewed as reproducing societies' class systems (Slee, 2018; Freire, 2005), where some will thrive while others will fail (Artiles, 2003). In a world where exclusion is a social phenomenon, part of almost every society (Slee, 2018), this is perhaps not surprising.

This brings the discussion to another challenge for inclusive education – the question of whether or not schools should be laden with the responsibility of challenging what are engrained and exclusionary societal structures (Bregman, 2017; Apple, 2015). It is schools to which this job has fallen, although this was not the original intent of those advocating for inclusive education. Rather, inclusive education, whatever definition it is operating within, is about systemic reform. The Salamanca Statement (1994) recognised this – "education systems should be designed and educational programmes implemented to take into account the wide diversity of these characteristics and needs" (p. viii) – yet many governments, in the ensuing years since, have placed the responsibility for the implementation of inclusive education at the feet of schools (Thomson, Lingard, & Wrigley, 2012). While schools are at the coalface of educational delivery and absolutely have a role to play in the development and enactment of inclusive practices, it cannot be done successfully without systemic reform. Otherwise, students for whom the system was not originally designed and established (see Connell, 1980, for an interesting discussion on the history of schooling), are at risk of being made to fit the system, rather than the system being flexible and malleable enough to meet the needs of every individual student. This raises the challenges of providing relevant curriculum and pedagogy (the what and how), resourcing (the who), and facilities (the where), that ensure access for all students.

The issues presented in this chapter demonstrate the breadth and complexity of the challenges, paradoxes, and ambiguities that inclusive education has encountered for the duration of its journey, and continues to face as its very existence and worth is questioned and challenged by many, including practitioners, researchers, and policy makers (Boyle & Anderson, 2019; Slee, 2018). It is perhaps unsurprising then to find that many nations have stagnated in their progress towards fully inclusive systems, and for some, the number of students accessing education in separate or segregated facilities is on the increase, once again (Boyle & Anderson, 2019). This is happening not only through traditional 'special school' or 'special education unit' service provisions, but also as a result of the increasing number of selective public schools, as exist in the UK and Australia (Slee, 2018), and the increase in numbers of students being home schooled (English, 2019). Paradoxically, this is all occurring under the umbrella of inclusive education, as it remains within the pages of these nations' educational policies (Slee, 2018).

Armstrong's (2017) assertion that inclusive education is a 'wicked problem' would be difficult to challenge, particularly when viewed as an educational construct that is struggling to exist within the current political, social and cultural climate. Armstrong (2017) concludes his paper with these words:

> (P)rogressive initiatives to address today's wicked problems in special and inclusive education are unlikely to make headway without addressing the underpinning beliefs and behavioural motivations – as well as political forces – which currently sustain them. Change it seems cannot be

> unidimensional to succeed in schools but must be adopted across the political, social, cultural, psychological and behavioural dimensions which make up the everyday, routine fabric of complex educational institutions. (p. 5)

It is indisputable that any solutions to resolve the myriad of challenges, paradoxes, and ambiguities that exist within inclusive education are going to be just as complex as the problems themselves. But this does not mean solutions should not be sought. To find a starting place, the problems need to be acknowledged, then understood in a deep and coherent way, for without this progress in the right direction will not be made. This book is an attempt to add to the discourse of inclusive education, by engaging in a genuine and honest discussion about some of the current global issues and controversies surrounding the construct, and how, if at all, inclusive education can move on from these.

3 Interrogating Inclusion

This book explores inclusive education from different perspectives through three distinct, but related, parts. The first looks at some of the big questions currently missing from the educational discourse through a philosophical lens – what is 'inclusive education' in the current climate, and what does this mean for those who are leading its charge? The second part interrogates aspects of why inclusive education has not become the prevailing model of education delivery, despite decades of it being at the forefront of educational policy and rhetoric. The book concludes with a look at what is happening in schools themselves, where much of the responsibility (rightly or not) for enacting inclusive practices has been placed. Its design allows readers to dip into particular sections, or to read it from beginning to end, with each chapter being a complete discussion in itself.

Part 1 begins with a chapter that provides a provocative discussion on what constitutes 'good' education in an era of competition and inequity. Drawing from philosophers (such as Plato and Socrates) and educational theorists (such as Dewey, Freire, Apple), Anderson and Boyle pose challenging questions which invite the reader to rethink the value and purpose of education, and its ability to be an agent of social change. More importantly, the authors appeal for a reconsideration of the purpose of schooling in a time of increasing inequality, and for a reengagement with the debate about what 'good' education should look like in today's world.

In Chapter 3 Anderson and Boyle continue the critical discussion of the notion of good education by analysing how neo-liberalism has impacted education. Biesta's three-domain model of educational purpose guides their endeavor to disentangle the complexities of what it means to provide 'good' education for *all*. They contend that the educational discourse evident in school policies, with its sole focus on effective instruction that places strong emphasis on evidence and practices that work and bring about measurable outcomes, is problematic as it detracts our attention from questions such as "*what* are students learning?" and "*why* are they learning?" and "*who* are they learning it from?" The authors conclude that inclusive education holds firm promise for bridging the achievement gap between students, and thereby contributing to fairness and equity in education.

The final chapter in this part considers the challenges encountered by school leaders committed to serve inclusion in a neo-liberal education system where high stakes assessment, ability grouping and exclusionary practices are the prevailing phenomena. Mac Ruairc's proposition is for "leadership practice to be reimagined" in the framework of cultural politics. If leaders view themselves and their staff as cultural workers constantly questioning and reflecting on their practice with the consideration that social conditions reproduce barriers and inequality in their schools, they will lead transformative action framed by the "politics of recognition" of difference, where hearts and minds are synchronized with the vision of fair and inclusive schools.

Part 2 commences with a discussion that challenges the notion supported by passionate advocates of full inclusion. Kauffman, Anastasiou, Badar and Hallendeck suggest that if inclusion is to be redefined with greater clarity, then there is a need to abandon the binary between 'all' and 'not-all', thereby avoiding self-defeating statements that present a threat to the ideology of inclusion itself. The authors interrogate nine paths to full inclusion, from the dilemma of who is to be included, to the economic cost of inclusion, to the impact inclusive education has had on the field of special education. The authors declare their support for partial inclusion as a moral and ethical obligation, and as a realistic way forward for teaching all students with disabilities within the mainstream school.

In the next chapter, Waitoller uses his previous work on a three-dimensional definition of inclusive education to frame the discussion around what inclusive education is. The definition identifies the mission of inclusive education as a movement as being (i) to examine the distribution of opportunities for access and participation, (ii) the recognition of diversity in content, pedagogy and assessment, and (iii) the representation of marginalised groups in decision-making in education contexts and beyond. The author critically analyses how inclusive education is currently materialised in the context of neoliberalism, perpetuating injustice and inequity, and puts forward a framework to understand why this is, and how to move inclusion forward.

Chapter 7 focusses on whether the definition, assessment and intervention for students with dyslexia may disadvantage other students with reading difficulties who may not get the support they require in an inclusive environment. Elliot argues against cognitive evaluations, which are widely applied and create diagnostic categories that distinguish between dyslexic and non-dyslexic students by validating a diagnosis of dyslexia. The author responds to the controversy surrounding the value of diagnostic labels within inclusive education by strongly endorsing the RTI (Response to Intervention) model, which offers systemic support in response to need rather than to a label. Elliot recognises the need for students with dyslexia to receive appropriate instruction but is concerned with the education for all other students who do not meet the criteria for a dyslexia diagnosis.

Boyle, Anderson and Allen begin Part 3 with a discussion on teacher attitudes towards inclusion, and the critical role this plays in the successful implementation (or not) of inclusive practices. The authors examine factors which exert major influence on whether teachers develop positive or negative attitudes towards inclusion, and argue that teacher attitudes should be conceptualised, measured and evaluated as one of the critical aspects in a whole-school approach to the sustainable development of an inclusive school culture.

In Chapter 9 Page and Jones draw from recent research, and calls from politicians urging schools and teachers to enforce strict discipline methods as a means to improve student outcomes, to express their timely concern about the direction of classroom management in the Australian landscape. They point to the critical disconnection between their own philosophy and principles, and the classroom management practices pre-service teachers observe in their professional experience placements. The authors propose an alternative model for understanding and teaching classroom management that is aligned with a holistic conceptualisation of classroom management that acknowledges both classroom ecologies and student need.

Mays, Jindal-Snape and Boyle present Chapter 10 with a look at issues surrounding the transitions of students with additional support needs across the different stages of schooling and into post-school life. The authors highlight the importance of understanding interpersonal challenges for each student during the transition process, not just the academic ones, and as such emphasise the need for a "whole-person" approach that will respect the student's preferences, peer affiliations and needs. The authors propose a multi-level systemic approach which encompasses the perspective/voice of students, alongside a number of other measures that teachers can use to prepare students for their transitions, from a strengths-based viewpoint.

In Chapter 11, Mavropoulou, Railey and Campbell present a discussion about the important role peers play in the successful experiences of students with ASD in inclusive school settings. The authors interrogate the research in this field and argue that poor peer relationships can have significant consequences for students with ASD, resulting in social isolation, loneliness and serious cases of bullying. Peer-mediated interventions, peer-awareness programs, school-wide bullying programs, and teacher understanding are unpacked and presented as methods that, when used together, can work to support successful peer relationships for students with ASD, which improve both social and academic outcomes for these students.

The next chapter, by Allen, Boyle and Lachlan, introduces the notion that a multi-systemic approach to the instruction of social skills will promote authentic social inclusion, especially for students on the autism spectrum who experience bullying and persisting difficulties in their social relationships, particularly at school. The central tenet of this approach is that individuals who sit in multiple layers around the individual student, such as peers, teachers, principals and parents, share responsibility for establishing and maintaining strong and positive social relationships, which in turn help build an atmosphere of belonging and connectedness in a mainstream school context.

The penultimate chapter presents a new model of teaching literacy (Integrated Group Reading), which offers support to Year 1 students grappling with learning to read. This model allows the delivery of support to be provided in the main by the classroom teacher within the context of the classroom and is therefore aligned with inclusive values and inclusive pedagogies. A key implication of this approach is that it contributes to professional development for inclusion as it equips teachers with advanced skills to support all students in their classes who have not mastered reading; the development of quality teaching practices that meet the needs of all students within the classroom is effective inclusive teaching.

Finally, Gaintza, Darretxe and Boyle present an analysis of the multi-tiered education system in the Basque Country, Spain, that has been designed to cater for the needs of diverse students. Schools operate in an inclusive framework, offering support within the broad general curriculum through the implementation of *ordinary specific measures* for students who need supplementary instruction. The authors engage in a critical discussion about this approach in light of the increasing numbers of students being enrolled in special education units, which they argue is a reflection of the gap in the Basque Country's education policy that favours alternative forms of schooling for students with special educational needs.

4 Conclusion

Inclusive education is sitting precariously within educational policies globally. There are some who believe that inclusive education 'is dead' as it has exposed itself to be an unattainable ideal (Imray & Colley, 2017, p. 1). Others, however, are still agitating for change, big change, that will enable education systems to deliver an education to all students, in an obtainable, inclusive way. Both of these viewpoints are argued in the pages ahead, providing the reader with opinions and ideas that may challenge, inspire or consolidate what it is they have come to this book with.

References

Allan, J. (2009). Teaching children to live with diversity: A response to 'Tocqueville on democracy and inclusive education: A more ardent and enduring love of equality than of liberty'. *European Journal of Special Needs Education, 24*(3), 245–247.

Anderson, J., & Boyle, C. (2019). Looking in the mirror: Reflecting on 25 years of inclusive education in Australia. *The International Journal of Inclusive Education, 23*(7–8), 796–810. doi:10.1080/13603116.2019.1622802

Apple, M. (2015). Reframing the question of whether education can change society. *Educational Theory, 65*(3), 299–315. doi:10.1111/edth.12114

Armstrong, D. (2017). Wicked problems in special and inclusive education. *Journal of Research in Special Educational Needs, 17*(4), 229–236. doi:10.1111/1471-3802.12402

Armstrong, D., Elliot, J., Hallett, F., & Hallett, G. (2015). *Understanding child and adolescent behaviour in the classroom.* Cambridge University Press.

Artiles, A. (2003). Special education's changing identity: Paradoxes and dilemmas in views of culture and space. *Harvard Educational Review, 73*(2), 164–202.

Boyle, C., & Anderson, J. (in press). Inclusive education and the progressive inclusionists. In U. Sharma & S. Salend (Eds.), *The Oxford research encyclopedia of education.* Oxford University Press.

Boyle, C., & Sharma, U (2015). Inclusive education – Worldly views? *British Journal of Support for Learning, 30*(1), 2–3. doi:10.1111/1467-9604.12077

Bregman, R. (2017). *Utopia for realists and how we get there.* Bloomsbury.

Connell, D. (1980). *A history of education in the twentieth century world.* Curriculum Development Centre.

Connolley, S., & Haussstätter, R. S. (2009). Tocqueville on democracy and inclusive education: A more ardent and enduring love of equality than of liberty. *European Journal of Special Needs Education,* 24(3), 231–243. doi:10.1080/08856250903016714

Denniss, R. (2018). Dead right: How neoliberalism ate itself and what comes next. *Quarterly Essay, 1*(70), 1–79.

English, R. (2019, April 15). *Homeschooling is on the rise in Australia. Who is doing it and why?* Commentary in The Conversation, The Conversation Media Group, Melbourne, Australia. Retrieved from https://theconversation.com/homeschooling-is-on-the-rise-in-australia-who-is-doing-it-and-why-110268

Freire, P. (2005). *Pedagogy of the oppressed* (30th ed.). The Continuum International Publishing Group Inc.

Imray, P., & Colley, A. (2017). *Inclusion is dead: Long live inclusion.* Routledge.

Lauchlan, F., & Fadda, R. (2012). The 'Italian' model' of full inclusion: Origins and current directions. In C. Boyle & K. Topping (Eds.), *What works in inclusion?* (pp. 31–40). Open University Press/McGraw Hill Education.

Loreman, T. (2014). Measuring inclusive education outcomes in Alberta, Canada. *International Journal of Inclusive Education, 18*(5), 459–483. doi:1080/13603116.2013.78822310

Niesche, R., & Keddie, A. (2016). *Leadership, ethics and schooling for social justice.* Routledge.

Norwich, B., & Black, A. (2015). The placement of secondary school students with Statements of special educational needs in the more diversified system of English secondary schooling. *British Journal of Special Education, 42*(2), 128–151. doi:10.1111/1467-8578.12097

Oldfield, J., Humphrey, N., & Hebron, J. (2015). Cumulative risk effects for the development of behaviour difficulties in children and adolescents with special educational needs and disabilities. *Research in Developmental Disabilities, 41*, 66–75.

Osiname, A. (2018). Utilizing the critical inclusive praxis: The voyage of five selected school principals in building inclusive school cultures. *Improving Schools, 21*(1), 63–83. doi:10.1177/1365480217717529

Schwab, S., Sharma, U., & Loreman, T. (2018). Are we included? Secondary students' perception of inclusion climate in their schools. *Teaching and Teacher Education, 75*(1), 31–39. doi:10.1016/j.tate.2018.05.016

Slee, R. (2018). *Inclusive education isn't dead, it just smelly funny.* Routledge.

Smit, T. (2016). *Eden.* Transworld Publishers.

Thomson, P., Lingard, B., & Wrigley, T. (2012). Reimagining school change: The necessity and reasons for hope. In T. Wrigley, P. Thomson, & B. Lingard (Eds.), *Changing schools: Alternative ways to make a world of difference.* Routledge.

Topping, K. (2012). Conceptions of inclusion: Widening ideas. In C. Boyle & K. Topping (Eds.), *What works in inclusion?* (pp. 9–19). McGraw-Hill.

UNESCO. (1994). *The Salamanca statement and framework for action on special needs education*. UNESCO.

UNICEF. (2013). *The state of the world's children: Children with disabilities – 2013*. Retrieved from https://www.unicef.org/sowc2013/

Yada, A., Tolvanen, A., & Savolainen, D. (2018). Teachers' attitudes and self-efficacy on implementing inclusive education in Japan and Finland: A comparative study using multi-group structural equation modelling. *Teaching and Teacher Education, 75*(1), 343–355. doi:10.1016/j.tate.2018.07.011

PART 1

Values, Philosophy and Debate about What Education Is in an Inclusive Context

CHAPTER 2

Including into What? Reigniting the 'Good Education' Debate in an Age of Diversity

Joanna Anderson and Christopher Boyle

> It would seem, Adeimantus, that the direction in which education starts a man, will determine his future life.
>
> PLATO, *The Republic*

∵

1 Introduction

The decision to write this chapter stems from an authentic unease about the absence of quality discourse amongst educators about the essence of our work – *education*. Every day in every classroom, teachers and other school staff work to deliver an education to students so they can grow to become knowledgeable, active and engaged citizens. Despite this, any discourse centred on the philosophical underpinnings of education and what it actually is, is conspicuously absent from the current global lexicon. Soltis (1968) expressed his unease about this almost four decades ago when he identified that educators:

> would be hard pressed if asked to spell out in simple words the ideas which are contained in such ordinary concepts of education as teaching, learning, or subject matter. Yet these very concepts are basic to any thought or discussion about education. (p. 2)

It is interesting to note that this concern was raised at a time when there was more discussion about education itself, through work such as that published by R. S. Peters, Robin Barrow and Mary Warnock, than there is today. Contemporary academics, such as Gert Biesta (2015, 2013a, 2013b, 20009, 2007 for his discussions about education) and Michael Apple (2016, 2017) are working to challenge this prevailing dearth of discourse on education, but it is proving difficult in the current educational climate. Despite the challenges, the pursuit

 | DOI: 10.1163/9789004431171_002

of quality discussion about education must persist. This is particularly relevant in the debate around inclusive education; how can we have a discussion about providing an education to all students, in an inclusive and meaningful way, if we do not consider what *education* is and what we are working to include students into?

The aim of this chapter is not to provide a prescriptive approach to education. Rather, it endeavours to reignite the discussion about education itself, to once again begin talking about what constitutes education – *good education* – for all students who are lucky enough to pass through a school gate.

2 The Importance of Education

Philosophers and educationalists have been writing about the part education has to play in strong and prosperous societies since Plato (2016) penned his Socratic dialogue *The Republic* around 380BC. Plato proposed the idea that education should be used to create both the good man (and woman) and the good citizen: 'true education, whatever that may be, will have the greatest tendency to civilize and humanize' (Book I, unpaginated). Although this debate has been raging for almost two and a half thousand years, there is still no unified understanding of what education should look like, how it should be enacted, or even what are the important things to be taught. All that has been settled is that education is something that societies need and that young people globally, regardless of circumstance, should be afforded the opportunity to engage in educational opportunities (UNESCO, 2015).

Education does not transpire within a vacuum, but rather works as part of the broader *social circumstances* in which it operates (O'Hear, 1981). In his work *The experimental ecology of education*, developmental psychologist Urie Bronfenbrenner (1976) conceptualised this as a 'nested system of structures' (p. 5), where the student sits at the centre and is surrounded by systems that incorporate the various environments that influence that student's education, from their home and classroom, to the global context in which they are living. For Western countries, that amounts to *systems* functioning within democracies, working under an umbrella of neoliberalism (Furlong, 2013). While the full impact of what this means for education is beyond the scope of this chapter (see Apple, 2017; Furlong, 2013; Bale & Knopp, 2012; Foster, 2011; Allman, 2001, for insightful discussions on the impact of neoliberalism on education), the popular presumption is that schools are 'agents of change that provide a means of social and economic mobility for poor and minoritized populations' (McMahon, 2013, p. 18). It is this premise that so often places education at the centre of the struggle to create a fairer, more equitable society. Evidence collected over the past three decades unquestionably identifies young people who receive a good education at both primary and secondary level as having more positive life outcomes, in terms of employment, health, and connectedness to and participation in their communities, than those who do not (Reardon, 2011; Wilkinson & Pickett, 2010). This is not just the case for those in developing nations. It is the case for everyone, in every nation across the globe.

3 Education as an Agent of Social Justice

'*Social justice* is a politically loaded term' and as such, any definition adopted has the capacity to manipulate or direct the discussion about an issue in a particular way (Shoho, Merchant, & Lugg, 2011, p. 37). Consequently, it is necessary to explore (albeit briefly) a number of ideas about what social justice is and what it is not. According to Rawls (2001), social justice refers to 'the basic structure of society, or more exactly, the way in which the major social institutions distribute fundamental rights and duties and determine the division of advantages from social cooperation' (p. 6). Miller's (1999) description of social justice as being 'how the good and bad things in life should be distributed among the members of a human society' (p. 1), illustrates a similar train of thought to that of Rawls. For a society to be considered socially just, the distribution of advantage must be carried out in a way that is of benefit to all. Conversely, social injustice can be simply described as 'inequalities that are not to the benefit of all' (Rawls, 1999, p. 54). In today's Western neoliberal world, the *division of advantage* is often measured in terms of income, as it is wealth that provides access to the necessities of life. In this sense, it could be argued that the world is currently moving towards becoming more socially just, as the past two decades have seen a drop in the inequity of income as distributed between nations; developing nations are receiving a higher percentage of the global income than ever before (World Bank Group, 2016; Rougoor & Van Marrewijk, 2015; Milanovic, 2012). Yet this trend is not reflected in the distribution of income within nations. Developing countries, who are earning a greater percentage of global income, do not distribute this in an equitable manner within their borders (Dastidar, 2012). Developed countries such as Australia, the United States of America, China, Sweden and Finland are not immune to this problem, and have all seen a growing divide between the income distributed to the wealthiest, and that received by the poorest in these countries (Milanovic, 2016). 'Income inequality is real and (it) is rising' (Marsh, 2011, p. 13).

Income distribution impacts on a community's capacity to create a socially just culture (Wilkinson & Pickett, 2010). Nevertheless, social justice is about more than just income distribution (Rawls, 1999). It 'implies a valuing of diversity' (Shoho et al., 2011, p. 37); an understanding and acceptance of diversity as part of the 'norm' within any society (Beachum, 2011). In this broader sense social justice can be described as being about 'equality, equity, fairness, acceptance of others, and inclusiveness' (Shoho et al., 2011, p. 48); it is about the distribution of, and access to, resources and services but it is also about the way people are treated and valued within a society. It is important to make reference here to why this is a necessary pursuit. Mounk (2017, pp. 163–164) encapsulates the work of the renowned American philosopher T. M. Scanlon to present five reasons (or classifications) as to why an egalitarian society is something to strive towards. These are described in Table 2.1.

Rightly so or not, education is often placed at the centre of the social justice debate. There is a conviction that a lack of education precipitates poverty and economic inequality, and therefore 'what will fix these ills is more and better education' (Marsh, 2011, p. 13). Recently, the Organization for Economic Cooperation and Development (OECD) (2012) reported that, 'an equitable education system can redress the effect of broader social and economic inequalities' (p. 15). The following year UNICEF (2013) described equitable education as 'the gateway to full participation in society' (p. 27). It is important here to identify the difference between the terms *education* and *equitable education*. While

TABLE 2.1 Five reasons for an egalitarian society

Reason	Description
Humanitarian	Sometimes, people suffer from hardships that are morally objectionable. The only, or the best, way of helping them is to take from those who have a lot.
Status	Sometimes, how citizens are treated, or what kind of material resources they have access to is objectionable because it marks them as having inferior status.
Domination	In many societies, those who have a lot come to acquire all kinds of official and unofficial power over those who have little.
Equality of opportunity	People who have a lot can find themselves in a cycle of self-sustaining privilege. They are able to undermine the fairness of political institutions, thereby ensuring that these pay greater attention to the powerful and wealthy than to those who are poor and powerless.
Just claim to equal resources	This is part of a wider obligation of governments to treat its citizens equally.

education is what is provided, *equitable education* assumes it is provided to all people. Field, Kuczera and Pont (2007) illustrated this point in more detail. They identified and described two dimensions of an 'equitable education'; the first, *fairness*, stipulates that personal and social circumstances (such as gender, ethnicity and socio-economic status) should not present obstacles to educational achievement, while the second dimension, *inclusion*, ensures that all individuals reach a basic minimum standard of education. The question then arises – is the equitable distribution of a basic education for everyone going to move society in a more socially just direction?

Apple (2015) explores this issue in a paper dedicated to the question of whether schools can change society. He concludes that it is a complex idea that raises more questions about schools and societies, as they currently exist, than can be answered readily. Laying the responsibility for societal change at the feet of education and its institutions, as governments, policy makers and international organisations (such as those mentioned above) have done, shifts the focus, or takes the onus of responsibility away from other aspects of current societal structures that need to be challenged within this debate (Apple, 2015). Economic power and social class are two such structures identified by Marsh (2011), who disputes the notion that education alone can change society. He contends that 'education bears far too much of the burden of our hopes for economic justice' (p. 18). Bregman (2017) concurs, stating that while education is a 'perceived silver bullet' (p. 55), unless other factors such as poverty are acknowledged and overcome, the current state of inequality is not going to change in any dramatic or sustained way.

Despite this, evidence does show that educational attainment is one construct that can lead to improved and better life outcomes – so whether or not education is able to create a more socially just world does not alter the fact that the equitable deliverance of education, a 'good' education, to all young people, is something worth striving for. The reasons for this are self-evident. Access to education has been shown to benefit everyone, both economically and socially. Those who receive an education are more likely to gain employment and to receive a higher income for their work, than those who do not (OECD, 2010); they contribute more in terms of tax to the government and in expenditure in the general economy. The educated also cost society less in terms of health, social welfare and spending on incarceration. Also of importance are the 'non-production' or social benefits of education, a concept that has been granted greater attention over the past decade or so (Lochner, 2011). Rawls (1999) described these benefits as stemming from the role education has in 'enabling a person to enjoy the culture of his society and to take part in its affairs, and in this way to provide for each individual a secure sense of his own worth' (p. 87). An interesting example of both the economic and social costs of education can be seen in the crime statistics. Crime has both an economic cost (the cost of the crime itself, the judicial process and of incarceration) and a social cost (the trauma caused by the crime). Evidence shows a direct causation between crime rates and levels of education (Machin, Marie, & Vujic, 2011). A study in the USA found that more than two thirds of the prison population in that country had not completed their schooling (Lochner, 2011). From this it can be surmised (as many have done) that increased access to and completion of education results in reduced rates of crime, improved health outcomes, better incomes, better access to services and more informed and engaged citizenry (Wilkenson & Pickett, 2010). Despite this there are still disparities across much of the globe between those who are accessing and completing their education and those who are not.

There is an assumption that in high-income countries, education is distributed equally. But this is not the case. In 2011 there were still 4% of children on the continents of Europe, the United Kingdom and the United States of America who were not accessing primary schooling, a figure that did not change from a decade earlier despite a commitment from governments that all children should be receiving an education (UNESCO, 2015). According to the UNESCO report, these children are likely to come from groups who are marginalised within their communities, such as those who are mobile (Travellers in Europe and the UK, or refugees), those who have a disability, or those who come from families on very low incomes. For the students who are accessing education, disparities also exist. A study conducted into education in the United Kingdom found that students from 'disadvantaged backgrounds', that is those from marginalised religious or ethnic groups, those with lower incomes, or those with poorer health status and/or access to services and facilities, generally attended lower performing schools, achieved lower academic outcomes during their schooling, and left school at a younger age (Ainscow et al., 2011). While it could be argued that this is only one study in one country, the OECD has found this relationship between schooling and social circumstance to exist in all education systems of the 30 nations belonging to that organisation (Kerr & West, 2010). Rawls (2001) identifies the reason for this as being that education favours 'certain starting places over others. These are especially deep inequalities' (p. 7). This is supported by a recent UNESCO (2015) report that identified a concerning trend – inequality in educational provision within countries has increased since 2000 with the 'poorest and most disadvantaged shouldering the heaviest burden' (p. i). The result? The gap in educational attainment between advantaged and disadvantaged learners is continuing to grow (Niesche & Keddie, 2016; Reardon, 2011).

Education systems have a responsibility to act as an agent of social justice through the equitable distribution of quality education to all students, a system that includes all and excludes none – inclusive education. UNICEF (2013) describes it in this way: 'If societies seek to reduce inequalities, they should start with the children best fitted to build an inclusive society for the next generation. Children who have experienced inclusive education can be society's best teachers' (p. 12). If there is any chance of this coming to be, it is important to understand the systems and institutions that deliver education as it is known today; it is important to understand schools.

4 The Creation of Institution

Today, schools (from kindergartens through to Universities) sit at the centre of the educational efforts across developing and developed societies globally (OECD, 2017). This is not a recent phenomenon. The institution of the 'school' has been in existence in various guises for millennia (Cole, 1950). In the time of Socrates, the once influential and progressive Greek city of Athens sanctioned the establishment of what today would be referred to as 'private' schools; educational institutions set up by individuals or groups of citizens where students were fed a curriculum of literacy, music and gymnastics in return for payment. In the two and a half thousand years since, many have advocated for the establishment of an accessible and effective education system for everyone, from Alcuin of York in the 700's, to the philosopher John Dewey at the turn of last century. By the beginning of the twentieth century schools, as educational institutions, had 'been deliberately set up on a large scale' (Connell, 1980, p. 2) throughout a substantial number of developed nations, many of which had some level of compulsory schooling. Today, compulsory schooling has become the norm (although there is disparity between starting and finishing ages), with a desire that all students across the globe have access to quality schooling, particularly in the primary years. Regrettably, this is a goal that is yet to be achieved.

For much of the world, the struggle to get all children into school classrooms continues (UNICEF, 2014). A report from the United Nations (2013) stated that 90% of the world's children in developing countries were receiving a primary school education, up 7% from 2000. Since then, the figure has remained static (for a myriad of reasons that are beyond the scope of this chapter – see the UN report for a discussion on this). As a consequence, approximately 57 million children throughout the developing world do not attend any type of formal schooling (UNICEF, 2014). In 2012, the then UN Secretary-General, Ban

Ki-moon, announced the 'Global education first' initiative, which had as its first priority to 'put every child in school' by the end of 2015. In a speech he delivered in the United States in 2014, there was an acknowledgement that there was still a long way to go with this initiative; 'I … want to see more action, more funding and many millions more children in school' (para. 22).

While this effort to increase the number of children enrolled in schools continues within developing countries, developed countries are grappling with their own problems. Student attendance, particularly within marginalised or minority groups, is a concern for many educational jurisdictions globally (Barlow & Fleischer, 2011; Rothman, 2001). The reasons for student absenteeism are complex. Variants such as age and locality affect student attendance rates, however low socio-economic status and ethnicity occur consistently as influencing factors (see Department for Education, National Statistics, 2013; Child Trends Data Bank, 2012; Purdie & Buckley, 2010, for discussions on factors influencing student absenteeism in the United Kingdom, Australia and the United States respectively), with these students being at a higher risk of complete disengagement from the educational system (Davies & Lee, 2006). Governments across many countries have identified absenteeism as a national concern and through the implementation of various policies and programs, are working to stem the tide of student absence (Davies & Lee, 2006).

With large amounts of energy and money being directed at getting children and young people into schools (throughout both the developing and developed world) it can be concluded that significant value is placed on what students will gain from attending school. If, as Connell (1980) outlines, schools reflect the 'social, cultural and political life … of contemporary human society' (p. 2), it is necessary to understand what role schools are expected to play in the development of young people as they grow to become participatory citizens. In other words, what is the purpose of schooling and what does it mean to receive an education?

5 The Purpose of Schooling

The question of what constitutes an education has been discussed and debated at length by philosophers for millennia, from Aristotle to Moore, and Rousseau to Dewey. Today the *purpose* of schooling is central to this debate, for it is within the confines of the school fence that governments, policy makers and educationalists work to deliver an education to their youngest citizens. To guide this, many countries describe the purpose of schooling within their contexts, through various law and/or policy documents. Johansson (2004) identified two consistent goals contained within these documents – 'passing on knowledge from one generation to the next and the upbringing of good and harmonious citizens who shall be able to take over and continue to develop our democratic societies' (p. 620). Despite these broad, overarching statements, 'the entire arena of the means and ends of education is as contentious now as it has ever been' (Apple, 2016, p. 129). This debate, although present since the inception of compulsory schooling more than a century ago, is reaching new heights in this global, neoliberal climate. Schools are very different places now to what they were one hundred years ago as they have developed and changed to reflect the socio-political zeitgeist of the present day. The appropriateness of the direction in which schooling has moved has been, and remains, contentious; does the purpose of schooling today align with current understanding of what education is and how the young within communities should receive it?

Since the 1980s schools, and the systems in which they operate, have undergone significant change under the influence of the dominant neoliberal global agenda. This has seen concepts such as competition, choice, growth, marketisation, standardisation, and improvement enter the educational discourse of many countries (Niesche & Keddie, 2016). As with any organisation or business operating under this agenda, success (or not) is measured through quantifiable output. Muller (2018) describes it like this: 'We live in the age of measured accountability, of reward for measured performance, and belief in the virtues of publicizing those metrics through "transparency"' (p. 16). For schools this has meant the introduction of accountability mechanisms such as standardised national and international tests (For example, Australia's NAPLAN testing, and the international tests TIMMS – Trends in International Mathematics and Science Study, and PISA – Programme for International Student Assessment), and teacher and principal performance standards. Within this context what can be easily measured counts (such as standardised test scores), and what is difficult to measure does not (such as a student's capacity to inquire and create). Many argue that the consequence of these accountability mechanisms for schools has been significant (see Muller, 2018; Apple, 2016; Sondel, 2016; Biesta, 2009; Cohen, 2006). Niesche and Keddie (2016) poignantly describe it as:

> delineating curriculum to focus on a narrow range of tested subjects, degrading pedagogy to a limited focus on instructional and rote larning, and reducing school and teacher value to their capacities to drive up student achievement on these subjects. (p. 16)

This narrowing of the curriculum does not align with what some see to be the purpose of schooling. R. S. Peters, a renowned British philosopher who has contributed much to this debate over the past half a century (Katz, 2010), espoused that education should be about the *whole man* (1970); a view shared by others who have written in the field over the millennia (For example, Plato in his work *The Republic*). As such, Peter's (1970) described it as 'incompatible with being narrowly specialised' (p. 6). Yet, as Niesche and Keddie (2016) outline above, this is precisely what has happened. This is reflected in (or perhaps dictated by) the policy that drives the delivery of schooling to many of the world's children and young people today. Cohen (2006) identifies the current state of play in schools as being 'driven by federal mandates' (pp. 201–202), where the sole focus is on improving literacy and numeracy standards, two of the areas consistently measured through the standardised testing regimes around the globe. While Cohen's paper focused on schooling in the United States, studies conducted throughout the world have noted similar shifts in the purpose of schooling (see Gilleylen et al., 2008, for a discussion on the UK; Shuayb & O'Donnell, 2008, for a detailed description of the purpose of schooling across five nations).

Adding further pressure to the work of schools over the past four decades has been the surge in the concept of 'market choice' within education systems across the globe. Proponents of this concept argue that it provides a freedom of 'choice', providing parents with the opportunity to choose the school that best suits the needs of their children. However, this presupposes two conditions; firstly that parents are in a position to make a credible decision about the quality (or not) of their children's schooling (Hutchings, 2017) and secondly that they have the financial and social means to send their children to the school of choice. The notion of choice laced with the concept of quality has heavily contributed to the metrification of education through measures such as the creation of league tables which inevitably create a very narrow and simplistic view of individual schools (Hardy & Boyle, 2011). On the other side of the debate there are those who argue that this system only perpetuates the problem of the widening educational gap between the 'haves' and the 'have nots', and given the evidence, it is an argument that is hard to dismiss. Schools performing at the lower end of the scale have a disproportionately high number of students from disadvantaged backgrounds, while higher performing schools attract students from privileged backgrounds (Niesche & Keddie, 2016). It is worth clarifying here what is meant by the term 'disadvantaged'. Rather than relating to any particular state of being, disadvantage refers to the incapacity of any individual or group to attain self-sufficiency as a result of one or more barriers. Mayer (2003) describes these barriers as including 'unavailability of resources, inaccessibility to resources, the society's regard for a group, government and corporate practices, and certain conditions of the group itself' (p. 3).

While education is considered to be a tool that can combat the barriers faced by disadvantaged groups, there are those who believe that the current state of schooling across the globe perpetuates rather than removes these obstacles.

This thinking is not new. Freire, a Brazilian educator and philosopher (who it should be noted was exiled from his homeland in 1964 after serving a prison sentence for being a 'revolutionary and an ignorant' (Gerhardt, 1993, p. 439), spent his life trying to change the systems of education that he described as perpetuating oppression. In his seminal work *Pedagogy of the oppressed*, first published in 1968, Freire (2005) expressed a deep concern for those within society who he named as the 'oppressed' (who today might be referred to as the 'disadvantaged'). He argued that the education being provided to them by those with the power to control it – the 'oppressors' – was perpetuating their position of oppression rather than providing them with the educational prowess to rise above their current status and find what he described as 'freedom and justice' (p. 44). Freire (2005) blamed 'neoliberal fatalism' for this, an agenda 'informed by the ethics of the market, an ethics in which a minority makes most profits against the lives of the majority. In other words, those who cannot compete, die' (pp. 25–26). Freire was not the only educationalist of his time to express these concerns. In 1979 Harris, an educational philosopher penned his thoughts about the state of education:

> *we* give our children a distortive and misrepresentative way of perceiving and knowing the world; a structured misrepresentation of reality, which favours one section of society and works against the interests of other sections, and yet does not seem to be that way. (p. 165)

The construct of power must, if only briefly, be brought into the discussion here. The concerns of Freire and Harris are grounded in the idea that the power relationship between those providing the education and those receiving it are not equal. This is a point that would be futile to argue as education is a 'socially constructed entity, and these social constructions are based on struggles of power between different paradigms, vocabularies and communities of research in all sorts of constellations' (Romer, 2011, p. 762). It would be easy to throw one's hands up and give in to the fact that many of the current systems of education across the globe are inherently flawed, particularly when, as Artiles (2003) emphatically proclaims: 'Schools organize activities, define roles for teachers and students, and create rules to privilege nondisabled middle-class students. Procedures and other institutional processes are orchestrated to instil in students particular (affective, cognitive) dispositions that reproduce their status in society' (p. 181). Despite this, hope must be placed in the idea of emancipation through education, as ultimately 'people should have the power to shape the social processes that fulfil their human rights rather than being merely the passive recipients of it' (Gilabert, 2015, p. 211). This should be the inherent purpose of education, the purpose of schooling.

Depending on which side of the neoliberal fence one sits, it may be considered either a fortuitous or a sorrowful state that the concerns raised by Freire and Harris are still being written about by educationalists and philosophers in the 21st century. As noted briefly at the beginning of this section, one of the major concerns being espoused about the work of schools today is around what has happened (and is still happening) to the curriculum that students are being taught. There is a general agreement within the literature that the past few decades has seen a constricting of the curriculum globally, with the work of schools today 'more and more being constructed as the effective production of pre-defined 'learning outcomes' in a small number of subjects or with regard to a limited set of identities' (Biesta, 2013b, p. 2). Sondel (2016) lays blame for this at the feet of the market-based system in which educational institutions now operate. He argues that the purpose of teaching (and as a consequence the purpose of schooling) has shifted to now be about 'the production of assessment data' (p. 172), collected generally from three subject areas (English, Mathematics and Science), albeit in a very narrow and often contentious way; it goes without saying that assessment data like this can only be collected on aspects of these curriculum areas that are quantifiably measurable. Apple (2017) believes the reason for this shift in the purpose of schooling is relatively simple – schooling is now about the production of human capital. In a world that relies upon economic growth and competition to survive, schools must work to 'produce a skilled and competitive labor force' (Artiles, 2003, p. 166). Implied in this notion is the concept of 'winners and losers' (Artiles, 2003); if schools are focusing on a narrow set of curricula that is quantifiably measured, some students are going to do better than others. Some will win and some will lose. Some will complete their schooling, go on to further education and finally land stable high paying jobs, and others will not gain employment at all. Some will have their culture, their identity, their status within society bolstered, while others will lose their sense of belonging (Sondel, 2016; Biesta, 2015). It is easy to draw the conclusion that those for whom the education system works are going to be the 'winners'. It is those students who do not fit within the narrowing confines of what is delivered within schools today under the banner of 'education', who are losers. Apple (2016) concurs, 'the basic ends and means of education are becoming so limited that education (perhaps "training" is a better word?) is increasingly only about serving an increasingly unequal economy' (p. 131).

The majority of current schooling systems are not working; they are not meeting the needs of all of the world's young people. Consequently, there is an urgent need for the educational discourse to be brought back to that ambitious but necessary question – what does it mean to provide a 'good education'? This is a debate that, since the 70's, has been somewhat forgotten. However, as nations across the globe face many new and unpredictable challenges, it is one that must be reignited (Potthoff et al., 2009).

6 Inclusive Education and the 'Good Education' Debate

Since the publication of the Salamanca Statement (UNESCO) in 1994, a growing number of organisations and nations have championed inclusive education as the right and acceptable way to educate all students (Pellicano, Bolte, & Stahmer, 2018). Despite these decades of acceptance, actually defining the term inclusive education and identifying what it should look like has proven more difficult, so much so that some have suggested that those in the field should stop trying to define the construct of inclusive education, and begin the process of delivering it (Pellicano, Bolte, & Stahmer, 2018; Slee, 2013). It is not surprising then that education systems globally have struggled with the implementation of inclusive practices (Schlessinger, 2018; Slee, 2018; Anderson & Boyle, 2019). In fact, many systems still provide segregated classroom and school settings for students with particular educational needs (see the work of Anastasiou & Kauffman, 2010; Warnock, 2010; Zigmond, Kloo & Volonino, 2009 for arguments about why this is necessary), and in countries such as Australia, the rates of students being excluded from school all together are increasing (Anderson & Boyle, 2019). Despite these inconsistencies and seemingly contradictory practices, inclusive education is still the prevailing philosophy for the education of all students in the majority of countries around the world; though it is not yet considered a moral human right (Gordon, 2013).

Inclusive education raises questions about the 'ethical norms and standards of justice' that education systems work by as they consider the educational needs of every, unique student (Reindal, 2016, p. 9). Should they be guided by a moral imperative to provide an inclusive education, no matter the needs of the student (Gordon, 2013)? While this question is too big to answer here, it does bring to the fore the notion that inclusive education is grounded in the philosophy that human diversity is something to be valued, and should be considered part of the bigger social justice debate (Thomas, 2013), in which education is already a major player.

As discussed earlier in this chapter, research supports the notion that better educated people have better life outcomes, and with this comes stronger community engagement and connection. Schools are at the centre of this push towards more socially just societies. Mulcahy (2008) maintains that 'if school is considered the preparatory stage of education … schooling must have the same educational objectives for all children without exception' (p. 76). Dewey (1916), more than a hundred years ago, described the best way to develop a strong society was to educate students in social groups made up of individuals from many different backgrounds with many different interests, where the interaction between these individuals was full and free. Mulcahy (2008) and Dewey (2016) both present arguments that education must be delivered in an equitable manner to all students for it to be an effective part of the broader shift towards a more socially just world. Unfortunately, education has not proved itself to be the social leveller that so many promised as the gap between the haves and have nots has continued to grow (Niesche & Keddie, 2016).

This raises serious questions about who is setting the 'agenda (for) and defin(ing) the terms of' education (Biesta, 2013a, p. 8). Really, what grounds are there for saying that 'one form of life', as is depicted and experienced within schools, is better than another (Hirst & Peters, 1970, p. 41)? It could be argued that the current system, rather than levelling the field and providing new opportunities, actually duplicates and reinforces the existing disparities in wealth, power and opportunities of different groups, or at least does not challenge it (Gilabert, 2015; Romer, 2011; Freire, 2005). After all, if a student is expected to perform poorly, either socially or academically, due to a characteristic of their being, then they are likely to meet this expectation (Gadsen, Davis, & Artiles, 2009). This concept of power is an important one.

> Power and privilege shape tangible and intangible aspects of the educational system such as the goals of education, the curriculum, and the organizational structures and processes of schools. If the role of power and privilege is not examined explicitly, we run the risk of perpetuating longstanding inequalities suffered by members of other minority groups. (Artiles, Harris-Murri, & Rostenberg, 2006, p. 264)

While further exploration of this particular issue is beyond the scope of this chapter, when considered with each of the other points raised about the current educational climate, a set of provocative questions need to be asked when talking about inclusive education. Is the current education system one that is worth being included into? Is it a system that everyone wants to be included into? If not, then should they be forced to participate in it? (Mac Ruairc, 2013).

7 Conclusion

To answer these questions with the deserved integrity would involve a much deeper exploration of the system and those it purports to educate than it is possible to present here. Rather, this chapter has attempted to demonstrate the need for a reigniting of the debate about what 'good education' is, particularly when looking at it through the reflective lens of inclusive education. Current educational discourse and policy are imbued with paradoxical values and colliding agendas (Furlong, 2013), and many of these are in *fundamental contradiction* to inclusive education (Hall, Collins, Benjamin, Nind, & Sheehy, 2004). Despite all of this, Reindal (2016) argues that this debate and reflection is absolutely paramount, as any work to create a more inclusive environment for all students will require 'the transformation of the philosophy, values and practices of entire educational systems' (Artiles et al., 2006, p. 260) – it will require the delivery of 'good' education.

References

Ainscow, M., Chapman, C., Dyson, A., Gunter, D., Hall, D., Kerr, K., McNamara, O., Muijs, D., Raffo, C., & West, M. (2011). *Insight 2, Social inequality: Can schools narrow the gap?* British Educational Research Association.

Allman, P. (2001). *Critical education against global capitalism: Karl Marx and revolutionary critical education.* Bergin & Garvey.

Anastasiou, D., & Kauffman, J. (2010). Disability as cultural difference: Implications for special education. *Remedial and Special Education, 33*(3), 139–149. https://doi.org/10.1177/0741932510383163

Anderson, J., & Boyle, C. (2019). Looking in the mirror: Reflecting on 25 years of inclusive education in Australia. *International Journal of Inclusive Education, 23*(7–8), 796-810. https://doi-org.ezproxy.une.edu.au/10.1080/13603116.2019.1622802

Apple, M. (2015). Reframing the question of whether education can change society. *Educational Theory, 65*(3), 299–315. https://doi.org/ 10.1111/edth.12114

Apple, M. (2016). Introduction to "the politics of educational reforms". *The Educational Reform, 80*(2), 127–136. https://doi.org/10.1080/00131725.2016.1135382

Apple, M. (2017). What is present and absent in critical analyses of Neoliberalism in education. *Peabody Journal of Education, 92*(1), 148–153. https://doi.org/10.1080/0161956X.2016.1265344

Artiles, A. (2003). Special education's changing identity: Paradoxes and dilemmas in views of culture and space. *Harvard Educational Review, 73*(2), 164–202. https://doi.org/10.17763/haer.73.2.j78t573x377j7106

Artiles, A., Harris-Murri, N., & Rostenberg, D. (2006). Inclusion as social justice: Critical notes on discourses, assumptions, and the road ahead. *Theory into Practice, 45*(3), 260–268. https://doi.org/10.1207/s15430421tip4503_8

Bale, J., & Knopp, S. (2012). *Education and capitalism: Struggles for learning and liberation*. Haymarket Books.

Barlow, J., & Fleischer, S. (2011). Student absenteeism: Whose responsibility? *Education and Teaching International, 48*(3), 227–237. https://doi.org/10.1080/14703297.2011.593700

Beachum, F. (2011). Culturally relevant leadership for complex 21st-century school contexts. In F. English (Ed.), *The Sage handbook of educational leadership: Advances in theory, research, and practice* (2nd ed., pp. 26–34). Sage.

Biesta, G. (2007). Why "what works" won't work: Evidence-based practice and the democratic deficit in educational research. *Educational Theory, 57*(1), 1–22. https://doi.org/10.1111/j.17415446.2006.00241.x

Biesta, G. (2009). Good education in an age of measurement: On the need to reconnect with the question of purpose in education. *Educational Assessment, Evaluation and Accountability, 21*(1), 33–46. https://doi.org/0.1007/s11092-008-9064-9

Biesta, G. (2013a). Interrupting the politics of learning. *Power and Education, 5*(1), 4–15. https://doi.org/10.2304/power.2013.5.1.4

Biesta, G. (2013b). *The beautiful risk of education*. Paradigm Publishers.

Biesta, G. (2015). What is education for? On good education, teacher judgment, and educational professional professionalism. *European Journal of Education, 50*(1), 74–87. https://doi.org/10.1111/ejed.12109

Bregman, R. (2017). *Utopia for realists and how we get there*. Bloomsbury.

Bronfenbrenner, U. (1976). The experimental ecology of education. *Educational Researcher, 5*(5), 5–15. https://doi.org/10.2307/1174755

Child Trends Data Bank. (2012). *Student absenteeism: Indicators on children and youth*. Author.

Cohen, J. (2006). Social, emotional, ethical, and academic education: Creating a climate for learning, participation in democracy, and well-being. *Harvard Educational Review, 76*(2), 201–237, 285. https://doi.org/10.17763/haer.76.2.j44854x1524644vn

Cole, L. (1950). *A history of education: Socrates to Montessori*. Rinehart & Company.

Connell, D. (1980). *A history of education in the twentieth century world*. Australian Curriculum Development Centre.

Dastidar, A. (2012). Income distribution and structural transformation: Empirical evidence from developed and developing countries. *Seoul Journal of Economics, 25*(1), 25–56.

Davies, J., & Lee, J. (2006). To attend or not to attend? Why some students chose school and others reject it. *Support for Learning, 21*(4), 204–209. https://doi.org/10.1111/j.1467-9604.2006.00433.x

Department for Education, National Statistics. (2013). *Pupil absence in schools in England, including pupil characteristics: 2011/2012*. Author.

Dewey, J. (1916). *Democracy and education: An introduction to the philosophy of education*. Macmillan.

Field, S., Kuczera, M., & Pont, B. (2007). *No more failures: Ten steps to equity in education*. OECD Publications.

Foster, J. (2011). Education and the structural crisis of capital: The U.S. case. *Monthly Review, 63*(3), 6–37.

Freire, P. (2005). *Pedagogy of the oppressed* (30th ed.). The Continuum International Publishing Group.

Furlong, J. (2013). Globalisation, neoliberalism, and the reform of teacher education in England. *The Educational Forum, 77*(1), 28–50. https://doi.org/10.1080/00131725.2013.739017

Gadsen, V., Davis, J., & Artiles, A. (2009). Introduction: Risk, equity, and schooling: Transforming the discourse. *Review of Research in Education, 33*(1), vii–xi. https://doi.org/10.3102/0091732X08330002

Gerhardt, D. (1993). Paulo Freire. *Prospects: The Quarterly Review of Comparative Education, 23*(3–4), 439–458.

Gilabert, P. (2015). Human rights, human dignity, and power. In R. Cruft, S. Liao, & M. Renzo (Eds.), *Philosophical foundations of human rights* (pp. 196–213). Oxford University Press.

Gilleylen, J., Hoogasian, J., Hunt, R., Johnson, E., Kristie, A., Landolfi, J., ... Schall, E. (2008). *The purpose of schooling: Beliefs and practices of educators in British schools* (TERC Documents, Paper 6).

Gordon, J. (2013). Is inclusive education a human right? *Journal of Law, Medicine & Ethics, 41*(4), 754–767. https://doi.org/10.1111/jlme.12087

Hall, K., Collins, J., Benjamin, S., Nind, M., & Sheehy, K. (2004). SATurated models of pupildom: Assessment and inclusion/exclusion. *British Educational Research Journal, 30*(6), 801–872. https://doi.org/10.1080/0141192042000279512

Hardy, I., & Boyle, C. (2011). My school? Critiquing the abstraction and quantification of education. *Asia-Pacific Journal of Teacher Education, 39*(3), 211–222. https://doi.org/10.1080/1359866X.2011.588312

Harris, K. (1979). *Education and knowledge: The structured misrepresentation of reality*. Routledge & Kegan Paul.

Hirst, P., & Peters, R. (1970). *The logic of education*. Routledge & Kegan Paul.

Hutchings, M. (2017). Accountability measures: The factory farm version of education. *The Psychology of Education Review, 41*(1), 3–15.

Johansson, O. (2004). Democracy and leadership – Or training for democratic leadership. *Journal of Educational Administration, 42*(6), 620–624. https://doi.org/10.1108/09578230410563629

Katz, M. (2010). R.S. Peters' normative conception of education and educational aims. *Journal of Philosophy of Education, 43*(S1), 97–108. https://doi.org/10.1111/j.1467-9752.2009.00734.x

Kerr, K., & West, M. (2010). *Insight 2: Social inequality: Can schools narrow the gap?* British Educational Research Association. Retrieved from https://www.bera.ac.uk/publication/social-inequality-can-schools-narrow-the-gap

Ki-Moom, B. (2014). *Speech given at the emergency coalition for education action.* United Nations.

Lochner, L. (2011). *Non-production benefits of education: Crime, health, and good citizenship* (Working Paper 16722). National Bureau of Economic Research. Retrieved from https://www.nber.org/papers/w16722

Machin, S., Marie, O., & Vujic, S. (2011). The crime reducing effect of education. *The Economic Journal, 121*(522), 463–484. https://doi.org/10.1111/j.1468-0297.2011.02430.x

MacRuairc, G. (2013). Including who? Deconstructing the discourse. In G. MacRuairc, E. Ottensen, & R. Precey (Eds.), *Leadership for inclusive education: Values, vision and voices* (pp. 9–18). Sense Publishers.

Marsh, J. (2011). *Class dismissed: Why we cannot teach or learn our way out of inequality.* New York University Press.

Mayer, S. (2003). *What is a 'disadvantaged group'?* Effective Communities Project Minneapolis.

McMahon, B. (2013). Conflicting conceptions of the purposes of schooling in a democracy. *Journal of Thought, 48*(1), 17–32. https://doi.org/10.2307/jthought.48.1.17

Milanovic, B. (2012). Global inequality recalculated and updated: The effect of the new PPP estimates on global inequality and 2005 estimates. *Journal of Economic Inequality, 10*(1), 1–18. doi:10.1007/s10888-010-9155-doi

Milanovic, B. (2016). Income inequality is cyclical. *Nature, 537*, 479–482. doi:10.1038/537479a

Miller, D. (1999). *Principles of social justice.* Harvard University Press.

Mishriky, M., Murphy, T., Preleski, L., Rigano, J., Schall E., & Zafrin, L. (2008). *The purpose of schooling: Beliefs and practices of educators in British schools* (TERC Documents, Paper 6). Retrieved from http://digitalcommons.uconn.edu

Mounk, D. (2017). *The age of responsibility: Luck, choice, and the welfare state.* Harvard University Press.

Mulcahy, D. (2008). *The educated person.* Rowman & Littlefield.

Muller, J. (2018). *The tyranny of metrics.* Princeton University Press.

Niesche, R., & Keddie, A. (2016). *Leadership, ethics and schooling for social justice.* Routledge.

OECD. (2010). *The high cost of low educational performance: The long-run economic impact of improving PISA outcomes.* OECD Publishing.

OECD. (2017). *The OECD handbook for innovative learning environments*. OECD Publishing. http://dx.doi.org/9789264277274-en

O'Hear, A. (1981). *Education, society and human nature: An introduction to the philosophy of education*. Routledge & Kegan Paul Ltd.

Pellicano, L., Bolte, S., & Stahmer, A. (2018). The current illusion of educational inclusion. *Autism, 22*(4), 386–387. doi:10.1177/1362361318766166

Peters, R. S. (1970). Education and the educated man. *Journal of Philosophy of Education, 4*(1), 5–20. doi:10.1111/j.1467-9752.1970.tb00424.x

Plato. (2016). *The Republic. The project Guttenberg eBook* (B. Jowett, Trans.). Penguin.

Potthoff, D., Mantle-Bromley, C., Clark, Kleinsasser, A., Badiali, B., & Baugh, S. (2009). *Finding a common purpose for schooling in the United States: Why do we educate in a democracy?* Work in Progress, Institute for Educational Inquiry, University of Washington. Retrieved from https://scholar.google.com.au/scholar

Purdie, N., & Buckley, S. (2010). *School attendance and retention of Indigenous Australian students: Issue paper No 1*. Australian Government.

Rawls, J. (1999). *A theory of justice*. Oxford University Press.

Rawls, J. (2001). *Justice as fairness: A restatement*. Belknap, Harvard.

Reardon, S. (2011). The widening academic achievement gap between the rich and the poor: New evidence and possible explanations. In G. Duncan & R. Murnane (Eds.), *Whither opportunity? Rising inequality, schools, and children's life chances* (pp. 91–116). Russell Sage Foundation.

Reindal, M. (2016). Discussing inclusive education: An inquiry into different interpretations and a search for ethical aspects of inclusion using the capabilities approach. *European Journal of Special Needs Education, 31*(1), 1–12. doi:10.1080/08856257.2015.1087123

Romer, T. (2011). Postmodern education and the concept of power. *Educational Philosophy and Theory, 43*(7), 755–772. doi:10.1111/j.1469-5812.2009.00566.x

Rothman, S. (2001). School absence and student background factors: A multilevel analysis. *International Education Journal, 2*(1), 59–68.

Rougoor, D., & Van Marrewijk, C. (2015). Demography, growth and global income inequality. *World Development, 74*, 220–232. doi:10.1016/j.worlddev.2015.05.013

Schlessinger, S. (2018). Reclaiming teacher intellectualism through and for inclusive education. *International Journal of Inclusive Education, 22*(3), 268–284. doi:10.1080/13603116.2017.1362598

Shoho, A., Merchant, B., & Lugg, C. (2011). Social justice: Seeking a common language. In F. English (Ed.), *The Sage handbook of educational leadership: Advances in theory, research, and practice* (2nd ed., pp. 35–55). Sage.

Shuayb, M., & O'Donnell, S. (2008). *Aims and values in primary education: England and other countries* (Primary Review Research Survey 1/2). University of Cambridge Faculty of Education.

Slee, R. (2013). How do we make inclusive education happen when exclusion is a political predisposition? *International Journal of Inclusive Education, 17*(8), 895–907. doi:10.1080/13603116.2011.602534

Slee, R. (2018). *Inclusive education isn't dead, it just smells funny*. Routledge Cavendish.

Soltis, J. (1968). *An introduction to the analysis of educational concepts*. Addison-Wesley Publishing Company Inc.

Sondel, B. (2016). "No excuses" in New Orleans: The silent passivity of Neoliberal schooling. *The Educational Forum, 80*(2), 171–188. doi:10.1080/00131725.2016.1135376

Thomas, G. (2013). A review of thinking and research about inclusive education policy with suggestions of a new kind of inclusive thinking. *British Educational Research Journal, 39*(3), 473–490. doi:10.1080/01411926.2011.652070

UNESCO. (2015). *Education for all 2000–2015: Achievements and challenges*. UNESCO Publishing.

UNICEF. (2013). *The state of the world's children: Children with disabilities – 2013*. Author.

UNICEF. (2014). *The state of the world's children: Every child counts – 2014*. Author.

United Nations. (2012). *Global education first initiative: The UN secretary-general's global initiative on education*. Author.

United Nations. (2013). *We can end poverty: Millennium development goals and beyond 2015, fact sheet*. UN Department of Public Information. Author.

Warnock, M. (2010). Special educational needs: A new look. In L. Terzi (Ed.), *Special educational needs: A new look* (pp. 11–45). Continuum.

Wilkinson, R., & Pickett, K. (2010). *The spirit level: Why equality is better for everyone*. Penguin Group.

World Bank Group. (2016). *Government expenditure on education, total (% of GDP)*. The World Bank.

Zigmond, N., Kloo, A., & Volonino, V. (2009). What, where and how? Special education in the climate of full inclusion. *Exceptionality, 17*(4), 189–204. doi:10.1080/09362830903231986

CHAPTER 3

'Good' Education in a Neo-Liberal Paradigm: Challenges, Contradictions and Consternations

Joanna Anderson and Christopher Boyle

1 Introduction

Perhaps there is no single answer to the question of what constitutes a 'good' education within schooling systems. If there were, one would hope that it would have been found by now. In his book looking at the big questions in life, contemporary philosopher Simon Blackburn gives an insight into the difficulties of answering this type of complex, philosophical question; 'There will be many answers in different contexts, rather than one big answer, and it is progress to realize this' (2009, p. 1). Nevertheless, it is an inescapable reality that education matters, and providing a 'good' education matters. So while there are still students for whom the current systems are failing (Mounk, 2017), the question must continually be placed in the way of those who are responsible for delivering education, from policy makers, to academics, to educators themselves. Why? Because, in the words of the late South African president Nelson Mandela, 'education is the most powerful weapon which you can use to change the world' (de Villiers, 2015, para. 1).

2 Neo-liberalism: A Brief Overview

It is important here, before getting too far into this discussion, to define what is meant by the term *neo-liberal* or *neo-liberalism*, and its relationship to education. Ross and Gibson (2006) cite neo-liberalism as the 'prevailing political economic paradigm' (p. 2) globally. It draws from 'proponents of neoclassical economics, social conservatives, libertarians and liberals' (Anderson & Donchik, 2016, p. 324) and the past thirty years has seen its 'language, ideas and policies' impact not only the economies of countries, but also their cultures (Denniss, 2018, p. 2). Glendinning (2015) defines neo-liberalism in the following way:

> (T)he outlook of a community of ideas that seeks the limitless extension of the norms of conduct of one domain of life to the whole of life. Its

 | DOI: 10.1163/9789004431171_003

> emancipatory claim is that it will achieve the optimal flourishing of the whole of life by co-ordinating and controlling it in terms dictated by the norms of that one domain. The guiding assumption of every neoliberal community of ideas is that human flourishing in life in general requires that one particular domain of life – the interests of one particular community of ideas – should rule. Neoliberalism in our time is, that is to say, understood as an economic neoliberalism. It is construed as an ideological conception that says every problem has a market solution or a solution within the logic of the market. (pp. 9–10)

The belief is that any market solution will be better than that which could be offered by any other, as 'the profit motive of companies, combined with consumers' ability to choose the product that suits them best, will result in the best possible social and economic outcomes' (Denniss, 2018, p. 33). In this sense, Apple (2017) describes the world as being like one 'vast supermarket' (p. 149), where consumers choice lays in what companies offer, without there being the option of any alternatives (Denniss, 2018). What does all of this mean for education?

Education is 'an inherently political act' (Aasen, Proitz, & Sandberg, 2014, p. 721) and has therefore been profoundly influenced by decades of working within a neo-liberal paradigm. This influence can be seen in the determining factors of such critical questions in education such as 'who', 'what', 'when', 'where' and 'how', being drawn from 'who ultimately gains the most from the ways that schools, the curriculum, and practices are organized and operated' (Aasen, Proitz, & Sandberg, 2014, p. 721). In this sense, education has come to be about those elements that are commonly attributed to neo-liberalism – marketisation, competition and profit (Apple, 2017). This chapter will interrogate the influence of these elements on education, but will also consider some other possibilities put forward by those who have a different view about where education should be heading. Neo-liberalism may have narrowed global policy agendas (Denniss, 2018) and as a result, pose a genuine threat to 'truly public education' (Apple, 2017), however 'the simple fact is that the world is full of alternatives' (Denniss, 2018, p. 17).

3 Good Education in the 21st Century

A 'good' education should expand 'everyone's freedom' to live better lives, through the development of the capacity to think for oneself (Warnock, 1973). Biesta and Safstrom (2011) describe it as 'a liberating process, a process aimed at the realisation of freedom' (p. 541). While the result of 'good' education should be equivalent for all, this does not dictate that everyone should receive the *same* education (Warnock, 1973). In fact it espouses an opposing notion. Noddings and Slote (2003) identify the inarguable fact that each community has a different set of traditions and values, therefore providing a universal or *one-size-fits-all* schooling system will not work. It is this notion of different sets of traditions and values that has made the seemingly simple task of defining what education actually is, and in turn what 'good' education is, problematic. To educate someone implies that something of value is being passed on, however what is considered to be of value is very different between individuals, communities and nations (Soltis, 1968). The result of this is that in the pursuit of providing a description or definition of education, a value-laden explanation is produced and anything value-laden will sit comfortably with some but not all. This simple notion lays bare the complexities of working to understand what it means to provide a 'good' education.

Education is inarguably influenced by what is considered to be 'valued' by society – politically, economically and also socially (O'Hear, 1981). Physical and menial work, and anything that is considered to be 'unskilled', is low paid and held in low regard by society (the reciprocity between these two concepts would be interesting to explore further). At the other end, professional and so-called 'high skilled' positions are rewarded by higher incomes and greater social status. As a consequence, curricula in many countries have, in recent years, shifted to contain greater amounts of 'academic' work, while the more traditional 'hands on' and creative subjects have disappeared. This has been precipitated by the development of standardised curriculum frameworks, such as those recently developed and implemented in Australia and the UK, where curriculum is an 'extrinsic imposition' rather than something that is designed by schools and their wider communities (Silbeck, 1984). Biesta (2010) attributes this 'academisation' of curricula to the political, economic and social influences of the past two decades, rather than having anything to do with what is 'good' for education.

Almost 40 years ago O'Hear (1981) warned that societies 'dismissed at their peril' this external influence on education. He argued that this influence would have ongoing and lasting ramifications. With the focus being directed towards a purely academic curriculum and subsequent standardised outcomes, schools do not always have the flexibility or capacity to provide what all of their students need. For those students seeking and able to engage with the academic curriculum, all is good. However, the story is different for students who do not fit this mould. For some, this type of education is inappropriate and may in fact alienate rather than engage, as Bantock (1963) candidly pointed out more than 50 years ago:

> Drag a lad ... through the process of education and what do you produce in him, in the end? A profound contempt for education and for all educated people. It has meant nothing to him but irritation and disgust. And that which a man finds irritating and disgusting he finds odious and contemptible. (p. 78)

The consequences of this can be significant, for both the individual and society (Mounk, 2017). But rather than questioning the ramifications of 'academiatising' the curriculum, governments are punishing the young people for whom the system does not work. In many countries, young people must be engaged in some type of formal education program or working, or they will be financially penalised as they cannot access any welfare support (see for example the Australian Governments 'earn or learn' policy; in England and in the majority of states in the USA, you must be either in education or working until age 18). These punitive systems have been put into place to keep young people at school, but do nothing to address the 'why' of these policies needing to be there in the first place.

Given this, perhaps the focus for governments should not be on dictating the 'what' (in other words standardising the curriculum), but rather on the 'how' – how can we deliver to all young people across the globe an education that is 'good' for them, one that gives them what they need to become engaged, contributing and content members of a healthy society? Biesta (2015) provides a contemporary approach to this question in his 'three domains of educational purpose'.

3.1 *Three Domains of Educational Purpose*

According to Biesta (2015), there are three domains of educational purpose, and each of these needs to be considered for education to be 'good' (see Figure 3.1).

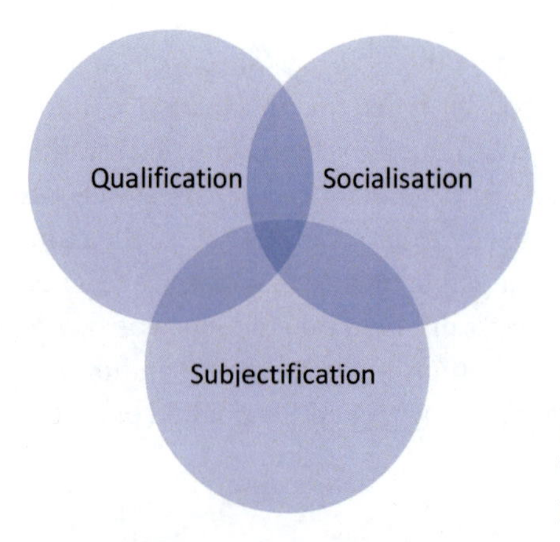

FIGURE 3.1
The three domains of educational purpose (from Biesta, 2015, p. 78)

Each of these domains has its own, very distinctive description, as provided in Table 3.1.

While it is acknowledged that this is one scholar's representation of the complex notion that is 'good' education, it does provide an illustration that aligns with work others have done in this area over the millennia (for example see Plato, 2016; Freire, 2005; Peters, 1970). Of significance is its assertion that the purpose of education must consider the whole person, both as an individual and as a member of the community/ies in which they live. The *domains of educational purpose* provide a model on which to begin the discussion on the complexities involved with trying to deliver a 'good' education, particularly under the current neo-liberal paradigm.

Where 'good' education fits within the context of Biesta's model will depend on what the needs of the particular child or young person and their community are. Nevertheless, this seemingly simple model makes a number of challenges to delivering a 'good' education glaringly apparent. The first challenge is the current educational climate, one that is replicated in many countries across the globe. Currently, the focus of education is on the domain of *qualification*, where there is excessive pressure on students (and teachers) to not only achieve to a set of standards, but to continually improve their results (Biesta, 2015). This expectation is set around a very narrow number of subject areas, and even within these subjects around a very narrow set of skills and understandings. Biesta (2015) believes that this strong focus on *qualification* is coming at the expense of the other two domains, meaning that students are not receiving all they need to, to be deemed to be getting a 'good' education.

TABLE 3.1 A description of the domains of educational purpose

Domain	**Definition**
Qualification	The transition and acquisition of knowledge, skills and dispositions. It allows people to 'do' something, it qualifies them.
Socialisation	The representation and initiation of people into traditions and ways of 'being and doing' – cultural, professional, political, religious traditions and so on. The way we identify with and are identified by these.
Subjectification	The positive or negative impact on a person of the education they receive, the qualities of being 'a subject' – autonomy, independence, responsibility, criticality and the capacity for judgment.

The focus on the *qualification* domain presents the second challenge – what content should be taught? This is an issue that could be a chapter in itself, however the important point to note here is that the content in education in many countries has become 'standardised', meaning there is set content that students are expected to be taught and set standards that students are expected to achieve, regardless of circumstances. An example of this can be seen in Australia, which is a country of eight educational jurisdictions, each with its own unique set of circumstances. In this multicultural nation students from countries all over the world learn alongside the nation's indigenous students, in classrooms situated in skyscrapers to single classroom schools hundreds of kilometres from anywhere. Students arrive at school each morning having come from a variety of communities and environments. The lived experiences, understandings and interests of these students vary greatly, as is to be expected. However once at school they are all delivered the same curriculum at the same time, and have the same expectations placed on them to achieve certain sets of standards at certain points during their schooling years. Australia is not the only country where this occurs; any system that operates using a standard set of curricula faces this issue. Mulcahy (2008) is sceptical of the intentions of those who make the decisions about standard curricula, the 'powerful interests' who dictate what is taught in schools. Author Thomas Frank (2016) also raises questions, describing education in the United States as being ruled by those he identifies as the 'political elite'. This area needs critical study. Artiles, Harris-Murri, and Rostenberg (2006) agree, arguing that questions need to be asked about the content being taught to students, and the way that it perpetuates rather than challenges current inequities in the education system, especially against those of minority racial and ethnic groups, and those with disabilities. Harris (1979) took this a step further and labelled the process of determining what will be 'included in' and what will be 'left out' of the curriculum as *political manipulation*. It is about what is valued by Frank's (2016) 'political elite' at a given point in time.

The final challenge to be discussed here is one that exists around the 'socialisation' domain. The very definition of this domain raises issues – what 'traditions and ways of 'being and doing' are students being initiated into? Each students' individual circumstances will dictate that the 'traditions and ways of 'being and doing' they experience or will experience as they grow will be unique in some way. Even if students live in similar circumstances, what this means and looks like in one community is going to be distinctive from what it means and looks like in another. This once again poses challenges for education systems that are insisting on delivering standardised curricula and standardised outcomes. As with the *qualification* domain, what is included into and excluded from this domain derives from what is valued at any given point in time by those with the power to make these decisions (Freire, 2005).

Controversy about what is included in or excluded from the curriculum, across each of Biesta's domains, is not new. Early last century Dewey (1934) acknowledged that different societies have different needs, and therefore it should be they who determine what is taught within their schools. Decades later Silbeck (1984) explored this notion further and developed the concept of 'school-based curriculum development'. Here, the 'planning, design, implementation and evaluation' (p. 2) of a curricula is undertaken by the school itself, not in isolation, but in conjunction with 'the larger educational environment, and the wider social and cultural environments' (p. 2). This way of thinking accepts Blackburn's (2009) theory that big questions, such as what constitutes a 'good' education, may not have a single, 'one size fits all' answer, and also negates many of the issues raised about education delivery in this section. Curriculum development undertaken by schools and their communities, with consideration of Biesta's three domains of educational purpose, may be one way of steering education towards that which could be considered to be 'good'; good for all students. Be that as it may, any shift towards this type of curriculum development and delivery is unlikely in the current global neo-liberal climate. There is a myriad of reasons for this and while it is not possible to explore all of them here, three of the most significant impacts of neo-liberalism on education, 'good' education, will be scrutinised: current educational discourse, measurement and education, and value. A failure to question the impact of these constructs on schooling presents a 'threat to the strive for good education' (Biesta, 2015, p. 84).

4 The Impact of Current Educational Rhetoric on 'Good' Education

There are two reasons why it is important to explore the changing use of language in educational rhetoric. First, words matter! Language plays a critical role in shaping the way things such as education, are understood (Denniss, 2018; Berg & Englund, 2014; Arduin, 2013), both by those working in the profession, and by society at large. A direct consequence of this, and the second reason for this exploration, is that language is used as a tool by those who want to affect change in the way something is understood (Kloch, 2012). It follows then that any change in educational rhetoric is going to have an influence on the way education is viewed and understood, and these changes have been made by those with the power to do so, in an effort to affect this change. Two examples of the changing language of education will be explored here: the shift from 'good' to 'effective' education, and the increasing use of the terms 'learning' and 'learner/s'.

Noticeably absent in contemporary rhetoric on educational policies and schooling systems is the term 'good' education. Instead, the term 'effective' education has become part of the vernacular used by governments, policy makers and now those working within educational systems. The significance of this new terminology can be seen in the establishment of centres such as the Institute for Effective Education (based at the University of York in the UK) and the biannual journal published since 2009 by Taylor & Francis entitled 'Effective Education'. While this may seem a small and insignificant shift, the move from talking about 'good' to talking about 'effective' education has worked to deviate the focus from *what* students are achieving, to one that is concerned with *whether or not* students are achieving; 'we no longer talk about the inherent value of educating our children, but of the increase in skills and productivity that their education will provide' (Denniss, 2018, p. 14). The logic behind this change in rhetoric sits within the context of the current neo-liberal agenda for education.

Effective education takes a 'technical and quantified' approach to policy and is focused on terms such as 'evidence-based' and 'what works' (Gorur & Koyama, 2013). This is in an attempt to 'impose order within a field that is complexified by the inter-related, the local, the specific and the idiosyncratic' (Gorur & Koyama, 2013, p. 634). Through the use of quantifiable evidence, the complicatedness of what happens in the classroom is sorted and factors are isolated to 'discrete and definitive' problems that can be *solved* using strategies from a 'what works' list. While this may seem a sensible way to look at educational improvement, it does expose a significant flaw of shifting the language from 'good' to 'effective' education, something Biesta (2015) has identified as being a 'mistake'. He describes the issue thus.

> The point here is that although 'effectiveness' is a value, it only refers to the degree in which a particular course of action is able to bring about a desired result, but it does not say anything about the desirability of the result. For this, we need to embed questions about effectiveness within a large discourse about what is educationally desirable – in other words, what makes education good. (pp. 80–81)

Along with the shift to talking about 'effective' education, has come what Biesta (2013) describes as the 'learnification of educational discourse and practice' (p. 5). Globally, educational conversations are about 'learning'; students have become 'learners', teachers have become those that must 'support' and 'facilitate' learning and schools have become 'learning environments'. On the face of it, this once again seems like reasonable language to use when talking about education. However, the impact of this is similar to the one discussed above. The 'learnification' discourse has shifted the focus of educational discussion from the questions that really matter – What are students learning?, Why are they learning?, and Who are they learning it from? In short, the discussion has moved away from the content, the purpose and the relationships of education (Biesta, 2015). This shift to talking about learning presupposes the assumption that all learning is inherently good and holds the same value (Biesta, 2013). It is easy to dispel this assumption. Can a child learning that their low socio-economic standing denies them access to some experiences be considered good? Can a young person learning how to make illicit drugs be considered good? Is learning about the capital cities of African nations as important or relevant as learning to be empathetic? Does learning about Quantum theory hold the same value as learning how to iron a shirt, or learning to be patient? The answer to all these questions is obviously no, not for the individual involved in the learning or for society as whole; the content, purpose and relationships of education matter. For this reason, 'the language of learning is *insufficient* for expressing what matters in education' (Biesta, 2015, p. 76).

A consequence of the current educational rhetoric is the need to measure. If the discourse is tied to the effectiveness (or not) of education, then the only way to know whether it is effective (or not) is to measure it. If the discourse is tied to student learning (or not) in education, then the only way to know whether students are learning (or not) is to measure. This has led to one of the most significant changes to education under neo-liberalism- the insatiable desire to measure (Muller, 2018).

5 The Paradox of Metrics

Neo-liberalism views all costs and benefits associated with any organisation, whether they are part of the free market or a government run institution, as being measureable (Denniss, 2018), and this impacts every facet of every organisation or institution operating within this paradigm (Denniss, 2018; Muller, 2018; Cukier & Mayer-Schonberger, 2013). Yet this idea is not a new one. In his latest book, Muller (2018) describes the introduction of this type of thinking into the realm of public administration. The mid 19th century saw legislation pass through parliament in Victorian Britain that reformed the structure of business. Not long after this, Robert Lowe, a liberal parliamentarian, recommended a 'new method for government funding of schools, which would be based on "payment by results"' (Muller, 2018, p. 29). The three areas to be measured were reading, writing and arithmetic. From the outset this approach of standardised measurement received criticism. Nevertheless, despite subsequent years of research and a growing body of evidence that refutes its effectiveness, the concept of 'education as machinery, tailored to the measurable production of reading, writing and computation' (Muller, 2018, p. 31) has ensued, and now forms a large part of much of the educational reform across the globe (Klenowski & Wyatt-Smith, 2012).

The question has to be asked – why, if something has been shown to be ineffective, does it still hold such sway over those with the power to develop and enact educational policy? Muller (2018) cites two main reasons. The first is centred on the concept of 'social trust', both in relation to the level of security those in positions of power feel about their status, and the trust that society has for those who are in these positions. If social trust is lacking, using quantitative standardised data to inform decision making 'replace(s) reliance on the subjective, experience-based judgments of those in power (Muller, 2018, p. 40), which in theory, should help to rebuild social trust. The second reason is accountability. Without a 'bottom line', not-for-profit organisations and institutions (such as schools) cannot be held accountable for success or failure. Developing and implementing standardised measures creates a 'substitute bottom line' (Muller, 2018, p. 42) by which these organisations and institutions can be held to account, particularly in relation to the funding they receive (Denniss, 2018).

As discussed in the previous chapter, education has been entrusted with the responsibility of preparing a nation's citizens to become active and contributing members who will work to 'improve the society' (Cramer, Little, & McHatton, 2018) in which they live. While there are those who consider this an unfair burden to place on a single construct without regard for the factors that impinge upon it (Muller, 2018; Goldstein, 2015), if education is perceived to be not driving improvement (with an acknowledgement that what this look likes for different groups with different agendas will be, unsurprisingly, different), then it must be reformed. Half a century ago, lobbying in the USA from an eclectic coalition of 'business groups concerned about the quality of the workforce; civil rights groups distressed by differential group achievement; and educational reformers disturbed by what they saw as the failure of public schools to educate, demanded national standards, tests and assessment' (Muller, 2018, p. 90). The ensuing time has seen education reform globally move towards greater standardisation and measurement (Cukier & Mayer-Schonberger, 2013), climaxing in what Muller (2018) describes today as 'metric fixation'. 'Metric fixation concerns the relationship between measurement and improvement' (Muller, 2018, p. 17), where there is a causational assumption that if something is measured, it will be improved. It should be noted here that what is being discussed is measurement that has 'high stakes'. That is, it has 'important consequences for test takers, on the basis of their performance' (UNESCO, 2018). The unfettered confidence that governments have placed in the ability of this type of measurement to drive improvement (Klenowski & Wyatt-Smith, 2012) has had 'significant impacts' on curriculum, pedagogy, and assessment, and consequently the work that teachers and schools do (Cramer, Little, & McHatton, 2018). It has become an evidence-based profession.

Recent years have seen a push from policy makers and governments for evidence-based practice, based on teachers becoming evidence-based professionals (Biesta, 2007). A belief exists that using a list of strategies that have been *shown to work* (what has become known as 'best practice') through the collection and collation of numerical data, will lead to improved student outcomes (Meyer, 2017). The conviction of this thinking can be seen in the adulation given to John Hattie for his work in 'Visible learning' (2008), where he constructed league tables of educational strategies in terms of their effectiveness (using the effect size measure), beginning with the *most effective* strategies for classroom teachers at the top and the *least effective* at the bottom. While there are those who lament this type of prescriptive pedagogy (see Veck, 2014), the success of this book has demonstrated a desire for a list of 'what works' – strategies that are *guaranteed* to improve student outcomes. Production of this hierarchy of strategies (whether by Hattie or anyone else), requires a tightly defined and quantifiable set of measures so that those things that work are easily discernible through the achievement of higher scores, and those that lead to poor levels of achievement can be labelled as ineffective. Fortuitously for Hattie, quantifiable data on educational achievement is readily available across much of the globe. Somewhat ironically, this is a result of the perceived need for accountability.

The sentiment that schools should be accountable for the work they do has been a feature of education systems around the world for a long time (Hutchings, 2017). However, what form this accountability takes has shifted across the centuries and decades, as the views and values of those with the political and cultural power to directly influence education, change. Neoliberalism has seen the adoption of the position that education should be managed as 'a productive system, in which inputs are transferred into outcomes', and it is these outcomes that are measured for their productivity and effectiveness to determine the quality of the schooling (Scheerens, Luyten, & van Ravens, 2011a, p. 36). As Muller (2018) succinctly describes it, educational '(p)erformance is … equated with what can be reduced to standardized measurements' (p. 17). Consequently, the quality of education is currently being critiqued through the lens of only those things that are 'objectively measureable and practically controllable' (Scheerens, Luyten, & van Ravens, 2011b, p. 4), which means what is measured is selected on this basis, rather than being selected because it accurately reflects a student's understanding or the quality of the education they are receiving (O'Neill, 2002). Muller (2018) identifies three problems associated with measuring in this way: (i) Measuring what is most easily measureable will rarely measure what is most important, or important at all; (ii) Measuring the simple when the outcome is complex leads to deceptive results; and (iii) Degrading information quality through standardisation strips away the context of what is being measured, such as the history, context, and meaning, and this results in information that appears more certain and authoritative than it actually is (pp. 23–24). This last point is echoed by Cukier and Mayer-Schonberger (2013), who caution a reliance on numerical data alone, as numbers 'are far more fallible than we think' (para. 2). An old adage springs to mind here – 'Not everything that can be counted counts, and not everything that counts can be counted'.

Many aspects of education cannot be measured. Unterhalter (2017) claims that this has created a tension between 'what is easily measurable, but may not be significant, and what is of major importance, but cannot be measured' (p. 2), with the latter being obscured or disregarded all together. There has been, and continues to be, much written about what is being missed because of the way student outcomes are being measured today (see any of the references from Biesta, Meyer or Hutchinson used in this section), and this is not the place for an in-depth discussion on the topic. Nevertheless, it is important. Why? Because the data being collected from students is being used to make what Meyer (2017) describes as 'far-reaching and often highly consequential pronouncements' (p. 18) about the quality of educational institutions and the work their educators do.

The measurement agenda is being driven by the global desire for educational improvement, improvement that can be seen in measureable student outcomes. In part, this is a result of the growing participation in, and reliance on, international comparative studies (Biesta, 2010), such as the *Progress in International Reading Literacy Study* (PIRLS), the *Trends in International Mathematics and Science Study* (TIMSS), and perhaps the most well-known and utilised, the *Program for International Student Assessment* (PISA). The OECD conducts PISA every three years to produce league tables that enable (and encourage) countries to examine their performance across narrow aspects of English, Mathematics, and Science through making comparisons with other countries, and tracking their own performance over time. The stakes attached to this test are high. Consequently, many countries have developed and implemented their own testing regimes in a bid to boost student achievement in the assessed areas (UNESCO, 2015). And why wouldn't they? The higher up the PISA table a country is, the more successful their education policy and systems are considered to be.

Unfortunately, there is a flip side to this agenda. Reliance on testing and assessment has impacted the work of all educators across all sectors of schooling; the culture of testing and assessing is evident in every classroom in every school across much of the world (Peim & Flint, 2009). Hursh and Martina (2016) even go as far as saying that schools are no longer places of shared and collaborative teaching and learning but are instead 'places where teachers and students focus on passing the tests' (p. 190). This focus on 'the test' has implications for the data these tests produce. Social psychologist Donald Campbell outlined his concerns in 1976, in what has become known as Campbell's Law (see Sidorkin, 2016, for a discussion on this). While this law pertains to the issue of using quantitative data for broader social change, he comments specifically on the challenge of using standardised testing in education:

> [A]chievement tests may well be valuable indicators of general school achievement under conditions of normal teaching aimed at general competence. But when test scores become the goal of the teaching process, they both lose their value as indicators of educational status and distort the educational process in undesirable ways. (p. 85)

This challenges the validity of any data drawn from high stakes testing, where the focus for schools is acquiring the best possible scores in the areas being measured, rather than on delivering what could be considered 'good' education.

Students are not the only ones who are being 'tested'. This appetite for improvement has led to the development of sets of standards for schools and the people who work within them, standards that are supposedly measureable and against which schools are audited. How this is actualised varies between countries (see Ehren, Perryman, & Skackleton, 2015, for a discussion on this in Europe, Baxter & Clarke, 2013, for a discussion on this in England, and Codd, 2005, for a discussion on this in New Zealand), though in each case the results of these audits are available for public viewing, whether in the form of league tables or reports. Whatever the form, the effect is the same – schools are working to ensure they are scoring well against the set standards, and if they do not, they have to do more to improve in these areas for the next round of audits. These types of standards are also set for systems at the national level. The OECD produces an annual report known as 'Education at a Glance', a document that compares around 40 nations against 30 measureable indicators. Gorur (2015) describes these indicators as statistics that are deliberately selected with the purpose of informing governments and policy makers about the state of their education systems; the standards in this publication are there to directly influence the educational debate, and in turn educational policy, at both a global and national level.

There can be little doubt that students, schools, educators and the systems they work within are being exposed to increased levels of accountability through ongoing assessment, in the form of student testing regimes, audit style evaluations for schools and teachers, and global performance league tables. While there are those who see this as a step in the right direction (Benjamin & Pashler, 2015; Roediger III, Putnam, & Smith, 2011), there are many who lament this regime of measurement, insisting it is moving education away from achieving its ultimate goal of being 'good'. Slee (2011), in his unmistakably frank manner, describes why:

> They (*educational power brokers and policy makers*) speak of teaching and learning and simultaneously distract students from their education with rote training for a battery of standardized tests ... Neo-liberal governments speak of educating flexible and adaptable students to become global citizens and restrict educational choices through narrow traditional curriculum. They emphasise the need for autonomous learners and disqualify the role of mistakes (or failure) in learning. They urge creativity and reify uniformity and standardization. (p. 4)

When viewed in this way it is not difficult to conclude that this measurement agenda has had a negative impact on both students and teachers alike (Hutchings, 2017). However, it is perhaps the consequences for those students and schools who are on the margins that are of most concern.

Globally, governments and organisations such as the OECD and UNESCO make claims that the measurement agenda will benefit not only high performing students and schools, but also those who are considered low performing. This is achieved, according to the rhetoric, through standard measures being able to identify where the shortfalls lay so that systems, schools and teachers can work to improve these areas for students. Research from England has found that schools that do raise their rates of academic achievement, as measured by high stakes systemic testing, also see success in other measured areas, such as student attendance rates and parent satisfaction data (Day, 2011). However, two points need to be made here. The first is that increases in student achievement tend to be fleeting; improved results are not sustained over longer periods of time (Muller, 2018). The second point is that schools that have achieved improvement in their results tend to be schools that were doing reasonably well in the first place (Muller, 2018). The consequences of the measurement agenda undoubtedly impact, most significantly, those students and schools who are low performing (Ainscow, 2010; Cramer, Little, & McHatton, 2018; Razer, Friedman, & Warshofsky, 2013).

As discussed previously, one of the effects of the measurement agenda has been the narrowing of what is delivered as curriculum and, consequently what is assessed. The way it is assessed has also been constricted. This phenomenon has narrowed the view of what is considered at a school, system and global level to be a high level of educational attainment. A result of this, whether deliberate or not, has been to 'discourage participation of learning of some groups of learners' (Ainscow, 2010, p. 75), particularly those who are interested in areas that sit outside those that fit the current depiction of educational success. Along with fewer academic disciplines being considered under the educational attainment umbrella, the increased reliance on standardised forms of assessment has led to fewer types of assessment being undertaken by students. The result of this has been twofold. Some students, for a myriad of reasons, cannot access or complete the assessments tasks at all, and therefore their data is not collected, which in turn means it is not counted. Other students, for reasons such as social class, disability, or ethnic background, cannot access the content of the assessment tasks in the same way as many of their peers. For this group of students, the data collected does not accurately reflect their ability in the areas being measured (Cramer, Little, & McHatton, 2018). For both groups of students, it can be argued that their 'voices' are not being heard when it comes to policy decisions being made using the data collected from these standardised assessments. Many regard them as students who are failing or low achieving, when rather it is the assessment regime itself that is failing these students (Fischman, DiBara, & Gardner, 2006).

Data that measures a very narrow set of standard outcomes across a very narrow set of curricula, and does not include all students in an adequate way in its collection process, is used by governments and policy makers to determine areas of educational need and future educational development (Meyer, 2017). In addition, this data has enabled the creation of national and international league tables with the highest performers at the top and the lowest at the bottom (Hardy & Boyle, 2011). This has ensured that a large number of 'the world's schools will always be wanting at various levels of deficiency' (Meyer, 2017, p. 19). In an era of educational choice for parents, schools and systems vie for positions that are higher up the league tables. The result of this is significant for 'low-attaining students, students who demand high levels of attention and resources, and those who are seen not to conform to school and classroom behavioural norms (Ainscow, 2010, p. 76). These students become 'unattractive' to 'higher performing' schools and as a result often end up attending schools that sit much lower down the league table. This cycle of low achievement is then perpetuated – poor results lead to 'poor performing' schools which in turn lead to poorer results and so on (Hutchings, 2017). Arduin (2015) describes the measurement agenda as 'a tool to compare and differentiate those who succeed from those who fail' (p. 108), and for those schools who fail, some form of sanction or penalty shall ensue (Muller, 2018; Cukier & Mayer-Schonberger, 2013).

For all of the reasons discussed here, Biesta (2010) concludes that 'the current culture of accountability is deeply problematic' (p. 59). This debate is not new. A century ago Dewey (1916) was arguing against the push for education to be viewed as a pure science, where a contrived set of standards was to be established and students measured against them (this was despite his desire that educators have a broad understanding of the sciences and their influence on education). 2000 years earlier his predecessor, Aristotle, was also espousing the belief that the most important things in nature (in us) could not be reduced to a set a quantities, but rather to understand them required, as described by Meyer (2017), 'sustained reflection and contextually sensitive discernment' (p. 18). Without this, 'it may alter the way we think about and practice education – from a civic good, anchored in liberal and emancipatory learning reflecting a community's historical and cultural commitments, to a global commodity, weighed, measured, and sold in the global marketplace' (Meyer, 2017, p. 19).

The critique of high stakes testing presented here does not assume that all data is bad. In fact, the opposite is true. 'Data can help improve things, if it's the right data used in the right way' (Cukier & Mayer-Schonberger, 2013, para. 18). Low stakes testing, where data is collected through various forms of assessment and judgment is allowed, can inform teachers of their students' progress and provide them with the information they require to make necessary adjustments to the curriculum and/or teaching methods (Muller, 2018). The inclusion of judgment is important here. Teachers, as professional educators, need permission to make judgments as '(u)ltimately, the issue is not one of metrics versus judgment, but metrics as informing judgment, which includes knowing how much weight to give metrics, recognizing their characteristic distortions, and appreciating what can't be measured' (Muller, 2018, p. 183).

The current reform agenda in education relies on data obtained from high stakes testing. This is despite growing bodies of research that show sustained improvement in results is not occurring, whether considering the achievements of individual groups of students, or in the 'closing of the gap' between the highest and lowest performers (Cramer, Little, & McHatton, 2018; Muller, 2018; Sidorkin, 2016; Klenowski & Wyatt-Smith, 2012). Yet governments continue to spend large sums of money on the development and re-development of standards and the testing regimes required to assess them, and the 'measurement continues unabated' (Muller, 2018, p. 98). Paradoxically, there may well be improvements in aspects that are not part of the current measurement regime, such as the creative arts, critical thinking, or the capacity to work collaboratively. Nevertheless the status quo remains, and data from high stakes assessment drives the prevailing education reform agenda. Any paradigm shift away from this will require a change in what societies, governments and the global community value in their education systems.

6 Value and 'Good' Education

The concept of value is ambiguous; on the one hand it can be used to refer to goods in terms of their worth, while on the other it can be used to describe conceptual notions such as Plato's ideas of 'the true', 'the good' and 'the beautiful' (Brezinka, 1994). An in-depth interrogation of value is beyond the scope of this chapter (see Hall, 1952, for an example of this) however it is necessary to provide a working definition for this discussion. The Oxford Dictionary defines value as being '(p)rinciples or standards of behaviour; one's judgment of what is important in life'. The determination of what is 'important' is influenced immeasurably by past histories, family, the Zeitgeist, group memberships and context-dependent experiences (Bergman, 1998). Values cannot be developed without direct influence from the situation in which one, or a society, finds itself (Williams, 1979). Values matter, in a big part because they 'serve as criteria for selection in action' (Williams, 1979, p. 16). This means that any shift in value is going to have consequences for 'the direction of societal development (Williams, 1979, p. 34). Understanding value in this way makes it clear that a reciprocal relationship must exist between what occurs as education and what is valued.

Education, as identified earlier in this chapter, has come to mean the 'knowledge and understanding' of something; something that is considered to be of value by society (Peters, 1970). In this sense, the influence of societal values on education can be clearly seen; if something is considered as being of value to know and understand by society, then it will become part of the education that its citizens receive. As Arduin (2015) puts it, 'societal values form the bedrock of an education system' (p. 106). Of course, there are many things that influence what society values, and while that needs to be acknowledged, it will not be explored here, except to share this sentiment of Furlong expressed so succinctly by Arduin (2015), 'the values that underlie a society's approach to, and definition of, education are inextricably political and, therefore, complex and ambiguous' (p. 107).

Understanding what society does value in education is not an easy task. Even if those with the authority over education systems seek this information, there is a strong chance that they will end up with something that 'represents values of adults rather than those of children and youth, or those of pupils a generation ago rather than those of the present day' (Cahn, 1970, p. 214). Current government policy makes the assumption that academic achievement is what is valued most highly in education by society (Jacob & Lefgren, 2007). This has created a need for the collection of evidence to ensure this is happening to the highest possible standard, leading to the current climate of standardisation and measurement. What is interesting here is that while the value attributed to academic achievement has led to a culture of standardisation and measurement for many educational systems, this has in turn had a significant impact on what is considered of value within education. It can be argued that what is now held up as being valuable in education has shifted over recent decades to fit what can be measured. This is a situation where society is valuing what it can measure rather than measuring what it values (Biesta, 2010). Warnock (1973) lamented the consequences of this more than four decades ago when she wrote, 'it must surely be putting the cart before the horse to argue for a certain kind of education on the basis of the examinations which are possible at the end of it' (p. 115).

Placement of value on things that are standard and measureable presents an issue for a construct such as education, which has been entrusted with the task (rightly so or not) of improving social inequality. Aristotle, as Peters (1966) cites, identified that '(in)justice results just as much from treating unequals equally as it does from treating equals unequally' (p. 118). These words, though penned millennia ago, identify a significant problem with value being placed on standards that can be easily measured – it assumes all students are equals, when in fact they are not (Cramer, Little, & McHatton, 2018). The reliance on data that treats all students as equals has led to education becoming an increasingly unequal construct, where the gap between the highest and lowest performers is increasing. This is in stark contradiction to the premise that education can help overcome, or at least reduce, inequalities within society. Until value shifts from the treatment of all students as equals to that of all students as individuals, the capacity for education to make a difference in a climate of growing inequality is negligible.

7 Conclusion

Despite the difficulties that the pursuit of 'good' education is facing under the neo-liberal reform agenda, it is clear that within this climate education is seen as something that is valuable, something that is worth pursuing. The money governments globally pour into their education systems every year attests to this. But this alone is not enough. 'Good' education must promote the growth and development of the whole person, with consideration of the community in which they live, so they have the opportunity to become contributing and content members of a healthy society. Peter's (1966) adds another element to this debate, the issue of fairness. Fairness raises issues not only about the quality of the education being delivered, but also about the distribution of its delivery. Is education being provided equitably? Is it fair? This question of fairness sits aptly at the end of this chapter, as fairness is, in itself, something that is 'intrinsically valuable, something worth wanting for its own sake' (De Marneffe, 2013, p. 52). The only way that the provision of education can be considered fair is by providing it in a way that is inclusive of everyone, regardless of his or her circumstance. This brings the discussion now into the realm of inclusive education.

References

Aasen, P., Proitz, T., & Sandberg, N. (2014). Knowledge regimes and contractions in education reforms. *Educational Policy, 28*(5), 718–738. doi:10.1177/0895904813475710

Ainscow, M. (2010). Achieving excellence and equity: Reflections on the development of practices in one local district over 10 years. *School Effectiveness and School Improvement: An International Journal of Research, Policy and Practice, 21*(1), 75–92. doi:10.1080/09243450903569759

Anderson, G., & Donchik, L. (2016). Privatizing schooling and policy making: The American Legislative Exchange Council and new political and discursive strategies of education governance. *Educational Policy, 30*(2), 322–364. doi:10.1177/0895904814528794

Apple, M. (2017). What is present and what is absent in critical analyses of neoliberalism in education. *Peabody Journal of Education, 92*(1), 148–153. doi:10.1080/0161956X.2016.1265344

Arduin, S. (2013). Implementing disability rights in education in Ireland: An impossible task? *Dublin University Law Journal, 36*, 93–126.

Arduin, S. (2015). A review of the values that underpin the structure of an education system and its approach to disability and inclusion. *Oxford Review of Education, 41*(1), 105–121. doi:10.1080/03054985.2015.1006614

Artiles, A., Harris-Murri, N., & Rostenberg, D. (2006). Inclusion as social justice: Critical notes on discourses, assumptions, and the road ahead. *Theory into Practice, 45*(3), 260–268. doi:10.1207/s15430421tip4503_8

Bantock, G. (1963). *Education in an industrial society*. Faber & Faber.

Baxter, J., & Clarke, J. (2013). Farewell to the tick box inspector? Ofsted and the changing regime of school inspection in England. *Oxford Review of Education, 39*(5), 702–718. doi:10.1080/03054985.2013.846852

Benjamin, A., & Pashler, D. (2015). The value of standardized testing: A perspective from cognitive psychology. *Policy Insights from the Behavioural and Brain Sciences, 2*(1), 13–23. doi:10.1177/2372732215601116

Bergh, A., & Englund, T. (2014). A changed language of education with new actors and solutions: The authorization of promotion and prevention programmes in Swedish schools. *Journal of Curriculum Studies, 46*(6), 778–797. doi:10.1080/00220272.2014.934718

Bergman, M. (1998). A theoretical note on the differences between attitudes, opinions and values. *Swiss Political Science Review, 4*(2), 81–93. doi:10.1002/j.1662-6370.1998.tb00239.x

Biesta, G. (2007). Why “what works” won’t work: Evidence-based practice and the democratic deficit in educational research. *Educational Theory, 57*(1), 1–22. doi:10.1111/j.1741-5446.2006.00241.x

Biesta, G. (2010). *Good education in an age of measurement: Ethics, politics, democracy*. Paradigm Publishers.

Biesta, G. (2013). Interrupting the politics of learning. *Power and Education, 5*(1), 4–15. doi:10.2304/power.2013.5.1.4

Biesta, G. (2015). What is education for? On good education, teacher judgment, and educational professional professionalism. *European Journal of Education, 50*(1), 74–87. doi:10.1111/ejed.12109

Biesta, G., & Safstrom, C. (2011). A manifesto for education. *Policy Futures in Education, 9*(5), 540–547. doi:10.2304/pfie.2011.9.5.540

Blackburn, S. (2009). *What do we really know? The big questions of philosophy*. Quercus.

Brezinka, D. (1994). *Beliefs, morals and education*. Avebury.

Cahn, S. (1970). *The philosophical foundations of education*. Harper & Row Publishers.

Codd, J. (2005). Teachers as ‘managed professionals’ in the global education industry: The New Zealand experience. *Educational Review, 57*(2), 193–206. doi:10.1080/0013191042000308369

Cramer, E., Little, M., & McHatton, P. (2018). Equity, equality, and standardization: Expanding the conversations. *Education and Urban Society, 50*(5), 483–501. doi:10.1177/0013124517713249

Cukier, K., & Mayer-Schonberger, V. (2013, May). The dictatorship of data. *MIT Technology Review: Global Panel*. Retrieved from https://www.technologyreview.com/s/514591/the-dictatorship-of-data/

Day, C. (2011). Building and sustaining successful principalship in an English school. In L. Moos, O. Johansson, & C. Day (Eds.), *How school principals sustain success over time: International perspectives* (Series Studies in Educational Leadership, Vol. 14). Springer Science + Business Media.

De Marneffe, P. (2013). Contractualism, personal values, and well-being. *Social Philosophy and Policy, 30*(1–2), 51–68. doi:10.1017/S0265052513000034

Denniss, R. (2018). Dead right: How neoliberalism ate itself and what comes next. *Quarterly Essay, 1*(70), 1–79.

de Villiers, D. (2015). *Mandela's belief that education can change the world is still a dream.* Commentary in The Conversation, The Conversation Media Group, Melbourne, Australia.

Dewey, J. (1916). *Democracy and education: An introduction to the philosophy of education.* Macmillan.

Dewey, J. (1934). Individual psychology and education. *The Philosopher, XII.* Retrieved from http://the-philosopher.co.uk/2016/08/individual-psychology-and-education-1934.html

Ehren, M., Perryman, J., & Skackleton, N. (2015). Setting expectations for good education: How Dutch school inspections drive improvement. *School Effectiveness and School Improvement, 26*(2), 296–327. doi:10.1080/09243453.2014.936472

Fischman, D., DiBara, J., & Gardner, D. (2006). Creating good education against the odds. *Cambridge Journal of Education, 36*(3), 383–398. doi:10.1080/03057640600866007

Frank, T. (2016). *Listen, liberal: Or, whatever happened to the party of the people?* Henry Holt and Company.

Freire, P. (2005). *Pedagogy of the oppressed* (30th ed.). The Continuum International Publishing Group.

Glendinning, S. (2015). Varieties of neoliberalism. *LSE 'Europe in Question' Discussion Paper Series, 1*(89). 1–38.

Goldstein, D. (2015). Quieting the teacher wars: What history reveals about an embattled profession. *American Educator, 39*(1), 14–17.

Gorur, R. (2015). Producing calculable worlds: Education at a glance. *Discourse: Studies in the Cultural Politics of Education, 36*(4), 578–595. doi:10.1080/01596306.2015.974942

Gorur, R., & Koyama, J. (2013). The struggle to technicise in education policy. *Australian Educational Research, 40*, 633–648. doi:10.1007/s13384-013-0125-9

Hall, E. (1952). *What is value?* Routledge & Kegan Paul Ltd.

Hardy, I., & Boyle C. (2011). My school? Critiquing the abstraction and quantification of education. *Asia-Pacific Journal of Teacher Education, 39*(3), 211–222. doi:10.1080/1359866X.2011.588312

Harris, K. (1979). *Education and knowledge: The structured misrepresentation of reality.* Routledge & Kegan Paul.

Hattie, J. (2008). *Visible learning: A synthesis of over 800 meta-analyses relating to achievement.* Routledge.

Hursh, D., & Martina, C. (2016). The end of public schools? Or a new beginning? *The Educational Forum, 80*(2), 189–207. doi:10.1080/00131725.2016.1135380

Hutchings, M. (2017). Accountability measures: The factory farm version of education. *The Psychology of Education Review, 41*(1), 3–15.

Jacob, B., & Lefgren, L. (2007, November). What do parents value in education? An empirical investigation of parents' revealed preferences for teachers. *The Quarterly Journal of Economics*, 1603–1637.

Klenowski, V., & Wyatt-Smith, C. (2012). The impact of high stakes testing: The Australian story. *Assessment in Education: Principles, Policy & Practice, 19*(1), 65–79. doi:10.1080/0969594X.2011.592972

Kloch, Z. (2012). Language and social change. Public communication, nation, and identity. *Psychology of Language and Communication, 16*(3), 253–267. doi:10.2478/v10057-012-0017-5

Meyer, D. (2017). The limits of measurement: Misplaced precision, phronesis, and other Aristotelian cautions for the makers of PISA, APPR, etc. *Comparative Education, 53*(1), 17–34. doi:10.1080/03050068.2017.1254981

Mounk, D. (2017). *The age of responsibility: Luck, choice and the welfare state.* Harvard University Press.

Mulcahy, D. (2008). *The educated person.* Rowman & Littlefield.

Muller, J. (2018). *Tyranny of metrics.* Princeton University Press.

Noddings, N., & Slote, M. (2003). Changing notions of the moral and of moral education. In N. Blake, P. Meyers, R. Smith, & P. Standish (Eds.), *The Blackwell guide to the philosophy of education.* Blackwell Publishers.

O'Hear, A. (1981). *Education, society and human nature: An introduction to the philosophy of education.* Routledge & Kegan Paul Ltd.

O'Neill, O. (2002). *BBC Reith lectures 2002: A question of trust.* Retrieved from http://www.bbc.co.uk/radio4/reith2002/

Peim, N., & Flint, K. (2009). Testing times: Questions concerning assessment for school improvement. *Educational Philosophy and Theory, 41*(3), 342–361. doi:10.1111/j.1469-5812.2008.00438.x

Peters, R. S. (1966). *Ethics and education.* George Allen & Unwin Ltd.

Peters, R. S. (1970). Education and the educated man. *Journal of Philosophy of Education, 4*(1), 5–20.

Plato. (2016). *The Republic. The project Guttenberg EBook* (B. Jowett, Trans.). Penguin.

Razer, M., Friedman, V., & Warshofsky, B. (2013). Schools as agents of social exclusion and inclusion. *International Journal of Inclusive Education, 17*(11), 1152–1170. doi:10.1080/13603116.2012.742145

Roediger III, D., Putnam, A., & Smith, M. (2011). Ten benefits of testing and their applications to educational practice. *Psychology of Learning and Motivation, 55*, 1–36. doi:10.1016/B978-0-12-387691-1.00001-6

Ross, D., & Gibson, R. (2006). *Neoliberalism and education reform.* Hampton Press, Inc.

Scheerens, J., Luyten D., & van Ravens, J. (2011a). Measuring educational quality by means of indicators. In J. Scheerens, D. Luyten, & J. van Ravens (Eds.), *Perspectives on educational quality: Illustrative outcomes on primary and secondary schooling in the Netherlands.* Springer.

Scheerens, J., Luyten, D., & van Ravens, J. (2011b). Perspectives on educational quality. In J. Scheerens, D. Luyten, & J. van Ravens (Eds.), *Perspectives on educational quality: Illustrative outcomes on primary and secondary schooling in the Netherlands.* Springer.

Sidorkin, A. (2016). Campbell's law and the ethics of immensurability. *Studies in Philosophy and Education, 35*(4), 321–332. doi:10.1007/s11217-015-9482-3

Silbeck, M. (1984). *School based curriculum development.* Harper & Row Ltd.

Slee, R. (2011). *The irregular school: Exclusion, schooling and inclusive education.* Routledge.

Soltis, J. (1968). *An introduction to the analysis of educational concepts.* Addison-Wesley Publishing Company Inc.

UNESCO. (2015). *Education for all 2000–2015: Achievements and challenges.* UNESCO Publishing.

UNESCO. (2018). *High stakes testing: Definition.* Retrieved from http://uis.unesco.org/node/334671

Unterhalter, E. (2017). Negative capability? Measuring the unmeasurable in education. *Comparative Education, 53*(1), 1–16. doi:10.1080/03050068.2017.1254945

Veck, D. (2014). Inclusive pedagogy: Ideas from the ethical philosophy of Emmanuel Levinas. *Cambridge Journal of Education, 44*(4), 451–464. doi:10.1080/0305764X.2014.955083

Warnock, M. (1973). Towards a definition of quality in education. In R. S. Peters (Ed.), *The philosophy of education.* Oxford University Press.

Williams, R. (1979). Change and stability in values and value systems: A sociological perspective. In M. Rokeach (Ed.), *Understanding human values: Individual and societal.* The Free Press.

CHAPTER 4

Headspace: School Leaders Working towards Inclusive Schools

Gerry Mac Ruairc

1 Introduction

This chapter seeks to examine the work of school leaders in leading schools in the direction of an inclusive culture, framed by the politics of recognition. The aim here is to create a difference-friendly school 'where assimilation to majority or dominant cultural norms is no longer the price of equal respect' (Fraser, 1996, p. 4). In a school context this can be challenging for leaders, teachers and school communities. Schools are often places where normalisation is a distinct part of the deliberative practice of schools (Graham & Slee, 2008). This coupled with the extent to which schools as institutions are often characterized by deeply sedimented practices (Laydar, 1997) can make change and innovation seem impossible. A seminal book by Labaree (2010) *Somebody has to Fail* provides a chilling account of the broad, persistent patterns of failure and success that characterise education more broadly. However, it can be more helpful to explore how school leaders advocate for a more inclusive type of school experience for children and young people. This chapter will begin by clarifying some issues in relation to the remit of leadership for inclusive schools, while the main body of the chapter seeks to examine both the exclusionary practice of schools and the manner in which schools deal with difference in an effort to help shape a way of thinking about school that might help the achievement of more inclusive school environments.

1.1 *What Are We Talking About?*

One of the things that is really important when talking about inclusion is the requirement to address the lack of clarity around what is meant by inclusive leadership. In this case it is necessary, from the outset, to make a distinction between leadership for inclusive schooling and inclusive leadership. In the case of the latter, the view in this chapter is that inclusive leadership is an organisational management style that can involve a whole range of practices. Included here are leadership characteristics such as good teamwork, good collaborative practice, and a commitment to distributed leadership, to name a few. Many

 | DOI: 10.1163/9789004431171_004

of these activities would characterise what is viewed in much of the literature as good leadership practice. Many of the identified practices with respect to distributed leadership can actually be encompassed within the notion of inclusive leadership (Gronn, 2000; Spillane, 2006; Harris, 2013). Essentially, what is meant here is a way of working as an inclusive leader in the day to day practice of involving staff in a range of ways. This does not mean, however, that this inclusive leader is actually working towards an inclusive type of school. Working for inclusion requires an ethical stance, a deliberative and reflexive development of a mindset that seeks to explore difference and diversity and to problematise what is done with difference and diversity in order to create an inclusive culture within an organisation. Both forms of leadership can be connected. Indeed, it is unlikely that an inclusive school is achieved unless inclusive leadership practice is part of the running of a school. Notwithstanding this, it is important to recognise that they are not the same. Consequently, when we discuss many of the different types of leadership that are outlined in the literature, many of them do not automatically lead to more inclusive schools and indeed many of them do not problematise many of the issues that need to be explicated in order to achieve this outcome (Lumby, 2012).

In any conversation about inclusion it is necessary to accept the notion that inclusion is a very complicated and complex idea that has been the subject of much criticism and contestation, and sometimes much opposition (Warnock, 2005; Allan, 2008; Florian, 2008). Clarity in relation to what inclusion means is not helped by a conflation with cognate ideas such as social inclusion or integration, often resulting in mixed and confused outcomes at every level of operation from policy to the minutiae of practice. Consequently, at the outset of a conversation about inclusion it is likely that protagonists are not always coming from the same set of assumptions about the substantive issues. When leadership for inclusive schools as an idea is mooted one would be well advised to assume that people come to this discussion with a range of preconceived notions of what meaning is intended. In this context, a range of discursive strategies that serve to close down discussion and debate can often allow the status quo to prevail. Comments such as 'it's all to idealistic' or 'that's all very well in theory but that won't work in my school' may well be familiar to the reader. Consequently, in exploring inclusion, it is sometimes necessary to work in the field of deconstructive forms of critical thinking and engagement where the search for solutions and answers is suspended and where dialogue and possibilities can prevail (Biesta & Stams, 2001). When viewed from this perspective closure isn't always possible, nor is it possible to be definitive about the range of strategies and procedures that can be used in schools for practice to become inclusive. At times, this can be difficult in a field of education that can be delimited by the search for classroom ready answers to very complex issues and compounded by a high level of moral closure (Goffman, 1956) about how to 'do education', and specifically in this case how to be an education leader. It is necessary to create a discursive space for ambiguity in schools and this is a key practice that leaders need to encourage, i.e. ways of working that opens up dialogic inquiry (Freire, 1970, 1997; Wells, 1999; Bahktin, 1981)

It might be helpful to proceed with some kind of working definition of how leadership for inclusive schooling can be understood. The purpose of this chapter is to focus on leadership for inclusive schools as an activity which enables and creates the conditions for the alignment of minds, hearts, purposes and resources in order to produce a more inclusive type of school experience for all. There is a concomitant need for leaders to ensure that this culture is constantly nurtured by an open, reflexive, pedagogically focused school culture. It is the task of leadership, therefore, in its broadest sense within a school to work within this framework and to ensure that it is this type of perspective that characterises leadership activity in school. This is a model of leadership that is deeply and critically engaged with the purposes of education. It is an organic intellectual activity in the purest Gramscian sense that seeks not only to understand the world but to transform it (Le Blanc, 2016). Many might argue that this way of working is overly normative, that it begins with a particular view of the world and mobilises capitals towards this end (Bush & Glover, 2014). It is true to say that there is a normative element to this type of focus. However, this is only a relative normativity, as an imperative for leadership the open, more inclusive perspective is deeply reflective and transformative (Shields, 2016). This process holds within it the achievement of a range of different outcomes depending on context – the idea of inclusive education provides direction rather than prescription and offers a space where leadership practice in schools can be reimagined in a number of ways.

1.2 *Discursive Legacies*

Debates relating to inclusion and the language relating to inclusion are somewhat problematic and create a particular set of discursive circumstances that need to be explicated. The first relates to the claim that much of the discussion around inclusion continues to overly rely on discourses emanating from special education literature. The single axis framework that underpins this work and subsequently mediates many discussions has not always been helpful to the broader inclusion debate (Corbet, 1996; Mittler, 2008). By frequently confining our explorations of inclusion to the consideration of learners with Special Educational Needs (SEN), we serve to narrow the concept and limit the potential of inclusion to transform school experience for all children. A related issue here is the manner in which discourses of the past continue to be carried in discourses of the present. This is particularly evident in the context of the paradigms that have framed the special education field. In this context, paradigms have moved from exclusion to segregation, from segregation to integration and now to inclusion. Since there is no clear cut 'end of an era' where all that went before is discarded (Foucault, 1977), and since practice takes on new paradigms slowly and through a process of a transformation of existing practice, current discourse and practices relating to inclusion, if and where they exist, hold residual ideas from each of the 'SEN eras'. This sometimes results in a conflation of ideas, which in turn contributes to confused models of both policy and practice. These confused views also appear in relation to dealing with other group differences; methods of dealing with religious diversity, for example, can be very exclusionary. Having a child sit and read at the back of a class while his or her peers engage in religious instruction is hardly good practice. Yes, the child is not 'doing' religion but they are 'othered' from their peers on the basis of their religious background. The result of this can impact the extent to which poor practice can be explicitly 'called' or named as such. By creating confusion around the notion of inclusion, a cover is provided for practice that can fall short of the mark. It has been argued (Slee, 2001; Allen, 2009; Mac Ruairc, 2013) for some time now to extend the discussion about the idea of inclusion beyond the SEN focus and align more clearly with the well-established view that inclusion is a broad construct and incorporates a range of differences that together form the diversity that exists within schools. In this way, it is possible to challenge many of the zones of exclusion that persist in education systems. This discourse provides a further platform on which to expose the extent to which schools resonate with dominant groups in society to the exclusion of other groups. Social class, for example, continues to be the primary determinant of success or failure for students and the exploration of this continues to be the focus of a considerable body of research (Reay, 2007, 2009; Laureau & Goyette 2014; Mac Ruairc, 2011a; Lynch et al., 2016). Other studies point to the alarming manner that sexuality and gender create unequal and sometimes very negative school experience for students (Neary et al., 2016; Neary et al., 2018).

1.3 *Defending Difference and Explicating Exclusion*

This chapter argues that what needs to be at the core of the issue of inclusion is the idea of difference, the manner in which difference is understood and the manner in which this understanding is incorporated into the way we teach, the way we assess, the way we run our schools and the way school is experienced by all students. In this context, leaders need to take on board the manner in which the concept of intersectionality (Anthias, 2008; Hill Collins et al., 2016) provides an insight into difference and diversity, creating a view of difference that is very complex and is rarely discussed in the education literature. A failure to deal with the idea of intersectionality and the multiplicative manifestations of the marginalisation (Anthias, 2008) that can occur for certain students again leads to an incomplete/flawed understanding of the students we have in our schools with the concomitant result that schools can, and do, continue to fail certain groups of students. It is not surprising therefore, that achieving an inclusive school system requires a radical shift in how we conceptualise schools and how we frame and develop the leadership of these schools. It is a reconceptualisation; what Slee calls a 'radical reconceptualization and reconstruction'.

> Inclusive schooling is concerned with the educational experiences and outcomes for all children. Since present forms of schooling routinely deny human rights and exclude students on the basis of race, ethnicity, gender, disability, sexuality, class – inclusive education is a project of reconceptualization and radical reconstruction. (Slee, 2001, p. 174)

This chapter proposes a way of working inclusion that forefronts the quest for a 'difference-friendly school'. This begins with recognition and respect for the multiple identities that teachers, children, young people and school communities bring to the classroom. What is key here is working with and valuing difference and meeting the inevitability of diversity with open minds and hearts. There are two elements encompassed in this approach and a consideration of both should provide for the foundation of a more inclusive school.

The first deals directly with diversity, how schools work with difference, and how and where it is identifiable, made visible and recognised. Key here is the response of the school leadership and the school community to this diversity, i.e. what happens when schools, leaders and teachers, encounter that which is 'other' to them. This process is mediated by a deeply personal component. In order for the opening up to happen individuals have engaged in deliberative reflexive action to confront personal biases and reformulate a professional stance that is applicable to, and facilitative of, an inclusive system. This is where the action of hearts and minds comes together, and without engaging in this type of transformative thinking (Shields, 2016) effort at inclusion will remain surface and perfunctory. The second and related component of the process is derived from the need to problematise exclusion in our schools. Whether we choose to admit it or not exclusion is embedded in our school systems – in the rituals, practices and outcomes that frame, to different and varying extents, all education systems. There are very few systems, if any, that can claim to be positioned outside the practices of exclusion when it comes to models of school practice. For the purpose of illustration this chapter will now focus on core examples of the type of sedimented types of exclusionary practice that often prevail. The first relates to the well-established practice of individualising failure within our education system. A core value, which is sometime tacit and implicit in systems rather than overt and explicit, is the persistence of meritocratic ideology in schools (Lampert, 2013). Within this construct the student becomes the source of failure. This value system has been applied to individual children, as well as to groups. In the context of SEN there has been a disability hunt (Baker, 2002), ongoing for years in search of a label to define the child. The diagnosis process is not in itself negative; in inclusive schools this label is used to support and build on the child's strengths and interests, however in less inclusive schools it can lead directly to a deficit view of a child or a group of children often through a process of essentialising and/or commodifying the child on the basis of SEN diagnosis (Kinsella & Senior, 2008; Senior, 2009). Another example of this type of exclusionary thinking is the manner in which the issue of sexuality and sexual differences in schools is often conflated with and confined to dealing with homophobic bullying (Greytak, 2016). This, albeit an important action, creates winners and losers – the bully and the bullied – and in many cases the only time that sexuality is mentioned in schools is in the context of bullying. Again, this type of practice locates the difference very firmly at the level of the individual student and places very little onus on the system to examine the practices that have marginalised this form of difference in the first instance.

The second issue relates to the prevalence of deficit thinking in the way different groups of students', such as travellers, Muslims, girls, boys, and so on, are discussed. While the literature in relation to profiling lower Socio-Economic Status groups in this way is both persistent and prolific, this is not the only group subjected to widespread deficit views. This deficit perspective can be a significant component in the categorisation of learners from multiple social groups. These binaries of 'us and them' rely for their production and reproduction to a large extent on what is valued in each individual school. A type of 'schools like ours' perspective that shapes what it is a school views as the most desirable type of student. In many ways, this is the sum of the parts of any school culture and the outcome can be specific and localised. Nonetheless, many schools' views coalesce with respect to how certain groups are perceived. The manner in which traveller children are included or not included in many Irish schools is a very clear case of schools arriving at a reasonably agreed view of the deficits embedded in traveller culture when read against the prevailing norms of many schools. The power of the norm here is significant. In creating or desiring an idealised centre schools develop an arsenal of techniques to monitor and 'police' learners' distance from this centre. The extent to which schools are structured on the assumption that we have a 'normal' child is a key imperative for leaders to challenge in developing inclusive schools. Challenging these views and the practice that emanates from these views together with providing alternatives to the assumptions and discursive strategies that frame this type of thinking is one of the core tasks of leadership focused on creating inclusive schools.

1.4 *Leadership for Leaders*

For many years now, working as a transformative leader (Shields, 2016) was the preserve of some heroic, charismatic types of school leaders who worked above and beyond what was expected in order to achieve very positive inclusive outcomes for the schools they led (see Wrigley, 2012; Thomson, 2007; Lingard, 2014). Imperatives for this type of approach are now identifiable in recent work on well-being and belonging (Smyth, 2015, 2016) and in some of the more recent work by the EU Commission (2018). The view that creating school spaces where children belong and where they feel they belong is ensuring that affective engagement with schools is now viewed as a key area of focus for schools (Bradshaw, 2016; Spratt, 2017). For these developments to provide a sustainable space for inclusive schooling it will be necessary to ensure that this drive toward well-being and belonging will incorporate the idea of intersectionality mentioned previously in this chapter. The idea that marginalisation is a multiplicative experience is essential (Donnor et al., 2016). Dealing with belonging cannot default to the single axis framework that has framed the work on SEN in school systems. If a child happens to be identified in a number of marginalised groups, e.g. a low SES, black, gay young man, the space that is created by this new focus on well-being needs to be adequately conceptualised so that all of the child belongs not just the bits the school chooses to recognise.

There are implications for the type of professional development that is provided for school leaders. In many cases professional development for leaders typically focuses on the 'nuts and bolts' of getting the tasks associated with being a principal done efficiently, focusing on how to deal with management and administrative tasks that can be easily 'covered' on 'time out, one off training days and at seminars. There is no doubt that paying attention to these tasks has a function in the overall support leaders are given. However, it can be argued that this is the easy bit. Programmes of this type can produce very achievable outcomes, however, the bigger ideas, such as those linked to inclusive schools, are much more difficult to deal with, and not so easily packaged into a few days' training. Not providing the type of professional learning that engages with the bigger questions runs the risk of not engaging with the real transformative potential of leadership. It is this potential that needs to be realised if schools are to become inclusive of all students. Leaders need to take on the big questions, not from a policy/normative/functionalist stance, but by engaging with a transformative perspective that changes the questions asked to produce different answers. School leaders, in their development, need to draw on robust research and scholarship in areas such as sociocultural theory, critical race theory, critical literacy and feminist pedagogies. Essentially, what is needed is strong robust scholarship that will cause leaders to problematise the status quo and current model of thinking in order to disturb the deeply sedimented practices in schools and within education systems that for too long have served too few.

Those who view this type of approach as anarchic will articulate a key defence against such a position very quickly. The challenge regularly draws on the idea that there is a need for schools to have a cohesiveness in order for them to function well and to create a safe, ordered learning environment. This requires the need for norms. However, leaders who are committed to a more inclusive school system need to be equipped with ways of working that moves the argument on from this 'common sense', 'natural order' position. Schools are good at defining, delimiting and reproducing the norm, they need to be led to a place where they can engage in a more critical analysis of what the norms are, where they come from, whose interests they serve and who they marginalise.

Leading inclusive schools shares many of the aspirations of other related or cognate endeavours that focus on issues such as social justice, equity, equality and other discourses that share a commitment to creating a better, more sustainable world. While this may be normative, it is a different kind of normative, one that dreams and transforms rather than seeks to curtail and reduce. It is not coming from the same place and scholarship that produces a list of desirable leadership behaviours or practices that will yield particular outcomes – the transferrable epistemologies (Gunter, 2006), of so many 'how to do school leadership' manuals. Nurturing this type of leader requires a different approach because there are no easy answers. There are no recipes. Rather, this requires an intellectual engagement with a much more complex set of discourses and perspectives that reflect a recognition of a view of school leadership that is complex to its core. Not only because of the intensification of the work of school leadership brought about by neoliberal reform, but because of the core task of the formation of children and young people that should be a defining imperative for all leadership practice in schools.

There are many contributing factors to achievement of an inclusive school. Many practices are context specific and are often diverse and nuanced, filtered by individual leaders with different constraints and opportunities for action. Such is the evolving and iterative nature of the situated activity that takes place in the unique social settings (Layder, 1997) of each school community. Because the achievement of an inclusive school is an on-going deliberative process of understanding what inclusion is like, where it is missing and what is required to keep moving toward this outcome, will require on-going problematizing. As thinking and ideas move on, practice needs to be challenged and re-imagined. There has to be a fluidity inherent in this type of approach to leadership and this is challenging at many levels. It requires that leaders take on board the idea that education is a political process, deeply immersed in cultural politics. Important too for leaders is to recognise that they themselves, and all school staff, are cultural workers. Leadership for an inclusive school has to make space for a consideration of the broader social conditions within which school happens. Failure to do this greatly limits the reach of the educative process, creating or reproducing patters of inequality and exclusion. Not taking account of the cultural circumstances of children and young people runs the risk of not helping children deal with the world in which they live, leaving them without the prerequisites necessary to engage proactively with their social worlds so as to enhance their own sense of belonging to a world they have been helped to understand. Central to this for leaders in inclusive schools is a commitment to learning and deliberative, reflexive focus on developing the pedagogical core (OECD, 2015) of the school. It is here that the transformative power of pedagogy can be realised, and consequently, it is where leaders need to become more and more visible and more effective. Leading learning in a school could be viewed as a prerequisite for ensuring that a school is working towards creating a more inclusive culture. It is in the classroom that inclusion is realised – this does not mean that classrooms are left to work it out themselves. The task of leadership here is to support teachers to create inclusive classrooms. In order for this to happen this means that leaders need to know and understand what is happening in classrooms.

This task is not easy, positioned as schools are in a world where demands are placed on schools to perform in particular ways and to deliver and make visible outcomes derived from predetermined norms and expectations. The much-critiqued neoliberal work has impacted the manner in which school and school leaders approach the idea of inclusion. A high stakes accountability culture can often create the demand for the commodification of children and for the creation of hierarchies of children that can in turn help the school perform to a particular outcome. The resurgence of streaming, banding and setting in schools is a response to this type of pressure that labels and packages children in an exclusionary zone for treatment. The dark side of leadership indicates that schools sometimes engage in practices that are far from laudable in order to ensure the most desirable profile for a school. A good example of how patterns of exclusion continue to persist can be seen in the manner in which gender remains an issue for inclusion. Gender still segregates and, despite widespread developments in the field, some fundamental traditional views in relation to gender and patterns of participation in education prevail, either tacitly in terms of teachers' assumptions, or explicitly in terms of particular forms of practice that continue to exist in schools (Smyth et al., 2011; Lodge & Lynch, 2003).

2 Conclusion

In some ways the task of inclusion is only beginning. There are many existing structures in the school systems that present a highly stratified, segregated system on the basis of age, class, gender, language, religion and sometimes race/ ethnicity. In Ireland, for example, we have catholic schools, church of Ireland schools, Muslim schools, schools teaching though the medium of Irish, junior primary schools, senior primary schools, Socio Economic Status (SES) disadvantaged schools, educate together schools, voluntary secondary schools, and Education Training Board (ETB) schools. The list is long and growing, and this presents a structural dilemma for inclusion and how we think about inclusion. We divide up our school population in almost every conceivable way and then ask of schools to include. These systemic structures create a sense that there are spaces for certain types of children, thereby creating a structurally exclusionary framework that is sustained by exclusionary norms, creating very real challenges for leaders committed to creating an inclusive school. Finally, while there is a hope that each leader will leave their mark on a school, there is often a desire to preserve the school as it is, to make sure that what the school has always stood for, prevails. This is often at the core of the job description for an incoming school leader. This requirement is often packaged in the seemingly benign indisputable language of tradition, particularly in the case of more prestigious, middle-class schools. The task of leadership in these cases often becomes preserving the privilege always enjoyed by the students in these schools. More recently, upholding the religious ethos of a school, another form of tradition, has become a task of leadership in Irish schools. An example of this in Catholic schools is a reviewed focus in the appointment of leaders who will commit to upholding the religious ethos of the school. Recent controversies in Ireland around the control and governance of most of the schools signifies clearly how this renewed focus on tradition is impacting on the creation of exclusionary practice at the stage of admission to schools – before the children ever takes his or her seat in the classroom. This provides a very recent indicator of just how far there is to travel on this journey toward inclusion.

References

Allan, J. (2008). *Rethinking inclusive education: The philosophers of difference in practice*. Springer.

Anthias, F. (2008). Thinking through the lens of translocational positionality; An intersectionality frame for understanding identity and belonging. *Migration and Social Change, 4*(1), 4–19.

Antonio, A., Astin, D., & Cress, C. (2000). Community service in higher education: A look at the nation's faculty. *Review of Higher Education, 23*(4), 373–398.

Baker, B. (2002). The hunt for disability: The new eugenics and normalization of school children. *Teacher's College Record, 104*(4), 663–703.

Bakhtin, M. (1981). *The dialogic imagination: Four essays*. University of Texas Press.

Biesta, G. J., & Stams, G. J. J. (2001), Critical thinking and the question of critique: Some lessons from deconstruction. *Studies in Philosophy and Education, 20*, 57–74.

Bradshaw, J. (2016). *The well-being of children in the UK*. Polity Press.

Bush, T., & Glover, G. (2014). School leadership models: What do we know? *School Leadership & Management, 34*(5), 202–208.

Collins, P. H., & Bilge, S. (2016). *Intersectionality: Key concepts*. Polity Press.

Corbett, J. (1996). *Bad-mouthing: The language of special needs*. Falmer Press.

Donnor, J. K., Dixson, A. D., Rousseau Anderson, C., Howard, T. C., & Navarro, O. (2016). Critical race theory 20 years later. *Urban Education, 51*(3), 253–273.

EU Commission. (2018). *European ideas for better learning: The governance of school education*. Directorate-General Education, Youth, Sport and Culture Schools and Multilingualism.

Evans, J., & Lunt, I. (2005) Inclusive education: are there limits? In K. Topping & S. Maloney (Eds.), *The RoutledgeFalmer reader in inclusive education* (pp. 41–55). RoutledgeFalmer.

Florian, L. (2008). Special or inclusive education, future trends. *British Journal of Sociology of Education, 35*(4), 202–208.

Foucault, M. (1977). *Discipline and punish: The birth of the prison*. Penguin.

Fraser, N. (1996, April 30–May 2). *Social justice in the age of identity politics: Redistribution, recognition, and participation*. The Tanner Lectures on Human Values Stanford University.

Freire, P. (1970). *Pedagogy of the oppressed*. Continuum Books.

Freire, P. (1997). *Pedagogy of the heart*. Continuum.

Goffman, E. (1956). *The presentation of self in everyday life*. University of Edinburgh, Social Sciences Research Centre.

Graham, L. (2006). *Discourse analysis and the critical use of Foucault*. Australian Association for Research in Education.

Graham, L., & Slee, R. (2008). An illusory interiority: Interrogating the discourse/s of inclusion. *Educational Philosophy and Theory, 40*(2), 277–293.

Greytak, E. A., Kosciw, J. G., Villenas, C., & Giga, N. M. (2016). *From teasing to torment: School climate revisited: A survey of U.S. secondary school students and teachers*. GLSEN.

Gronn, P. (2000). Distributed properties: A new architecture for leadership. *Educational Management Administration Leadership, 28*(3), 317–338.

Gunter, D. (2006). Knowledge production in the field of educational leadership: A place for intellectual histories. *Journal of Educational Administration and History, 28*(2), 205–215.

Harris, A. (2013b). Distributed leadership friend or foe? *Educational Management Administration & Leadership, 41*(5), 545–554.

Kinsella, D., & Senior, J. (2008). Developing inclusive schools: A systemic approach. *International Journal of Inclusive Education, 12*, 651–665.

Labaree, D. F. (2012). *Somebody has to fail*. Harvard University Press.

Lampert, K. (2016). *Meritocratic education and social worthlessness*. Plagrave Macmillan.

Lareau, A., & Goyette, K. (2014). *Choosing homes, choosing schools*. Russell Sage Foundation.

Layder, D. (1997). *Modern social theory*. Routledge.

Le Blanc, P. (2016). *From Marx to Gramsci: A reader in revolutionary marxist politics*. Haymarket Books.

Lingard, B. (2014). Re-articulating social justice as equity in schooling policy: The effects of testing and data infrastructures. *British Journal of Sociology of Education, 35*(5), 710–730.

Lumby, J. (2013). Distributed leadership: The uses and abuses of power. *Educational Management Administration and Leadership, 41*(5), 257–277.

Lynch, K., Baker, J., & Lyons, M. (2016). *Affective equality: Love, care and injustice*. Palgrave Macmillan.

Morrell, R., Davies, L., Lynch, K., Crean, M., & Subrahmanian, R. (2007). Gender, schooling and global social justice: Review symposium. *British Journal of Sociology of Education, 28*(6), 797–813.

Mac Ruairc, G. (2009). Language, socio-economic class and educational underachievement. In S. Drudy (Ed.), *Education in Ireland: Challenge and change*. Gill and Macmillian.

Mac Ruairc, G. (2011a). Where words collide: Social class, schools and linguistic discontinuity. *British Journal of Sociology of Education, 32*(4), 541–561.

Mac Ruairc, G. (2011b). They're my words – I'll talk how I like! Examining social class and linguistic practice among primary-school children. *Language and Education, 25*(6), 535–559.

Mittler, P. (2008). Planning for the future: Planning for the 2040s: Everybody's business. *British Journal of Special Education, 35*(1), 3–10. https://doi-org.ezproxy.une.edu.au/10.1111/j.1467-8578.2008.00363.x

Neary, A., & Cross, C. (2018). *Exploring gender identity and gender norms in primary schools: The perspectives of educators and parents of transgender and gender variant children.* University of Limerick and the Transgender Equality Network of Ireland.

Neary, A., Irwin-Gowran, S., & McEvoy, E. (2016). *Exploring homophobia and transphobia in primary schools.* University of Limerick and Gay and Lesbian Equality Network.

OECD. (2015). *Schooling redesigned: Towards innovative learning systems.* OECD Publishing.

Reay, D. (2006). The zombie stalking English schools: Social class and educational inequality. *British Journal of Educational Studies, 54*(3), 288–307.

Reay, D., Hollingworth, S., Williams, K., Crozier, G., Jamieson, F., James, D., & Beedell, P. (2007). A darker shade of pale? Whiteness, the middle classes and multi-ethnic inner city. *Schooling Sociology, 41*(6), 1041–1060.

Senior, J. (2009). ADHD: Inclusion or exclusion in mainstream Irish schools? In S. Drudy (Ed.), *Education in Ireland: Challenge and change.* Gill and McMillan.

Shields, C. M. (2016). *Transformative leadership: A primer.* Peter Lang.

Slee, R. (2001). Social justice and the changing directions in educational research: The case of inclusive education. *International Journal of Inclusive Education, 5*, 167–177.

Smyth, E. (2015). *Wellbeing and school experiences among 9- and 13-year-olds: Insights from the growing up in Ireland study.* NCCA.

Smyth, E. (2016). Social relationships and the transition to secondary education. *The Economic and Social Review, 47*(4), 447–472.

Spillane, J. P. (2006). *Distributed leadership.* Jossey-Bass.

Spratt, J. (2017). *Wellbeing, children and education: A critical analysis of wellbeing discourses in schools.* Springer.

Thomson, P. (2007). Leading schools in high poverty neighbourhoods. In D. T. Pink & G. D. Noblit (Eds.), *International handbook of urban education* (Vol. 2). Springer.

Warnock. M. (2005). *Special educational needs: A new look.* Philosophy of Education Society of Great Britain.

Wells, G. (1999). *Dialogic inquiry: Towards a sociocultural practice and theory of education.* Cambridge University Press.

Wrigley, T. (2012). Pedagogies of transformation: Keeping hope alive in troubled times. *Critical Studies in Education, 53*(1), 95–10.

PART 2

What's Gone Wrong? Why Are We Not More Inclusive?

CHAPTER 5

Becoming Your Own Worst Enemy: Converging Paths

James M. Kauffman, Dimitris Anastasiou, Jeanmarie Badar and Betty A. Hallenbeck

1 Introduction

Many of us have experienced becoming our own worst enemies. We wonder how it happened. Often, we can figure out how, or at least understand how others have done so. Sometimes, we cannot or do not figure out how it happened. Sometimes we can predict that other people are very likely to become their own enemies. We see them going down paths leading eventually to destruction or abandonment of their own goals. We want to warn them, but warnings are often ignored.

Becoming our own worst enemies is gradual. The nightmare scenarios we create for ourselves often develop over a period of years or decades. The process is insidious, like a disease with symptoms that are at first ambiguous, easily mistaken for or confused with normal processes. It is very hard for true believers to see the likely collapse of their movement, to change course before it is too late, not to scoff at those who see a high probability of disaster ahead. True believers do not doubt that the path leads to a good end. We are among the doubters about full inclusion, meaning the inclusion of all (meaning ALL) students in the regular classroom and probably the elimination of every form of *specially* designed instruction (*special* education). We note here that the full inclusion notion varies, but some supporters of full inclusion pursue the elimination of special education teachers' support even in the general education classroom (see Anastasiou, Gregory, & Kauffman, 2018, for commentary).

Misleading, inclusion-focused, intemperately romanticized rhetoric regarding the education of children with disabilities in many nations is worrisome. The United Nation's *Convention on the Rights of Persons with Disabilities* (CRPD) is a case in point (Anastasiou et al., 2018). We are struck by the possibility, and the relatively high probability, that many advocates of including *all* students in general education may be well down the paths people follow to become their own worst enemies (e.g., see Hornby, 2014; Imray & Colley, 2017; Kauffman, Anastasiou, & Maag, 2017). Our concern is that advocacy for inclusion might

 | DOI: 10.1163/9789004431171_005

become so extreme that the progress we have made in partial inclusion is reversed.

Our purpose in this chapter is to suggest nine converging paths that seem to us to lead supposedly radical intellectual movements to the unfortunate end of becoming their own worst enemies, whatever the matter in question might be. That is, we have tried to think about how certain behavior and attitudes toward "hot button" issues, besides inclusion, have not only created vehement disagreement but eventually become their own greatest enemies. We suggest paths seeming to us to lead to the demise of social movements or ideologies. These nine paths lead to what we see as counterproductive extremes, dissolution of the movement, sometimes even to regression or consequences opposite of those intended. We know there are other paths as well.

2 Converging Paths

The paths we discuss are interconnected and interdependent, like a maze of crossing and converging roads. Some routes may converge before the end point of self-destruction or regression. Our purpose is merely to suggest some of the most obvious paths people follow, only to find they have created a backlash or tidal wave that destroys a change they were hoping would be permanent.

2.1 *Drawing Clear and Extreme Lines*

Drawing lines to separate things into categories is necessary to make sense of the world. No matter what the "things" are (e.g., times, events, sizes, ages, colors, abilities, duties, privileges, rights) we categorize and label them by the lines we draw and what we call them (Harnad, 2005). Sometimes these lines are very sharp or bright, but sometimes they are ambiguous or fuzzy. One path to becoming your own worst enemy is making the line exceedingly sharp, bright, or clear with no possible ambiguity or nuance. That is, make the matter black or white, on or off, good or bad, such that there is, for example, no gray. In anti-miscegenation laws, the "one drop" rule made "race" classification a matter of supposedly complete clarity. "One drop" of blood – any ancestry whatever other than that considered "white" – was sufficient to prohibit marriage of a "pure white" person to a "colored" person (Smedley & Smedley, 2005) or sufficed to make someone sink to a rank below that of the "common white", as is reflected in the French nineteenth-century novella *Les Epaves* by Madame Charles Reybaud (Sollors, 1997) and the contemporary American novella, *The Color of Integrity* by Patricia L. Pullen (2017; also search the Internet for "one drop rule"). Anti-miscegenation was, fortunately, overcome as a result of (a) the defeat of Nazi Germany and the horrendous experience of its racial state, which tried to restructure society along clear-cut racial-ideological lines (Burleigh & Wippermann, 1991), (b) the 1967 U.S. Supreme Court decision in Loving versus Virginia (Pullen, 2017), and (c) the civil rights movement in the United States.

In the matter of inclusion, the clearer the line between inclusion and non-inclusion (or inclusive and not inclusive) and the clearer it is that there are to be *no* exceptions, the more likely it is that one can find a fault, see an enemy, or make an accusation. Thus, "all means all" (i.e., presumably "all" means *no* exceptions) is a way of making the line as clear as possible. Suggesting that "inclusion" in general education means being taught as part of the general group, not a group pulled aside or an individual taught one-on-one, is a way of making the line defining inclusion brighter. Insisting that "inclusion" means being at or near the center of the classroom, not on the spatial periphery, is another way of defining inclusion with less ambiguity.

We think of this path toward becoming your own enemy as reducing the issue to a binary: e.g., yes-no, on-off, black-white, all-not all. Making a question or issue binary is often combined with other paths leading in the same direction. It reduces the issue to either-or judgments, sharpening divisions (e.g., consider the pro-life/pro-choice binary). Furthermore, the reduction of complex issues to binaries is a disturbing trend away from critical thinking or deep analysis of complex problems. Viewing issues that are highly intricate as binary is another step towards replacing meaningful discussion with tweets, a habit allowing flabby thinking to become even more atrophied.

Moreover, in many cases of extremism, the binary is not symmetrical – one extreme is not matched by an equal and opposite extreme. For example, some people advocate prohibition of abortion in *all* or very nearly all cases. No one we know of advocates abortion in *all* or very nearly all cases or even abortion without limitations. In the inclusion debate, some do advocate inclusion in *all* or very nearly all cases, but we know of no one who advocates inclusion in *no* or almost no cases. Extremism typically dies of its own weight, having become an enemy of itself and having accomplished a kind of self-evisceration (e.g., Lysenko's genetics in Stalinist times; Stanchevici, 2017). But until they are recognized as self-defeating, extremely intolerant ideologies typically end in catastrophe and/or create a great deal of social injustice. That is, although a movement may have equality or social justice as a goal, the binary ensures that social *in*justice will be done in at least some cases.

2.2 *Bypassing Dilemmas of Judgment*

The definition of "inclusion" may require judgment, but other issues of judgment also arise, and to the extent that judgment of any part of the issue can be eliminated the issue seems simpler. If the judgment required is a binary – e.g., simply yes or no, did or did not, guilty or not guilty – then the judgment can be relatively simple and straightforward. Ambiguity, as typically involved in disability issues, makes judgment harder. Furthermore, allowing judgment introduces the possibility of error (Hastie & Dawes, 2010; Lewis, 2017; Lipsky, 2010).

Errors of judgment may be false positives or false negatives – that is, a judgment of yes or positive when no or negative is correct; or a judgment of no or negative when yes or positive is correct. But, some judgments can be precluded by a policy of uniform, invariant decisions such that the only judgment required is binary: yes/no, did/did not.

A jury may well hear conflicting or ambiguous testimony in a trial, but nevertheless be charged with returning a binary: guilty or not guilty. A teacher may well need to consider multiple factors in coming to a conclusion that a student does or does not need a particular support or meet a particular criterion (Lipsky, 2010). Nevertheless, the "cognitive load" may be lightened by eliminating the necessity of some judgments (Hastie & Dawes, 2010). Thus, one can eliminate judgments by, for example, prohibiting abortion in *all* cases, prohibiting *any* possession of alcohol, disallowing *any* amount of a proscribed substance, having *zero* tolerance (e.g., for something considered a drug or weapon), or requiring placement in general education in *all* cases. The problem is one of social justice. To the extent that judgment is allowed, it is highly likely that some individuals will make bad or mistaken judgments (Hastie & Dawes, 2010; Lipsky, 2010). But to the extent that judgment is *not* allowed, instances of social injustice are made certain because of variability in individuals' characteristics and circumstances. Although cognitive uncertainty may cause psychological pain, its denial can be cruel (see Hastie & Dawes, 2010). The dilemma is important to recognize, but a certain route to becoming one's own enemy is to deny judgment in favor of a uniform policy, one not open to question. Many examples of this can be found in the literature of school discipline involving zero tolerance, a once popular policy in schools and communities that has been largely abandoned because even enthusiastic supporters of the policy followed it to predictable disasters, such as children being punished for doing the right thing or for something they did not understand was wrong (see Lewis, Mitchell, Johnson, & Richter, 2014).

Judgment presents a true dilemma, for there will be disappointing, if not agonizing, outcomes whether judgment is allowed or disallowed. Allowing judges to use discretion in sentencing people brought before the law will sometimes result in what many people see as outrageous miscarriages of justice (Lipsky, 2010). But uniform sentencing is certain to be unjust sometimes.

In the field of medicine, there is a strong trend away from the use of narcotic pain relievers, even for individuals who would clearly benefit from these medications. It appears that we are more comfortable with some individuals receiving inadequate pain relief than we are with the possibility that one individual might misuse a pain medication in the future. This issue has been inappropriately presented as a binary to the detriment of the most needy patients in any hospital. So determined are the anti-opiate crowd that narcotics must be avoided that even hospice doctors are having difficulty procuring adequate pain medication for people in the final weeks of their lives. The rationale for this cruel practice is that opiate use carries an unacceptable risk of future addiction, even among patients who will be dead within a matter of weeks (see Hallenbeck, 2003).

In special education, allowing exceptions to the inclusion imperative risks someone making a bad decision, either to include or not to include a student in a general education classroom. Disallowing exceptions ensures absolutely that social justice will not be done in some cases – unless, of course, inclusion is by definition considered to represent social justice in all cases, regardless of any other consideration or consequence.

2.3 *Ignoring Economic Consequences of Policy*

One fact often not considered in social policy is that the wealthy can, almost always, buy what they want regardless of social policy, but the poor, nearly poor, and/or socially disadvantaged typically must conform to the policy as written. Thus, policies that affect options, choices, or judgments are likely to have greater consequences for the poor than the rich. We see this play out in access to health care, mental health care, abortion, gun rights, and education. A path leading to becoming one's own enemy disregards such disturbing economic considerations.

Economic consequences apply to both restriction and expansion of choice. That is, prohibition of choosing a traditional special education setting often does not prohibit people who have many financial resources from exercising their choice outside the boundaries of the law in a free market economy (Anastasiou et al., 2018). For those with few economic resources, the legal expansion of choice may be meaningless because they do not have the means necessary to exercise their choice in a meaningful way (i.e., they may not have the resources necessary to choose a school, a health-care plan, or the purchase of an option ostensibly given to them by law).

We do see extreme concentration of wealth and growing economic inequalities as significant social problems of our time (Piketty, 2014; Piketty & Saez, 2014). The most important thing to consider when living in a new *Gilded Age* – an era of deeply socially stratified societies and powerful forces pushing toward rising economic inequality (Beardsley et al., 2017; Piketty & Saez, 2014) – is how proposed social policies play out in various socioeconomic groups. Including *all* students with disabilities in general education is likely to play out differently in different socioeconomic strata. Blindness to the powerful forces of marketizing public education of people with disabilities (e.g., vouchers, charter schools, academies, multi-academy trusts, and free schools in England) can create a paradox. That is, a policy making individual needing a market can be used as license to spur *de facto* what pro-inclusion policy-makers ostensibly hate (exclusion).

2.4 *Flirting with Irrationality*

Rationality has its limits; irrationality has none. This was perhaps most obviously on display to the world in the early days of the Trump presidency when the term "alternative fact" was coined to describe falsehood. True believers in an ideology see that policy as having no rational limits. They peddle "alternative facts" that rational analysis of data do not support. A path virtually certain to lead to becoming your own enemy is to see rationality as relatively unimportant and limitations as mere human constructions.

In special education, "postmodern" notions that rationality and the scientific method are remnants of an oppressive past seem to have fueled the tendency to claim that full inclusion can ignore rational objections. Cautions are interpreted as misapprehensions and attempts to justify the unjustifiable. The ideology of full inclusion is presented as having no limits imposed by rationality or evidence (see Hornby, 2014; Imray & Colley, 2017). The so-called "neurodiversity movement" that frames autism, ADHD, mental disorders, dyslexia, and other disorders as simple neurological differences rather than disabilities and rejects the very idea of treatment is the logical consequence of the irrational denial of disability for the sake of a social constructionist philosophy and the romance of full inclusion (Anastasiou & Kauffman, 2011; Kauffman et al., 2017; cf., Armstrong, 2010; Farber, 2012; Rentenbach, Prislovsky, & Gabriel, 2017; Strauss, 2013). "Neurotypical" may indeed accurately describe the typical development of the central nervous system, but that does not mean all variations of neurological development are equal. Mind-related and/or severe disabilities are far from being minor, statistically typical neutral, or harmless (Anastasiou, Kauffman, & Michail, 2016).

Claims of limitlessness and irrationality are extremely likely to be exposed as false. Irrationality and claims of limitlessness or literal all-inclusiveness often become their own enemies, eventually requiring acknowledgement of their own demise. In the long run, reason and replicable evidence have greater odds to prevail (Sagan, 1997). When someone clings to irrationality, perhaps in the name of what is considered morally superior or because it is among the tenets of an ideology or religion, it seems highly probable that they are on a path leading nowhere or to eventual humiliation. Religions seem impervious to rationality, but other forms of ideology are less robust.

2.5 *Oversimplifying the Complex*

Some things are relatively simple, but often what seems simple is actually quite complex. We are well advised to seek simplicity but, at the same time, distrust it (Bunge, 1962). Apparent simplicity can mask an underlying complexity that someone must acknowledge and understand to work successfully with or on a given matter.

Perhaps the most fatuous notion underlying the ideology of full inclusion is that a change of the *place* of instruction is key to improving special education. That notion is perhaps best captured by the following quotation:

> "Place" is the issue ... *There is nothing pervasively wrong with special education.* What is being questioned is not the interventions and knowledge that has [sic] been acquired through special education training and research. Rather, what is being challenged is the location where these supports are being provided to students with disabilities.
>
> Special education needs to be reconceptualized as a support to the regular education classroom, rather than as "another place to go". Recent research suggests that what is so wrong about special education is the stigma and isolation that result from being removed from the regular education class for so long. We now have the effective strategies to bring help to the student rather than removing the student from the enriching setting of the regular education class. (Blackman, 1992, p. 29, original emphasis)

This and other claims for full inclusion (e.g., Sailor & McCart, 2014) suggest a simple solution to special education's faults in all cases – change the place it happens, and – voila, it is better! The place of instruction is certainly an important consideration, but realities suggest that improving special education involves much more than place and that a diversity of places is required to make special education what it should be, that places other than the general education classroom are required in some cases for best results (Kauffman & Hallahan, 1997). Furthermore, special education is not conceptualized as a place, and it has never been so conceptualized by scholars.

Full inclusion as absolutist ideology suggests that there is one primary dimension of special education – that first and foremost is place, with other aspects or dimensions of special education being subsumed. Instruction and the individual's instructional needs may well be deemed important, but not as important as the place in which instruction and supports are provided. IDEA (the Individuals with Disabilities Education Act of 2004 and its predecessors dating from 1975) demands that the dominant issue be appropriate education and that place of instruction be of secondary importance – and that one cannot assume that the most appropriate instruction can occur only in one type of place (see Bateman, 2007, 2017; Endrew, 2017; Lemons, Vaughn, Wexler, Kearns, & Sinclair, 2018; Martin, 2013; U.S. Office of Education, 2017; Yell, Katysiannis, & Bradley, 2017).

Actually, addressing the instructional and support needs of all children with disabilities is very complex regardless of where it occurs, and the place of instruction is one important issue. Making place the dominant issue is a way of masking complexity somewhat, nullifying the complexity of place by making it unidimensional or binary so that place is removed from consideration, for there are simply no appropriate alternative environments in any case (e.g., Laski, 1991). A certain path to becoming our own enemy is oversimplification.

2.6 *Claiming Moral Superiority*

Proponents of full inclusion feel morally obligated to include all students with disabilities in general education so that no student is discriminated against – so that students with disabilities are presumably afforded all the opportunities any other student has. The moral imperative that proponents of full inclusion feel is based on the premise that all individuals, regardless of personal characteristics, are to be treated equally, not "segregated" in any way. Their premise is that disability is merely one of many forms of diversity, and that treating people differently because of their diversity is discriminatory. Because the U.S. Supreme Court found that "separate is inherently unequal" in cases involving skin color or parentage (or because another nation's highest court made a similar finding), proponents of full inclusion conclude we have a moral obligation to include students with disabilities in the same school and classroom they would be in were they not to have a disability (e.g., see Stainback & Stainback,

1991). Claiming the moral high ground, particularly when ignoring ethical problems that complicate the moral claim, is a common path to becoming one's own enemy.

The illogic of equating disabilities and skin color in matters of "segregation" and "integration" in education seems obvious. Certainly, racial segregation is morally unjust. But treating all students alike in education, regardless of their abilities or disabilities, violates not only a moral responsibility to treat students fairly but ethical principles of meeting individual educational needs (e.g., the beneficience principle). A balance between moral and ethical principles must be found, as Berg (2003–2004) explained. But exercising both the moral and the ethical dimensions of inclusion requires nuance, something not attainable without considering both. Claiming moral superiority simply because students are physically "integrated" allows proponents of full inclusion to claim the moral high ground while giving less attention to ethical treatment or pretending that students are having their needs fully met such that ethical standards have been given full consideration. In such a dogmatic approach, rightness is always goodness, and feedback from policy consequences is ignored. Full inclusion as a moral dogma excludes finding out what works and what does not, what is right or wrong, except by reference to its own moral code (see Bunge, 1989, p. 210).

2.7 *Demonizing Dissent*

Wholesome and beneficial social interactions require tolerance of and respect for those who dissent. Vilification of dissenters on "hot button" issues has become common, if not de rigueur, in the USA's Trump administration. Sometimes, dissenters (e.g., regarding religious affiliation, guns, homosexuality) are killed or seriously injured by those who hold an opposite view.

One path to destroying what one holds dear is vilification of an alternative point of view by labeling it as something it is not or using an inaccurate analogy, especially if the label or analogue is one that arouses strong emotion. Describing special education that involves instruction in a place other than the general education classroom as "segregation" is one such tactic. True, "segregation" has multiple meanings and can be a necessary and benign process, but it is a word likely to arouse strong emotion because of its use to describe racism.

Sometimes, leaders of a public policy recommendation become more extreme in their rhetoric when dissent arises, believing that they will move followers toward the extreme they advocate. However, such leaders, who initially distinguish themselves by taking extreme positions, eventually may become so fanatical or rabid in their advocacy that they alienate many or most of their followers. Perhaps this has happened in the case of the National Rifle Association (see Valentine, 2017). Certainly, it is something that can happen in special education when vilification of dissenting views and/or ad hominem arguments are used.

We hope not to be misunderstood here, as dissent *can* itself be unacceptable – become advocacy for something morally or ethically questionable or even horrific. Dissent, like various forms of diversity and other issues, can be misunderstood and misused to try to justify injustice. We realize that our dissention is with the ideology of full inclusion, but our judgment is that total or full inclusion results in injustice in some cases, if not in many. Moreover, we realize that the dissention of those who promote the idea of full inclusion is with the notion of a full continuum of alternative placements. Thus, dissent itself requires judgment.

2.8 *Losing Focus*

The focus of special education initially was – and has been until relatively recently – access to appropriate instruction. The first and foremost requirement of federal law since its inception has been FAPE (free, appropriate public education; see Bateman, 2007; Yell, Crockett, Shriner, & Rozalski, 2017). That focus seems to have gotten lost, and inclusion seems to have become the preoccupation of educators in many nations of the world (see Anastasiou et al., 2018; Kauffman et al., 2017; Kauffman & Badar, 2014).

People sometimes risk obscurity or becoming their own enemies by emphasizing something secondary or trivial. Imagine what would happen if hospitals were designed with the same level of emphasis on place as some would have us employ in schools! None of us would likely be satisfied with a hospital that had only general medical wards, eliminating such special places as intensive care units, maternity wards, and oncology centers, arguing that they "separate out" and "stigmatize" the patients who are "relegated" to them. The needs of students with disabilities, the nature and quality of instruction, particularly its appropriateness for the individual student, seems to us of primary importance. Of clearly secondary importance is the issue of the place it is provided. This is true according to law, but it is also true when the ethics of special education and a multifaceted social justice principle are considered (see Anastasiou et al., 2018; Anastasiou, Kauffman, & Michail, 2016; Bateman, 2007, 2017).

2.9 *Ignoring History*

Lessons of history are often mentioned but seldom learned. Often, those who ignore history argue that we are in a different era, that relevant things have changed, and that a proposition that once failed will now succeed (or vice versa). Sometimes, history is revised or distorted such that the lesson supposedly to be taught is twisted to represent an untruth or contradiction. Someone may claim that decades of research indicate inclusion has good outcomes for all students, but others see the history of inclusion quite differently:

> ... educational inclusion despite a constantly changing and liquid definition, has not been achieved in any country under any educational system despite some 30 years of trying. It was no doubt a valiant and laudable attempt to ensure justice and equity but its failure must now be addressed. Inclusion has become a recurring trope of academic writing on education; it is trotted out as an eternal and unarguable truth, but it is neither. It doesn't work, and it never has worked. (Imray & Colley, 2017, p. 1)

We note here that at least one nation of the world claim to have achieved the goal of full inclusion (e.g., Italy; see Anastasiou, Kauffman, & Di Nuovo, 2015; Anastasiou & Keller, 2017). In some nations of the world, full inclusion presents particular problems, especially given the nature of the country's system of education (e.g., Ahrbeck, Badar, Felder, Kauffman, & Schneiders, 2018; see also Anastasiou et al., 2018). The meaning of full inclusion seems to vary among nations, and the implications of movement toward full inclusion differs with the history of a nation's education system (Anastasiou & Keller, 2011, 2017).

Powers (2017) and others (e.g., Earley, 2006) have described the abject failure of deinstitutionalization in the USA in the twentieth century. They describe how jails and streets have become the default "mental health system" following decades of hyperbole and false claims about the transformation offered by community mental health centers and psychoactive drugs. Deinstitutionalization is a sad story of overzealous rhetoric and denial of realities. People with mental disorders and their families have paid a high cost in the unavailability of alternative services, not only in community mental health centers but institutional care as well. We hope that 50 years hence no one will be able to write something like the following paragraph about reform involving special education (a paraphrase of Powers, 2017, pp. 156–157, writing about attempted reform of mental health services).

The wave of educational reforms, its crest ridden by zealous ideologues, myopic politicians, and cynical bureaucrats, achieved a bungled "liberation" of students with disabilities. It sent many students away from imperfect special education and into the fickle mercies of general education classrooms supposedly designed to accommodate *all* children. The "transformation" achieved by these reforms was based on the assumption that universal design for learning and differentiation or multi-tiered systems of supports and new concepts and labels for educational failure and special education would change everything. The restructured ("fully inclusive") classrooms and the new concepts (e.g., not "deficits", only "diversity" and "differences") and labels (e.g., say "differently abled;" replace "special education" with "systems of supports") did not meet all students' needs. Instead, the reforms launched a crisis in American schooling, one unimaginable even in the days when most students with disabilities got "special education" in "segregated" classes or schools.

Ignoring relevant history and rejecting its lessons of unintended consequences is a common path leading toward becoming your own enemy. True, the history of one thing or social movement is not the history of another, and it is tempting to deny analogies, supposing that history does not and will not yield a similar result for the movement or ideology in question. And, of course, parallels can be deceiving. As some have observed, history may not repeat itself but it rhymes (i.e., exact replications may not occur, but the issues and outcomes may be quite similar).

3 Conclusion

We have suggested several paths people might take to becoming their own worst enemies: (a) drawing especially clear and extreme lines, (b) neglecting or rejecting matters of judgment, (c) ignoring or downplaying the economic consequences of policy, (d) abjuring rationality and flirting with irrationality, (e) offering simple solutions to complex problems, (f) claiming moral superiority while ignoring competing moral and ethical principles, (g) demonizing dissenting views, (h) losing focus on what is most important, and (i) ignoring history. We see all of these either playing out or on the margins of acceptance by the special education community, auguring problems ahead.

Undoubtedly, the probability that we are wrong is substantial, even if low; the probability that we are correct may be high, but we know it is not 1.0. Imray and Colley (2017) have pronounced inclusion dead, and they refer to full inclusion, not the partial inclusion they clearly support, along with Hornby (2014), Warnock (2005), and many others. In fact, the subtitle of Imray and Colley's book is "Long Live Inclusion". No one of whom we are aware rejects all inclusion of students with disabilities in general education; we and everyone we know or have read support inclusion that makes sense, and we all recognize that such inclusion is not only required by U.S. law but a moral and ethical obligation. We fear that proponents of full inclusion – total and complete, without exception, all meaning literally all – will become their own worst enemies and threaten to "pull the house down around us", endangering the progress made in rational, judgmental inclusion. Too many have forgotten that "the disgrace is that we have come to believe that special education is so *not-special* that it can be delivered by a generalist, busy teaching 25 other students" (Zigmond & Kloo, 2017, p. 259). We believe another disgrace is the ideology that the general education classroom must be made the place where the most effective special education can be provided for all students.

Many radical intellectual movements have had unenviable fates (e.g., Lysenkoism, Rousseauvian or romanticized education; see Mosenthal, 1989; Stanovich, 1993), but no two have followed precisely the same routes to exactly the same consequences. We can trace the failure of the prohibition movement in the USA, its ostensible victory, and its abandonment after it became so clearly unworkable. We do not know that attempts to prohibit abortion will suffer a similar fate, but those attempts and their fate may rhyme with that of the prohibition of alcohol. We observe the mental health carnage created unintentionally by the policy of deinstitutionalization (which had noble intentions), and we do not know that similar wreckage would follow a policy of full inclusion. Our era has been described as one in which the "stars are in alignment" (Sailor & McCart, 2014). Ours is also the era in which Imray and Colley (2017) pronounced full inclusion dead. Others (e.g., Hornby, 2014; Warnock, 2005) have noted the advisability of partial inclusion tempered by the realities of teaching and learning. We would rather be guided by science and reason than by romanticism or "pure" but crude ideology (Bunge, 2017; Stanovich, 1993).

References

Ahrbeck, B., Badar, J., Felder, M., Kauffman, J., & Schneiders, K. (2018). Fachbeitrag: Totale inklusion? Fakten und Überlegungen zur situation in Deutschland und den USA [Technical paper: Total inclusion? Facts and considerations on the situation in Germany and the USA]. *Vierteljahreszeitschrift für Heilpädagogik und ihre Nachbargebiete (VHN)* [*Quarterly Journal for Special Needs Education and Neighboring Areas*], *87*(3), 218–231. doi:10.2378/vhn2018.art23d

Anastasiou, D., Gregory, M., & Kauffman, J. M. (2018). Commentary on article 24 of the CRPD: The right to education. In I. Bantekas, M. Stein, & D. Anastasiou (Eds.), *Commentary on the UN Convention on the rights of persons with disabilities* (pp. 656–704). Oxford University Press.

Anastasiou, D., & Kauffman, J. M. (2011). A social constructionist approach to disability: Implications for special education. *Exceptional Children, 77*, 367–384. doi:10.1177/001440291107700307

Anastasiou, D., Kauffman, J. M., & Di Nuovo, S. (2015). Inclusive education in Italy: Description and reflections on full inclusion. *European Journal of Special Needs Education, 30*, 429–443.

Anastasiou, D., Kauffman, J. M., & Michail, D. (2016). Disability in multicultural theory: Conceptual and social justice issues. *Journal of Disability Policy Studies, 27*, 3–12. doi:10.1177/1044207314558595

Anastasiou, D., & Keller, C. (2011). International differences in provision for exceptional learners. In J. M. Kauffman & D. P. Hallahan (Eds.), *Handbook of special education* (1st ed., pp. 773–787). Routledge.

Anastasiou, D., & Keller, C. (2017). Cross-national differences in special education: A typological approach. In J. M. Kauffman, D. P. Hallahan, & P. C. Pullen (Eds.), *Handbook of special education* (2nd ed., pp. 897–910). Routledge.

Armstrong, T. (2012). *Neurodiversity in the classroom: Strength-based strategies to help students with special needs succeed in school and life*. ASCD.

Bateman, B. D. (2007). Law and the conceptual foundations of special education practice. In J. B. Crockett, M. M. Gerber, & T. J. Landrum (Eds.), *Achieving the radical reform of special education: Essays in honor of James M. Kauffman* (pp. 95–114). Erlbaum.

Bateman, B. D. (2017). Individual education programs for children with disabilities. In J. M. Kauffman, D. P. Hallahan, & P. C. Pullen (Eds.), *Handbook of special education* (2nd ed., pp. 87–104). Taylor & Francis.

Beardsley, B., Holley, B., Jaafar, M., Kessler, D., Muxi, F., Naumann, M., Rogg, J., Tang, T., Xavier, A., & Zakrzewski, A. (2017). *Global wealth 2017: Transforming the client experience*. The Boston Consulting Group.

Berg, H. (2003–2004). Bridging moral and ethical polarities in inclusive education. In N. L. Hutchinson (Ed.), *Graduate student symposium: Selected papers* (Vol. 2). Queen's University. Retrieved June 17, 2017, from https://qspace.library.queensu.ca/bitstream/handle/1974/15721/10.pdf?sequence=1

Blackman, H. P. (1992). Surmounting the disability of isolation. *The School Administrator, 49*(2), 28–29.

Bunge, M. (1962). The complexity of simplicity. *The Journal of Philosophy, 59*(5), 113–135.

Bunge, M. (1989). *Treatise on basic philosophy VIII: Ethics: The good and the right*. Kluwer.

Bunge, M. (2017). *Doing science in the light of philosophy*. World Scientific.

Burleigh, M., & Wippermann, W. (1991). *The racial state: Germany 1933–1945*. Cambridge University Press.

Earley, P. (2006). *Crazy: A father's search through America's mental health madness*. Penguin.

Endrew F. v. Douglas County School District RE-1, 137 S. Ct. 988. (2017).

Farber, S. (2012). *The spiritual gift of madness: The failure of psychiatry and the rise of the mad pride movement*. Inner Traditions.

Hallenbeck, J. L. (2003). *Palliative care perspectives*. Oxford University Press.

Harnad, S. (2005). To cognize is to categorize: Cognition is categorization. In H. Cohen & C. Lefebvre (Eds.), *Handbook of categorization in cognitive science* (pp. 19–44). Elsevier.

Hastie, R., & Dawes, R. M. (2010). *Rational choice in an uncertain world: The psychology of judgment and decision making* (2nd ed.). Sage.

Hornby, G. (2014). *Inclusive special education: Evidence-based practices for children with special needs and disabilities*. Springer.

Imray, P., & Colley, A. (2017). *Inclusion is dead: Long live inclusion*. Routledge.

Kauffman, J. M., Anastasiou, D., & Maag, J. W. (2017). Special education at the cross-road: An identity crisis and the need for a scientific reconstruction. *Exceptionality, 25*, 139–155. doi:10.1080/09362835.2016.1238380

Kauffman, J. M., & Badar, J. (2014). Instruction, not inclusion, should be the central issue in special education: An alternative view from the USA. *Journal of International Special Needs Education, 17*, 13–20. doi:10.1080/09362835.2017.1283632

Kauffman, J. M., & Hallahan, D. P. (1997). A diversity of restrictive environments: Placement as a problem of social ecology. In J. W. Lloyd, E. J. Kameenui, & D. Chard (Eds.), *Issues in educating students with disabilities* (pp. 325–342). Lawrence Erlbaum Associates.

Laski, F. J. (1991). Achieving integration during the second revolution. In L. H. Meyer, C. A. Peck, & L. Brown (Eds.), *Critical issues in the lives of people with severe disabilities* (pp. 409–421). Paul H. Brookes.

Lemons, C. J., Vaughn, S., Wexler, J., Kearns, D. M., & Sinclair, A. C. (2018). Envisioning an improved continuum of special education services for students with learning disabilities: Considering intervention intensity. *Learning Disabilities Research and Practice, 33*, 131–143.

Lewis, M. (2017). *The undoing project: A friendship that changes our minds*. Norton.

Lewis, T. J., Mitchell, B. S., Johnson, N. W., & Richter, M. (2014). Supporting children and youth with emotional behavioural disorders through school-wide systems of positive behaviour support. In P. Garner, J. M. Kauffman, & J. Elliott (Eds.), *The Sage handbook of emotional and behavioural difficulties* (2nd ed., pp. 373–384). Sage.

Lipsky, M. (2010). *Street-level bureaucracy: Dilemmas of the individual in public service* (expanded ed.). The Russell Sage Foundation.

Martin Jr., E. W. (2013). *Breakthrough: Federal special education legislation 1965–1981*. Bardolf.

Mosenthal, P. B. (1989). The whole language approach: Teachers between a rock and a hard place. *The Reading Teacher, 42*, 628–629.

Piketty, T. (2014). *Capital in the twenty-first century*. Harvard University Press.

Piketty, T., & Saez, E. (2014). Inequality in the long run. *Science, 344*(838), 838–843. doi:10.1126/science.1251936

Powers, R. (2017). *No one cares about crazy people; The chaos and heartbreak of mental health in America.* Hachette.

Pullen, P. L. (2017). *The color of integrity.* James Kauffman.

Rentenbach, B., Prislovsky, L., & Gabriel, R. (2017). Valuing differences: Neurodiversity in the classroom. *Phi Delta Kappan, 98*(8), 59–63.

Sagan, C. (1997). *The demon-haunted world: Science as a candle in the dark.* Headline.

Sailor, W. S., & McCart, A. B. (2014). Stars in alignment. *Research & Practice for Persons with Severe Disabilities, 39*(1), 55–64. doi:10.1177/1540796914534622

Skiba, R. J. (2002). Special education and school discipline: A precarious balance. *Behavioral Disorders, 27,* 16–19.

Smedley, A., & Smedley, B. D. (2005). Race as biology is fiction, racism as a social problem is real. *American Psychologist, 60,* 16–25. doi:10.1037/0003-066X.60.1.16

Sollors, W. (1997). *Neither black nor white, yet both: Thematic explorations of interracial literature.* Oxford University Press.

Stainback, W., & Stainback, S. (1991). A rationale for integration and restructuring: A synopsis. In J. W. Lloyd, N. N. Singh, & A. C. Repp (Eds.), *The regular education initiative: Alternative perspectives on concepts, issues, and models* (pp. 223–239). Sycamore.

Stanchevici, D. (2017). *Stalinist genetics: The constitutional rhetoric of T. D. Lysenko.* Routledge.

Stanovich, K. E. (1993). Romance and reality. *The Reading Teacher, 47,* 280–291.

Strauss, J. N. (2013). Autism as culture. In L. J. Davis (Ed.), *The disability studies reader* (4th ed., pp. 460–484). Routledge.

U.S. Department of Education. (2017, December 7). *Questions and Answers (Q&A) on U.S. Supreme Court case decision Endrew F. v. Douglas County School District Re-1.* U.S. Department of Education.

Valentine, M. (2017, June 18). The NRA wants policies that most gun owners don't: The group alienates its members as it seeks new enemies. *The Washington Post,* B1, B4.

Warnock, M. (2005). *Special educational needs: A new look* (Impact, No. 11). Philosophy of Education Society of Great Britain.

Yell, M. L., Crockett, J. B., Shriner, J. G., & Rozalski, M. (2017). Free appropriate public education. In J. M. Kauffman, D. P. Hallahan, & P. C. Pullen (Eds.), *Handbook of special education* (2nd ed., pp. 71–86). Routledge.

Yell, M. L., Katysiannis, A., & Bradley, M. R. (2017). The individuals with disabilities education act: The evolution of special education law. In J. M. Kauffman, D. P. Hallahan, & P. C. Pullen (Eds.), *Handbook of special education* (2nd ed., pp. 55–70). Routledge.

Zigmond, N., & Kloo, A. (2017). General and special education are (and should be) different. In J. M. Kauffman, D. P. Hallahan, & P. C. Pullen (Eds.), *Handbook of special education* (2nd ed., pp. 249–261). Taylor & Francis.

Zweers, I., Tick, N. T., Bijstra, J. O., & van de Schoot, R. (2019). How do included and excluded students with SEBD function socially and academically after 1.5 year of special education services? *European Journal of Developmental Psychology.* doi:10.1080/17405629.2019.1590193

CHAPTER 6

Why Are We Not More Inclusive? Examining Neoliberal Selective Inclusionism

Federico R. Waitoller

1 Introduction

In this chapter, I engage with one of the questions posed by the editors of this book: Why are we not more inclusive? To answer this question, I argue, it is imperative that scholars, activist, parents, students, and practitioners engage in a critical examination of *actual existing neoliberalism* (Brenner & Theodore, 2002) and its global and local influence in the deployment of an inclusive education agenda. I do not argue neoliberalism is the *only* reason for inclusive education shortcomings. Yet, neoliberalism has been the dominant economic, cultural, and political ideology in many developing and developed countries, significantly impacting how education is conceptualized, implemented, and measured (Apple, Kenway, & Singh, 2005). In the following sections, I define inclusive education and review the status of inclusive efforts. Then, I examine various aspects of actual existing neoliberalism and their implications for an inclusive education agenda.

2 Inclusive Education

Inclusive education emerged as a movement concerned with the exclusion of students from *minoritized backgrounds* (Harper, 2012) from quality educational opportunities. I use the term students from *minoritized backgrounds* to signify the social construction of marginalization and subordination in institutions around the globe. Students and families are not born as a part of a minority group (i.e., racial, ethnic, gender, caste, minorities and students with dis/abilities[1] and those living in poverty) nor are they a minority group in every social context; they are minoritized by social and institutional arrangements that sustain exclusion and perpetuate dominant cultures and ways of being (Harper, 2012).

Inclusive Education has become a buzzword required in the discourse of any effort towards equity, becoming a dulled and vague concept (Slee, 2010).

 | DOI: 10.1163/9789004431171_006

Broadly speaking, inclusive education focuses on increasing access and participation in education for *all* students, valuing and recognizing diversity, creating a sense of belonging, and improving the achievement and learning of all students (Ainscow, Booth, & Dyson, 2006; Artiles, Kozleski, Dorn, & Christensen, 2006). Despite these commonalities, inclusive education has been a global movement with multiple faces and contested meanings (Clough, 2000). Indeed, at the core of the inclusive education movement there are many discourses that differentially favour certain justice paradigms over others (Rizvi & Lingard, 1996; Skrtic, 1991) and tensions emerge between efforts to address various forms of injustice (Waitoller & Kozleski, 2015; Waitoller & Pazey, 2016).

To address this conceptual ambiguity around the definition of inclusive, I use Waitoller and colleagues' (Waitoller & Artiles, 2013; Waitoller & Kozleski, 2013) definition that crystalizes the struggles for inclusive education around three dimensions of justice (Fraser, 2009). Inclusive education is defined as

> an ongoing struggle toward (a) the redistribution of access to and participation in quality opportunities to learn [the redistribution dimension], (b) the recognition and valuing of all students' differences as reflected in content, pedagogy, and assessment tools [the recognition dimension], and (c) the creation of more opportunities for non-dominant groups to advance claims of educational exclusion and their respective solutions [the representation dimension]. (Waitoller & Artiles, 2013, p. 322)

Struggles for social justice based on redistribution focus on the economic aspects of justice and aims to address injustices based on misdistribution, wherein social and material privileges are bestowed on a small group of already privileged people (Young, 1990). Youth with dis/abilities, for instance, have experienced numerous injustices based on misdistribution, such as lack of funding for social services and denial of access to public schools, among others.

Struggles for justice based on recognition focus on the cultural aspects of justice. Students with dis/abilities have also experienced numerous injustices based on misrecognition. For instance, the cultural identities of students with dis/abilities have been and continue to be undervalued and addressed from a deficit and medical perspective. This takes particular significance for those students with dis/abilities who come from other minoritized background (e.g., race, language, and class; Artiles, 2003). Inclusive education efforts have aimed to change school cultures, creating spaces in where everyone belongs and is valued.

Struggles for justice based on representation focus on the political dimension of justice. Injustices based on misrepresentation emerge when people are denied the opportunities to define exclusion and its corresponding solutions. Students with dis/abilities and their families, particular those from minoritized background, have been denied opportunities to be meaningful participants in instances of decision-making that affect their lives in education and beyond.[2]

3 Inclusive Education Progress: A Tale of Selective Inclusivity

There has been some encouraging data suggesting progress towards universal inclusive education. Access to pre-primary, primary, and secondary education services is expanding around the globe. For instance, there was an increase of 64% since 1999 in young children under the age of five attending schools (UNESCO, 2015). Countries around the globe have increased their enrolment ratios in primary schools, with encouraging examples such as Burundi and Niger who experienced a 50% and 37% increase in enrolment, respectively (UNESCO, 2015). Similarly, the gross enrolment ratios for secondary education have also increased rapidly since 1999. For instance, Indonesia has almost double the ratio of enrolment in secondary schools, and Afghanistan, China, Ecuador, Morocco, and Mali have increased these ratios by 27% (UNESCO, 2015).

Despite this overall increase in access to education, inequities have become more pronounced. Globally, the access gap to pre-elementary education between young children living in urban wealthy areas and children living in poverty and rural areas, particularly children from minoritized backgrounds has increased (Brito et al., 2014). Students from the poorest households made less progress in completion rates than those from wealthier backgrounds, widening the gap of educational access and achievement. Relatedly, child labour is still the higher in poor countries (23%) when compared to more affluent ones (6%; ILO, 2013).

In addition, inequities within countries have remained or increased in many cases. For instance, within the same country, completion rates of students from the poorest households have increased at a smaller rate than those rates for students from wealthier household (UNESCO, 2015). In Argentina, test scores in Spanish and mathematics have increased overall but only in more wealthy municipalities (Galiani et al., 2008). When access to secondary schooling becomes universal, it is usually accessed first by advantaged groups and then by marginalized ones, increasing overall rates of disparities as this differentiation affects the transition to higher education (UNESCO, 2015). In some countries, like Colombia and Pakistan, gaps in access to secondary education between children from the poorest and wealthiest households have remained the same since the early 2000s. In other countries, such as the Laos Democratic Republic, the gap on access to secondary education between rural and urban students has increased by 13% in a ten-year period (UNESCO, 2015).

In India, there has been an increase in children's access to schools and in the quality of learning opportunities provided to children. However, students from minoritized background have not experienced this increase (Singal & Jeffery, 2011). These inequities are associated to the geographical distribution of opportunities. Children in rural areas are significantly more likely to be out of school (Singal & Jeffery, 2011). Twenty percent of villages in India, which tend to be smaller, more distant from major roads, and populated predominantly by lower caste groups, host 75 % of all children out of school in the country.

Students with dis/abilities continued to be "spaced out" from education (Armstrong, 2003), and even more so when dis/ability status interacts with other marginalized gender, class, immigration, and ethnic statuses. For instance, in Western Africa girls with dis/abilities faced increased discrimination and isolation from educational opportunities and are at risk of abuse and sexual violence (Coe, 2013). In the U.S, though rates of inclusion in the general education classroom have increased overall, racial and language minorities with dis/abilities are less likely to be included in the general education classroom than their White peers identified with the same dis/ability category (Office of Special Education Programs, 2015).

Considering these examples, it is difficult not to question how efforts that aim to dismantle educational exclusion contribute to furthering inequities. This question compels advocates, researchers, police makers, and practitioners to understand inclusive education as situated practice, in which the implementation of inclusive efforts is shaped and appropriated according to the local activity and its associated tools and discourses (Greeno, 2006; Waitoller & Pazey, 2016). From this vantage point, it is critical to examine actual existing neoliberalism (Brenner & Theodore, 2002) and its differential impact on education.

3.1 *Actual Existing Neoliberalism*

Neoliberalism is an economic, cultural, and political ideology for capital expansion that has permeated into most aspects of human life in developing and developed countries (Ball, 1997). From an economic standpoint, neoliberalism aims to redistribute wealth and social goods through the privatization and de-regularization of services and unleashing market forces in all sectors of human activity, including education (Harvey, 2005). From a cultural standpoint, neoliberalism has shaped human relations. It is an identity and ontological project that aims to shape individuals into *homo economicus:* individuals who are defined in economic terms as market-rational and entrepreneurs who strive to increase productivity and capital in all aspects of social life (Brown, 2003). From a political standpoint, neoliberalism has been a tool to increase the control of the wealthy and powerful (Harvey, 2005). Democracy is weakened in favour of more efficient ways to conduct public business, as the public sector is portrayed as a failing system. In contrast, the market is depicted as innovative, unbiased, and capable of solving longstanding inequities. Thus, managerial top-down approaches to decision-making are privileged to increase efficiency and effectiveness and implement "what works" practices (Ball, 2003). Considering its economic, cultural, and political aspects, neoliberalism aims to shape the discourse of justice based on distribution, recognition, and representation that are at the core of the inclusive education movement.

Yet, it is important to not fall in totalizing and overgeneralizations, but engage in analysis of *actual existing neoliberalism* (Brenner & Theodore, 2002). That is, neoliberalism needs to be understood (much like inclusive education) as a complex, hybrid, and paradoxical project, where implementation is shaped by local histories, geographies, and socio-cultural contexts. Thus, an analysis of the impact of neoliberalism on inclusive education efforts needs to be sensitive to such contextual differences.

Since the 1970s, neoliberal measures have been implemented all over the globe, sometimes in whole packages and sometimes by pieces (Brenner & Theodore, 2002). Following neoliberal rationales, education systems around the world have moved towards a market model of education. Even countries with a history of strong social democracies like Sweden have implemented neoliberal measures in education (Berhanu, 2008). The neoliberal logic establishes that by producing and inspecting data on academic achievement, administrators and parents can make school comparisons and make informed decisions (Apple, 2007). While administrators may decide to close schools due to underperformance or under enrolment, parents make decisions about where to enrol their children, which can also affect the enrolments and academic performance of schools. Thus, educational outcomes, particularly those reflected in high-stakes assessment scores such as Program for International Student Assessment (PISA), or national or state level assessments, serve as measures of and assurances that a quality education is available to all students. It is unsurprising, thus, that standardized testing to measure and compare countries, schools, and students has grown dramatically both globally and locally. From 1990 to 2013, these assessments increased globally by 200%, from 276 to 479 (Benavot & Köseleci, 2015). Latin-American, the Caribbean and the

Asia and Pacific regions have been areas in where standardized assessment has flourished (Benavot & Köseleci, 2015).

Examining major aspects of actual existing neoliberalism can further our understanding of the disparate results of inclusive education efforts discussed above. Thus, I advance a framework to understand *neoliberal selective inclusionism*. By inclusionism, I refer to the activity of including children and youth with dis/abilities into social institutions (e.g., schools) without altering the institutions' norms of belonging and being, and neoliberal fantasies of normative productive bodies (Mitchell, 2015). This inclusionism is also selective; it only provides access for those bodies whose differences are integrable to normative practices. I organize actual existing neoliberalism major aspects around the three dimension of justice that have been at the core of the inclusive education movement: redistribution, recognition, and representation (see Figure 6.1).

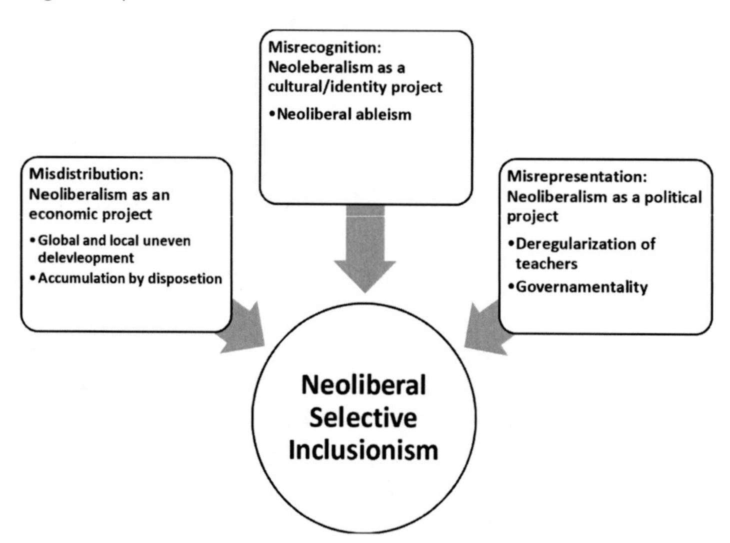

FIGURE 6.1 Model of neoliberal selective inclusionism

4 Unjust Geographies and Accumulation by Disposition: Exclusion Based on Misdistribution

Neoliberalism claims to redistribute quality educational opportunities for all students through market reforms, choice and competition. Yet, neoliberalism has contributed to increased inequities at least through two of its interrelated driving forces: (a) unjust geographies created by uneven geographical development and (b) accumulation by dispossession.

4.1 *Uneven Geographical Development*

Policies and practices based on neoliberal ideology have a profound impact on local and global space (Harvey, 2009). Neoliberalism intends to resolve social and economic problems through a 'spatial fix', appropriating and restructuring spaces for capital accumulation (Harvey, 2009). This capital expansion is achieved by an increasing role of national and global government bodies and, overtime, encompasses more and more of the population's resources (Soja, 1989). Yet capital investment is unevenly distributed, creating spaces of wealth and others of increasing poverty. This uneven distribution of resources is inscribed in the pre-existing unjust geographies of countries and cities, disproportionately affecting students from minoritized background.

These inequitable forms of development not only have marked differences among countries but also within major urban centres as cities try to become global competitors (Sassen, 2005). For instance, cities like Chicago in the US and Hyredabad in India have experienced a restructuring of their urban space (Lipman, 2011; Kamat, 2011). Efforts in Hyderabad to make the city into a global competitor have combined state-promoted urban development strategies and higher education efforts that intensified caste and socioeconomic inequities between Hyderabad and the region in which this city is located: Telangana (Kamat, 2011). While Hyderabad has received significant state and private investment from its neighbourhood region, Andhra, the remaining of Telangana has experienced shrinkage of public higher education funding resulting in higher fees for students (Kamat, 2011).

In Chicago, efforts to become a global city have also included urban development strategies that encompassed educational policies (Lipman, 2011). Through gentrification processes, White and also African American and Latino middle-class professionals claim and occupy certain urban spaces in which poor and working-class racial minorities lived. Yet, while some low-income communities experience rapid change and displacement due to gentrification, others show the opposite: multi-generational poverty and a lack of economic development over many decades. Interestingly, areas with the potential of being gentrified have been the locales of school closings; these schools are later open as selective enrolment, charter schools (I discuss this schools in the next section) or as specialty schools to attract middle class professionals (Lipman, 2011).

In 2013, Chicago Public Schools closed an unprecedented amount of schools: 50. Over 80% of the total students impacted by the school closings were African American. This number represented over one quarter of all African America children living in Chicago between the ages of 5 and 14 (Radinsky & Waitoller, 2013). Further, the average proportion of students with dis/abilities in the closed schools was 17%: a higher proportion than the one found in the remaining schools (13%; de la Torre et al., 2015). Indeed, one third of the closed schools had special education programs serving African American students with extensive support needs (i.e., autism, intellectual disabilities, multiple disabilities, sensory impairments).

Thus, the production of space for capital development is endemic to neoliberalism (Brenner & Theodore, 2002). Understanding uneven geographical development helps to understand the uneven impact of inclusive efforts across locales. Education policy has been a tool for uneven geographical development (Lipman, 2011). The state has been a main actor in the production of unjust education geographies by disinvesting in traditional public schools and then closing them. This creates new markets for private/public partnerships such as those materialized in charter and private schools. Thus, I turn now to discuss how capital is accumulated through the dispossession of public educational opportunities from minoritized communities.

4.2 *Accumulation by Dispossession*

Related to the uneven distribution of capital and resources is what Harvey (2005) calls *accumulation by dispossession.* That is, accumulation of capital and resources in the hand of a few is achieved by the disposition of public land and resources paired with an engineered shrinking of the welfare state (Harvey, 2005). Through privatization of public goods such as education, neoliberal policies aim to fix educational inequities. The assumption is that by unleashing market forces, educational inequities will be dismantled through privatization and competition.

Accumulation by dispossession is clearly evidenced in rapid and continuous global growth of the private education sector, which has been rising in numerous countries, particularly in middle and high-income countries (UNESCO, 2015). In Sweden, private enrolment grew almost 10% as a result of government policy favouring school choice and market models of schooling (UNESCO, 2015). Charter schools in the U.S are particularly proliferated in urban areas where low-income racial and linguistic minorities lived. Charter schools are publicly funded, but privately-run schools that are supposed to increase the competitiveness of education markets. Charter school campuses have more than doubled from 2003 to 2014. There are now over 6,500 charter campuses in comparison to 3000 in 2003, serving over 2.5 million students. Similarly, England and Sweden have experienced a similar growth of public/private partnerships in education. Modelled after charter schools in the U.S, both countries have adopted *Free Schools* (Wiborg, 2015). These schools are funded by the government but are privately run. They have the abilities to set their own pay for teachers, change the length of the school day, and they do not have to follow the national curriculum. The outcomes of these public/private partnerships have been inconclusive at best and have furthered inequities at worst. On the one hand, research on student achievement in U.S charter schools has shown mixed effects, and it is difficult to tease out why some charter schools are more successful than others or in what conditions are more successful (Berends, 2015). On the other hand, charter schools have increased racial segregation and withdrawn funding from already financially hurt traditional schools (Fabricant & Fine, 2012). Indeed, the U.S Office of Inspector General (OIG) found charter schools to be a financial risk for the U.S Department of Education and that there was a lack of accountability over how charter schools utilize federal funds (OIG, 2016).

Furthermore, charter schools enrolled lower proportions of students with disabilities, particularly those with more extensive support needs, than traditional public schools (Barnard-Brak, Schmidt & Almekdash, 2018; Waitoller, Maggin, & Trzaska, 2017). Research on the academic outcomes of students with dis/abilities is almost non-existent, and accounts of "steering away mechanisms" indicates that charter schools implicitly suggest that parents move their children to other schools (Welner & Howe, 2005). Steering away mechanisms can include, but are not limited to, charter schools communicating to parents that the school does not have the services the child required, denying an evaluation to identify students for special education, applying repetitive disciplinary measures to students (e.g., suspensions), or not providing services required in the students' IEP (Welner & Howe, 2005). These steering away practices have been motivation for several court cases against charter schools (e.g., Southern Poverty Law Center *v.* Pastorek, 2010). Thus, it is fair to conclude that charter schools have been cropping off services (Lacireno-Paquet, Holyoke, Moser, & Henig, 2002) for students who are more costly to educate and tend to not perform well on accountability assessments. These inequities forged by neoliberal policies have a spatial dimension as charter schools tend to be located in and serve low-income Black and Latino communities in the areas in which urban school districts have closed public schools. Thus, new unjust geographies are produced in already unjust socially produced spaces.

The privatization of education is not limited to wealthy countries such as England, Sweden, and U.S. Interestingly the education private sector has growth in urban slums due to lack of government policy and planning. People living in Urban Slums in India, Kenya, and Nigeria have experienced an expansion of low-fee private schools (Srivastava, 2006; Tooley & Dixon, 2003; Walford, 2013). Only 35% of students in Hyderabad, India, attend government schools. In Lagos, the rate is even lower (25%). Further, 40% of the poorest students living in Slums in Kenya attend private schools, a number that is increasing steadily. Private schools in urban slums have low fees, they do not receive help from the government, and they are usually underfunded. They can also be invisible in official records. The spatial dimension of these cases is also noteworthy. One of the reasons for the increase in private school attendance in the slums is that government schools tend to be on the edges of the slums. Thus, the lack of stable public schools closest to their household funnels the poorest children into private low-fee schools, whose families may not be able to pay for fees or buy uniforms.

5 Neoliberal Ableism: Exclusion Based on Misrecognition

Neoliberalism is not only an economic project, it is also a cultural and identity project (Ball, 2003). The neoliberal project aims to nurture productive workers who contribute to capital production and accumulation in the global economy. Children, youth and adults, are expected to overcome misfortunes and adopt ableist ideals that confine to a narrow and individualistic conception of personhood, privileging autonomy, independency, and entrepreneurship. Goodley (2014) named this identity project *neoliberal-ableism*, arguing that individuals become normalized through economic and social policy and judged by the neoliberal ideal of the human being. Any physical and mental inclination to interdependency creates grounds for anxiety and intervention as they are perceived as a threat to economic productivity (Shildrick, 2012).

The neoliberal cultural and identity project has had a profound impact on the implementation of inclusive education around the world. Inclusion has become a means to nurture the neoliberal subject. The project of inclusion is being leveraged to develop able and productive subjects. The assumptions are that students should be able, self-entrepreneur, productive, self-accountable, and willing to take leadership in the classroom (Goodley, 2014). Examples of the neoliberal cultural and identity project are found, for instance, in the new emphasis on college ready standards and assessments in the U.S., which focus on developing an independent and able labor force. In England, education policy embodies the neoliberal identity project, stating that children *with* special educational needs "desire to become like every other child – successful and independent" (DfE, 2011, p. 2).

Further, neoliberal informed educational practices view students as eternally lacking (Goodley, 2014), and demands a continuous inspection of students' deficits. Even when trying to move away from special education and deficit models, current educational practices generate new and more sophisticated sorting mechanisms based on deficit and medical models (Waitoller

& Kozleski, 2015). When school professionals ignore traditional dis/ability labels, new markers emerge such as "intensive", "strategic", "at benchmark", and "exceeding" students, in order to sort, quantify, and address ability differences. This is because new frameworks and practices for addressing student differences (e.g., Response to Intervention) continue to rely on a medical model of dis/ability that is coupled with new fine-tuned forms of assessment to monitor student progress (Waitoller & Kozleski, 2015).

In sum, exclusion is shaped by neoliberal practices in which assimilation and normalization are prerequisites to gain access to neoliberal informed institutions such as education (Mitchell et al., 2014). The overreliance on large-scale assessments to make global and local policy decisions has enforced normalcy through language and narrow assessment practices. This reduces valuable ways of knowing, doing and being, defining what it means to be able and educable. What can be and is measured trumps other deeper and more radical inclusive agendas and a new form of *global norming* (McDermott, Edgar, & Scarloss, 2011) emerges as ableism evolves.

6 From Government to Governance in Education: Misrepresentation

Neoliberalism shifts decision-making from government elected by citizens to governance from managers, judicial authority, and executive orders (Lipman, 2011). This shift constrains opportunities for teachers and families to participate in key instances of decision-making through two vehicles: (a) deregulating the teaching force and (b) reducing participation of students and parents to a political spectacle.

6.1 *Deregulating the Teaching Force*

The deregulation of teacher training and the dismantling of teacher unions has been at the centre of the neoliberal project of education in the USA (Apple, 2007). Neoliberalism pushes to weaken teachers' collective efforts so that top-down managerial decisions are swiftly implemented and with little resistance (Apple, 2007). For instance, alternate teacher training programs have gained momentum around the globe. National teacher certification and salary policies have been at the core of financial restructuring efforts pushed by the International Monterey Fund (IMF) and the World Bank (WB) since the 1990s (International Labor Organization, 2012). As part of austerity measures, these agencies have pushed governments to reduce teachers' salaries and to replace experienced teachers with more affordable and unqualified ones (ILO, 2012).

Such requirements from the IMF and WB also emphasized the increase of inspection and top-down administrative control over teacher practice, undermining the professional status of teachers.

Amid these pressures, contract teachers or those with alternate certifications are cost-effective solutions for teachers' shortage and local and national governments' shrinking budgets. Numerous countries have experienced an increase of contract teachers. In India, for instance, the hiring of contract teachers has expanded swiftly since the early 2000s, with significant variation across regions; in the 2013–2014 school year 47% of teachers in Jharkhand were contract teachers, in comparison to 2% in Karnataka (NUEPA, 2014). Rates of contract teachers in Niger has increased from 55% in 2002 to near 80% in 2008 (UNESCO, 2015); and in 2013, the percentage of contract teachers in Chile reached 20% (Kingdon et al., 2013).

Contract teachers tend to work in rural and remote locations. They experience poorer working conditions, lack of job security and lower salaries; they tend to be younger and have less training (particular in-service experience), making it less likely for them to include students with dis/abilities (Kingdon et al., 2013). This stratification of labor has resulted in low morale among contract teachers and high attrition (Chudgar et al., 2014).

Similarly, in the United States, organizations such as Teach for America (TFA) and other alternative routes have also increased their presence in schools, particularly in low-income urban schools. Now on its 25th year, TFA has placed over 42,000 teachers covering 52 regions (Scott, Trujillo, Rivera, 2016). TFA has also become a political movement aligned with the privatization of schools and with close ties to Foundations and political organizations aligned with neoliberal reforms in education (Scott et al., 2016). TFA has expanded outside the U.S. under the name of Teach for All, and now operates in 39 countries. The effectiveness of TFA graduates as measured by standardized assessments has been mixed (Vasquez-Heilig & Jez, 2014). TFA has also started a Special Education and Ability Initiative, which provides an extra year of experience for preservice teachers in inclusive classrooms. This short induction and training is problematic as students with dis/abilities have greater achievement when taught by special education trained and certified personnel (Feng & Sass, 2013).

Thus, the expansion of alternative routes to become teachers could explain the discussed increasing inequities amid efforts for inclusive education, as these teachers who have less training and expertise are disproportionally placed in rural and low-income urban areas. Interestingly, an effort to weaken the participatory power of teachers (i.e., injustice based on misrepresentation) has had implications for access to quality education for minoritized students (i.e., injustice based on misdistribution).

6.2 *Parent and Student Participation in Neoliberalism as Pollical Spectacle*

Parents' and students' right to participate in decision-making instances that affect their lives is paramount to achieve greater inclusivity. However, research has documented that asserting these rights tends to be a challenging task for parents from minoritized background. When these families' cultural repertoires are not valued and when they are perceived by school professionals as non-caring or "uneducated", their opinions and concerns could be dismissed, diminishing parents' and students' contribution to frame and advance potential solutions to the problems affecting them. In addition, due to their economic and cultural capital, White parents from affluent backgrounds are more likely than minoritized families to engage in legal struggles for educational services (Ong-Dean, 2009).

Building from these existing forms of inequities, neoliberalism adds another layer of injustice. Informed and driven by neoliberalism, school districts in urban centres in the U.S and other developed countries have shifted from having government elected by constituencies to governance by experts and managers. Public debate and participation have been replaced by an instrumental and strategic form of governance that values efficiency over democratic deliberation (Miller, 2007). For instance, in large urban centres in the U.S, such as New York City, Los Angeles, and Chicago, the mayor appoints the school board and the School District's CEO, which allows the government to enact school policy with little to no opposition. Through this shift towards governance, state and corporate leaders make decisions about school and other public institutions. At the grassroots level, participation within neoliberal ideology takes the form of appointed advisory boards that hear the grievance of citizens but have little power to make decisions, creating an illusion of democratic participation and leaving no mechanism to hold appointed school boards and CEO accountable for their actions (Lipman, 2011).

For instance, when the Chicago School Board members, appointed by the mayor, approved the closing of 50 schools in the 2013–2014 school year, the school district hosted countless hearings in school gymnasiums and churches that were packed by parents, students, and teachers. Through media outlets and briefs, the district officials argued that they were listening to constituents. Yet despite that parents, students, and teachers argued and pled for their schools, held candle light vigils, protests, public testimonies, and even though there was no evidence that the closings would improve the educational experiences of students, the school board decided unanimously to close all 50 schools. The hearings were no more than a political spectacle (Smith, 2004) in which decisions were previously made behind the stage curtain.

Similarly, Pazey and DeMathews (2016) documented this illusory inclusion of student voices in decision-making. Examining the experiences of students in a turnaround school, Pazey and DeMathews (2016) found that students with learning dis/abilities were not passive participants in neoliberal reforms. Students with dis/abilities fought hard to keep their schools open, by attending school board meetings and convincing board members to vote against the school closing. In a board meeting, one of the students expressed his frustration to the board:

> I want to tell you that I'm tired. I'm not tired of being a high school student. I'm not tired of showing my [school mascot] pride. I'm not tired of fighting for my school. I'm tired of showing up every month and feeling like it doesn't matter and you don't hear me. I'm tired of watching teachers stand up for me and then disappearing. I'm tired [of] parents taking their kids out of my school because they think it's turning into a charter school and shutting down next year. (Pazey & DeMathews, 2016, p. 25)

Students felt the forceful stigmatization of accountability discourses that labeled them and their schools as deficient. Their voices and those of their family members were given a space to grieve and complain, but these opportunities were no more than a political spectacle (Smith, 2004).

7 Conclusion

In this chapter, I have grappled with one of the questions posed by the editors of this book, "why are we not more inclusive?" I examined the main aspects of actual existing neoliberalism and its impact on education as a starting point to answer such a question. Neoliberalism has shaped inclusive education's radical agenda into a selective inclusionism that provides access to practices based on neoliberal ableism for a selected group of students (Mitchell, 2015). Selective inclusionism does not disrupt normative frameworks and includes some bodies to exclusionary practices at the expense of excluding those whose differences are deemed as not integrable. The analysis presented in this chapter is by no means exhaustive. Other aspects of neoliberalism (e.g., the role of non-profits and philanthropic organizations to name some) are beyond the scope of this chapter but should be considered when examining the impact of the neoliberal project on inclusive education. Future research should continue to examine how neoliberalism shapes inclusive education policy and practice as it interacts with pre-existing forms of injustices inscribed by global and local geographies, empirically testing the framework advanced in this chapter to understand neoliberal selective inclusionism.

Notes

1 I purposely write dis/ability with a slash to denote dis/ability not as an individual trait, but rather a social construction – the product of cultural, political, and economic practices This understanding does not deny biological and psychological differences, but emphasizes such differences gain meaning, often with severe negative consequences (e.g., segregation), through human activities informed by norms. Dis/ability is also an identity marker, which includes ways notions of ability are relied upon and constructed in tandem with other identity markers (e.g., gender, race, and language).

2 See Waitoller and Annamma (2016) for an expanded discussion of the relationship and tensions among these dimensions of justice and their materialization at the intersections of race, ethnicity, gender, class, and dis/ability.

References

Ainscow, M., Booth, T., & Dyson, A. (2006). *Improving schools, developing inclusion.* Routledge.

Apple, M. D. (2001). *Educating the "right" way: Markets, standards, God, and inequality.* RoutledgeFalmer.

Apple, M. D. (2007). Ideological success, educational failure? On the politics of no child left behind. *Journal of Teacher Education, 58*(2), 108–116.

Apple, M. D., Kenway, J., & Singh, M. (2005). *Globalizing education: Policies, pedagogies, & politics.* Peter Lang.

Armstrong, F. (2003). *Spaced out: Policy, difference, and the challenge of inclusive education.* Springer.

Artiles, A. J. (2003). Special education's changing identity: Paradoxes and dilemmas in views of culture and space. *Harvard Educational Review, 73,* 164–202.

Artiles, A. J., Kozleski, E. B., Dorn, S., & Christensen, C. (2006). Learning in inclusive education research: Re-mediating theory and methods with a transformative agenda. *Review of Research in Education, 30*(1), 65–108.

Ball, S. J. (1997). Policy sociology and critical social research: A personal review of recent education policy and policy research. *British Educational Research Journal, 23*(3), 257–274.

Ball, S. J. (2003). The teacher's soul and the terrors of performativity. *Journal of Educational Policy, 18*(3), 215–228.

Barnard-Brak, L., Schmidt, M., & Almekdash, M. D. (2018). Enrollment of students with disabilities in charter schools: Contemporary national and state level findings. *Education Policy Analysis Archives, 26*(43). http://dx.doi.org/10.14507/epaa.26.3276

Benavot, A., & Köseleci, N. (2015). *Seeking quality: Growth of national learning assessments, 1990–2013*. Background paper for EFA Global Monitoring Report 2015.

Berends, M. (2015). Sociology and school choice: What we know after two decades of charter schools. *Annual Review of Sociology, 41*(15), 159–180.

Berhanu, G. (2008). Ethnic minority pupils in Swedish schools: Some trends in over-representation of minority pupils in special educational programs. *International Journal of Special Education, 23*(3), 17–29.

Brenner, N., & Theodore, N. (2002). Cities and the geographies of "actually existing neoliberalism". *Antipode, 34*(3), 349–379.

Britto, P. R., Yoshikawa, D., van Ravens, J., Ponguta, L. A., Reyes, M., Oh, S., ... Seder, R. (2014). Strengthening systems for integrated early childhood development services: A cross-national analysis of governance. *Annals of the New York Academy of Sciences, 1308*, 245–255.

Brown, D. (2003). Neo-liberalism and the end of liberal democracy. *Theory & Event, 7*(1), 1–25.

Chudgar, A., Chandra, M., & Razzaque, A. (2014). Alternative forms of teacher hiring in developing countries and its implications: A review of literature. *Teaching and Teacher Education, 37*, 150–161.

Clough, P. (2000). Routes to inclusion. In P. Clough & J. Corbett (Eds.), *Theories of inclusive education* (pp. 1–32). Sage.

Coe, S. (2013). *Outside the circle: A research initiative by plan international into the rights of children with disabilities to education and protection in West Africa*. Plan West Africa.

de la Torre, M., Gordon, M. F., Moore, P., & Cowhy, J. (2015). *School closings in Chicago: Understanding families' choices and constraints for new school enrollment*. University of Chicago Consortium on Chicago School Research.

DfE. (2011). *Support and aspiration: A new approach to special educational needs and disability: A consultation*. Stationary Office Limited. Retrieved from http://webarchive.nationalarchives.gov.uk/20130401151715/ https://doi.education.gov.uk/publications/eorderingdownload/green-paper-sen.pdf

Fabricant, M., & Fine, M. (2012). *Charter schools and the corporate makeover of public education: What's at stake?* Teachers College Press.

Feng, L., & Sass, T. R. (2013). What makes special-education teachers special? Teacher training and achievement of students with disabilities. *Economics of Education Review, 36*, 122–134. http://dx.doi.org/10.1016/j.econedurev.2013.06.006

Fraser, N. (2009). *Scales of justice: Reimagining political space in a globalizing world*. Polity Press.

Galiani, S., Gertler, P., & Schargrodsky, E. (2008). School decentralization: Helping the good get better, but leaving the poor behind. *Journal of Public Economics, 92*(11–11), 2106–2120.

Goodley, D. (2014). *Dis/ability studies: Theorizing disableism and ableism.* Routledge.

Greeno, J. G. (2006). Learning in activity. In R. K. Sawyer (Ed.), *The Cambridge handbook of the learning sciences* (pp. 79–96). Cambridge University.

Harper, S. (2012). Race without racism: How higher education researchers minimize racist institutional norms. *The Review of Higher Education, 36*, 9–29.

Harry, B., & Klingner, J. K. (2006). *Why are so many minorities in special education? Understanding race and disability in schools.* Teachers College Press.

Harvey, D. (2005). *A brief history of neoliberalism.* Oxford University Press.

Harvey, D. (2009). *Social justice and the city* (2nd ed.). The University of Georgia Press.

International Labor Organization. (2012). *Joint ILO–UNESCO committee of experts on the application of the recommendations concerning teaching personnel: Final report.* International Labour Office.

International Labor Organization. (2013). *Marking progress against child labour: Global estimates and trends 2000–2012.* International Labour Office.

Kamat, S. (2011). Neoliberalism, urbanism and the education economy: Producing Hyderabad as a 'global city'. *Discourse: Studies in the Cultural Politics of Education, 32*(2), 187–202.

Kingdon, G., Aslam, M., Rawal, S., & Das, S. (2013). *Are contract and para-teachers a cost effective intervention to address teacher shortage and improve learning outcomes?* EPPI-Centre, University of London.

Kozleski, E. B., Engelbrecht, P., Hess, R., Swart, E., Eloff, I., Oswald, M., ... Jam, S. (2008). Where differences matter: A cross-cultural analysis of family voice in special education. *Journal of Special Education, 42*(1), 26–35.

Lacireno-Paquet, N., Holyoke, T. T., Moser, M., & Henig, J. R. (2002). Creaming versus cropping: Charter school enrollment practices in response to market incentives. *Educational Evaluation and Policy Analysis, 24*(2), 145–158. doi:10.3102/01623737024002145

Lipman, P. (2011). *The new political economy of urban education: Neoliberalism, race, and the right to the city.* Routledge.

McDermott, R., Edgar, B., & Scarloss, B. (2011). Conclusion: Global norming. In A. J. Artiles, E. B. Kozleski, & F. R. Waitoller (Eds.), *Inclusive education: Examining equity in five continents* (pp. 223–235). Harvard Education Press.

Miller, B. (2007). Modes of governance, modes of resistance. In D. Leitner, J. Peck, & E. S. Shepard (Eds.), *Contesting neoliberalism: Urban frontiers* (pp. 223–249). Guildford Press.

Mitchell, D. (2015). *The biopolitics of disability: Neoliberalism ablenationalism, and peripheral embodiment.* The University of Michigan Press.

Mitchell, D., Snyder, S., & Ware, L. (2014). [Every] child left behind. *Journal of Literary & Cultural Disability Studies, 8*(3), 295–314.

NUEPA. (2014). *Elementary education in India progress towards UEE: Flash statistics DISE 2013–2014*. National University of Educational Planning and Administration.

Southern Poverty Law Center v. Pastorek, No. 10-ED-04049. (E.D. La. 2010).

Pazey, B. L., & DeMathews, D. D. (2016). Student voice from a turnaround Urban high school: An account of students with and without dis/abilities leading resistance against accountability reform. *Urban Education, 38*, 1–38. doi:10.1177/0042085916666930

Radinsky, J., & Waitoller, F. R. (2013). *Chicago public schools actions: Impact on students*. Chicagoland Researchers and Advocates for Transformative Education.

Rizvi, F., & Lingard, B. (1996). Disability, education, and the discourses of justice. In C. Christensen & F. Rizvi (Eds.), *Disability and the dilemmas of education and justice* (pp. 9–26). Open University Press.

Sassen, S. (2005). The global city: Introducing a concept. *The Brown Journal of World Affair, 11*(2), 27–43.

Scott, J., Trujillo, T., & Rivera, M. D. (2016). Reframing teach for America: A conceptual framework for the next generation of scholarship. *Education Policy Analysis Archives, 24*(12). Retrieved from http://epaa.asu.edu/ojs/article/view/2419

Shildrick, M. (2012). *Dangerous discourses of disability, subjectivity and sexuality*. Pagrave Mcmillan.

Singal, N., & Jeffery, R. (2011). Inclusive education in India: The struggle for quality in consonance with equity. In A. J. Artiles, E. B. Kozleski, & F. R. Waitoller (Eds.), *Inclusive education: Examining equity on five continents* (pp. 161–183). Harvard Education Press.

Skritic, T. M. (1991). The special education paradox: Equity as a way to Excellence. *Harvard Educational Review, 61*(2), 148–206.

Slee, R. (2010). Political economy, inclusive education, and teacher education. In C. Forlin (Ed.), *Teacher education for inclusion: Changing paradigms and innovative approaches* (pp. 13–22). Routledge.

Smith, L. M. (2004). *Political spectacle and the fate of American schools*. Routledge-Falmer.

Soja, E. D. (1989). *Postmodern geographies: The reassertion of space in critical social theory*. Verso.

Srivastava, P. (2006). Private schooling and mental models about girls' schooling in India. *Compare, 36*(4), 497–514.

Tooley, J., Dixon, P., Shamsan, D., & Schagen, I. (2010). The relative quality and cost effectiveness of private and public schools for low-income families: A case study in a developing country. *School Effectiveness and School Improvement, 21*(2), 117–144.

United Nations Educational, Scientific, and Cultural Organization (UNESCO). (2015). *Education for all 2000–2015: Achievements and challenges*. United Nations Educational, Scientific, and Cultural Organization.

U.S. Department of Education, Office of Inspector General. (2016). *Nationwide assessment of charter and education management organizations: Final audit report*. U.S. Department of Education. Retrieved from http://www2.ed.gov/about/offices/list/oig/auditreports/fy2016/a02m0012.pdf

U.S. Government Accountability Office. (n.d.). *Charter schools: Additional federal attention needed to help protect access for students with disabilities*. U.S. Government Accountability Office. Retrieved from https://www.gao.gov/assets/600/591435.pdf

U.S. Government Office of Special Education Programs. (2015). *35th annual report to congress on the implementation of the Individuals with disabilities education act, 2013*. U.S Department of Education.

Vazquez-Heilig, J., & Jez, S. J. (2014). *Teach for America: A return to the evidence*. National Education Policy Center.

Waitoller, F. R., & Artiles, A. J. (2013). A decade professional development research in inclusive education: A critical review and notes for a research program. *Review of Educational Research, 83*(3), 319–356. doi:0034654313483905

Waitoller, F. R., & Kozleski, E. B. (2013). Working in boundary practices: Identity development and learning in partnerships for inclusive education. *Teacher and Teaching Education, 31*, 35–45.

Waitoller, F. R., & Kozleski, E. B. (2015). No stone left unturned: The emergence of new capitalism in inclusive education reform. *Education and Policy Analysis Archives, 23*(18).

Waitoller, F. R., Maggin, D. M., & Trzaska, A. (2017). A longitudinal comparison of enrollment patterns of students receiving special education in Urban neighborhood and charter schools. *Journal of Disability Policy Studies, 28*(1), 3–12.

Waitoller, F. R., & Pazey, B. L. (2016). Examining competing notions of social justice at the intersections of highs-stake testing practices and parents' rights: An inclusive education perspective. *Teachers College Record, 118*(4).

Walford, G. (2013). Low-fee private schools: A methodological and political debate. In P. Srivastava (Ed.), *Lowfee private schooling: Aggravating equity or mitigating disadvantage?* (pp. 199–213). Symposium Books.

Welner, K., & Howe, K. (2005). Steering toward separation: The policy and legal implications of "counseling" special education students away from choice schools. In J. Scott (Ed.), *School choice and student diversity: What the evidence says* (pp. 93–111). Teachers College Press.

Wiborg, S. (2015). Privatizing education: Free school policy in Sweden and England. *Comparative Education Review, 59*(3), 473–497.

Young, I. M. (1990). *Justice and the politics of difference*. Princeton University Press.

CHAPTER 7

The Dyslexia Debate and Its Relevance to Inclusive Education

Julian Elliott

1 The Dyslexia Debate

If one wants to ensure that inclusion operates effectively, it is surely a wise course of action to ascertain whether a given child's problems in school are a consequence of a pre-existing condition of one kind or another. To do this, it would seem essential that highly trained experts are made available to undertake this task. Given an accurate diagnosis, we might assume that teachers will, as a consequence, be better placed to understand the nature of the child's problems and act accordingly to help to overcome these. Given this, it is hardly surprising that many parents whose children are struggling to learn to read, are eager to explore whether their children are dyslexic. For many in this position, a primary task is to access the services of a gifted reading specialist who is capable of using recondite expertise, together with a variety of specialist assessment tools. Once a determination of dyslexia has been made, it is widely believed that teachers and other professionals can put into place specialist intervention programmes geared to help such children overcome their difficulties. It is further widely believed that a diagnosis of dyslexia can help to unlock additional resources for those with this complex condition.

Of course, at a simplistic level, the more we know about a child's strengths and difficulties, the more likely we are to be able to help them overcome their educational challenges and fulfil their potential. But does arriving at a diagnosis of dyslexia actually assist in this? The answer is, of course, it all depends what we mean when we use the term dyslexia. Unfortunately, there is little consensus in this respect.

One of the key difficulties of the dyslexia debate (Elliott & Grigorenko, 2014) is that while much of the scientific community understands dyslexia as a term synonymous to that of reading disability (that is, a difficulty in decoding text), many professional and advocacy groups consider the term to refer solely to a subset of those who encounter decoding problems. To illustrate this distinction, consider Emma, a ten-year-old child reading at an age equivalent level of six years. Assuming that she does not have a substantial intellectual disability

 | DOI: 10.1163/9789004431171_007

or a sensory (visual or hearing) impairment, Emma's performance on standardised reading tests would clearly mark her as a suitable participant to be recruited for genetic, neuroscience or psychological studies of the underpinnings of dyslexia. To such researchers, Emma would typically be described as dyslexic on the grounds that:

> … dyslexia represents the lower end of a normal distribution of word reading ability. (Peterson & Pennington, 2012, p. 1997)

Contrast this perspective with operations in the sphere of educational practice and lay understandings. Here, parents are often advised to explore whether their daughter's reading problems stem from an underlying dyslexic condition. To achieve such a determination, they will likely be informed that she would need to be given a thorough psychological examination using a range of cognitive tests. Only then could a decision be taken as to whether she has dyslexia, rather than a more general reading difficulty. This Manichean distinction is rendered more complex by the seeming unwillingness of many members of the scientific research community to acknowledge the dissonance between these two positions. For many academic researchers in this area, it seems that the power of the dyslexia construct with policymakers and the public is such that the inconsistencies are best ignored or dismissed as largely an irrelevance (Elliott, 2015a, 2015b).

Complicating this issue is a third school of thought. This maintains that dyslexia is a much wider and more pervasive condition than merely referring to poor decoding and spelling. According to those who espouse such views, while dyslexia is often manifested by literacy difficulty, it may also be evidenced by various cognitive difficulties such as poor working memory, speed of processing, attention and concentration, organisation and self-regulation. This understanding, particularly prevalent in further and higher education, leads to the belief of some professionals that dyslexia can be diagnosed on the basis of poor performance on one or more tests of these processes, even if the individual's literacy skills are adequate.

From the perspective of those who seek to ensure that inclusion operates effectively, the distinctions outlined above are of immense importance. If there is a meaningful difference between dyslexic and other poor readers, this needs to be made clear to teachers so they can provide suitably differentiated intervention programmes. If there is not a meaningful difference, why pursue such assessments? Either way, we need to consider how our current understandings and practices ensure that all children encountering reading difficulty receive the help and support they require. The rest of this chapter will seek to examine and reconcile these questions.

The conceptual flaws of the dyslexia construct have been examined elsewhere (Elliott & Grigorenko, 2014; Elliott & Nicolson, 2016). Accordingly, they will not be discussed in detail in this chapter. Table 7.1, however, demonstrates the many contrasting ways that this construct has been identified and understood. As can be seen, categories a to c reflect the position that all poor readers (i.e. decoders) can be considered to be dyslexic. Category d reflects the position that dyslexia is about more than just reading. Categories e–l reflect the position that those with dyslexia are a subset of a wider pool of poor readers.

TABLE 7.1 Differing understandings of who may be considered to have dyslexia

a	anyone who struggles with accurate single word decoding
b	anyone who struggles with accurate and/or fluent decoding
c	those who score at the lowest end of the normal distribution on an appropriate reading test
d	those for whom decoding is merely one element of a more pervasive dyslexic condition marked by a range of comorbid features. This can include compensated dyslexics who no longer present with a severe reading difficulty
e	those whose decoding difficulties cannot be explained in alternative ways (e.g. because of severe intellectual or sensory impairment, socio-economic disadvantage, poor schooling, or emotional/behavioural difficulty)
f	those for whom there is a significant discrepancy between reading performance and IQ
g	those whose reading difficulty is unexpected
h	those whose poor reading contrasts with strengths in other intellectual and academic domains
i	those whose reading problems are biologically determined
j	those whose reading problems are marked by certain associated cognitive difficulties (in particular, phonological, rapid naming, and verbal memory deficits)
k	those poor readers who also present with a range of symptoms commonly found in dyslexics (e.g. poor motor, arithmetical, or language skills, visual difficulties, and low self-esteem)
l	those who fail to make meaningful progress in reading even when provided with high-quality, evidence-based forms of intervention

SOURCE: ELLIOTT AND GRIGORENKO (2014)

While the reader is pointed to Elliott and Grigorenko (2014) for a thorough review of these issues, I will offer a few observations here that are particularly relevant for issues of inclusion.

1.1 *Dyslexia as a Biological Condition*

One of the principal arguments for differentiating between so-called dyslexic and other poor decoders is that dyslexia is primarily a biological condition. Certainly, research has shown that reading disability has a genetic component. Put simply, if a parent struggles with reading, there is a greater likelihood that their offspring will also demonstrate such a difficulty; such findings have been employed to suggest that dyslexia has a genetic basis (Nicolson, 2005). The reality of course is that this claim only works when dyslexia and reading disability are treated as synonymous constructs. Those who study the genetic background of dyslexia typically select, for their participant samples, those who self-report a history of reading problems, or who score poorly on reading tests. Thus, their research concerns the genetics of poor readers, not a subset of poor readers considered to be dyslexic. This is a critical, yet often overlooked, fact.

Similarly, neuroscience has shown that certain aspects of brain structure and functioning tend to differ for poor readers. While the claims resulting from neuroscience for education are often over-stated (Bowers, 2016; Im, Varma, & Varma, 2017), there is clear evidence from functional magnetic resonance imaging (fMRI) research that successful interventions for poor readers may result in changes in brain functioning. However, as is the case for genetics, it is essential to understand that these studies involve participants selected on the basis of their performance on reading tests (typically, the lowest 10–15%), not some kind of supposedly dyslexic subsample.

The implications of these misunderstandings for effective inclusive educational practice are highly significant. If those diagnosed with dyslexia are perceived as having a biologically-based problem while the 'garden-variety" decoding difficulties of others are seen as the product of adverse environmental factors (e.g. poor home environment, poor schooling or insufficient motivation, effort and engagement), a divide is created in which the former may be perceived as more deserving of help and support. Within such a scenario, struggling readers from socially disadvantaged environments would rarely be identified as dyslexic (Rutter, 1978), particularly if an additional criterion is that the difficulty should be 'unexpected'. Given current practices and understandings, exclusion from this diagnosis may serve to disadvantage them further.

However, even if we were to set aside the moral and ethical issues involved, a bifurcation into the nature and nurture explanation provides an overly simplistic picture of what is a far more complex reality. Often, and unsurprisingly, a family history of reading difficulty co-occurs with a home environment that is not maximally conducive to literacy acquisition. Furthermore, heritability estimates may vary between those who have experienced more or less favourable childhood experiences. Indeed, it is now understood that environmental experience in infancy can differentially affect subsequent brain structure and functioning (Jednoróg et al., 2012; Hackman, Farah, & Meaney, 2010). The reality is that it is not possible to divide poor readers up into clear biological sheep and environmental goats and we cannot meaningfully distinguish between a neurobiological versus environmental aetiology in respect of an individual who has performed poorly on a measure of reading (Fletcher et al., 2007; Rutter, Kim-Cohen, & Maughan, 2006).

Poor schooling is similarly a more complex explanation than it might first appear. Of course, the teacher is a critical influence in the child's acquisition of literacy, and poor teaching will be particularly problematic for children who find difficulty in this domain. Add to this, the particular approach to the teaching employed, and the struggling reader may be doubly disadvantaged. In respect of this latter component, Elliott and Grigorenko (2014, pp. 124–128) discuss the longstanding 'Reading Wars' between the proponents of structured phonics teaching and those advocating whole language approaches (Chall, 1996; Snow & Juel, 2005). In the former camp are situated 'traditionalists' who advocate, '... an approach to, or type of, reading instruction that is intended to promote the discovery of the alphabetic principle, the correspondences between phonemes and graphemes, and phonological decoding' (Scarborough & Brady, 2002, p. 236). In contrast, the 'progressives', contending that learning to read is essentially a natural process, even when there is no explicit or systematic instruction (Goodman, 1967, 1986), espouse approaches that de-emphasise structured skills-based approaches in favour of those that place greater weight upon reading for meaning. Research has now clearly shown that, irrespective of the supposed aetiology of their difficulty, poor readers are less able to discover letter-sound patterns and, for such individuals, explicit teaching of essential phonic skills and knowledge is essential (Calfee & Drum, 1986; Torgesen, 2004,) albeit within a broad-based literacy curriculum that includes reading for meaning (Torgerson, Brooks, & Hall, 2006). Crucially, a de-emphasis upon highly structured phonics teaching only really becomes problematic when it is applied to those who already have a difficulty. Thus, the child's pre-existing problem is exacerbated by poor teaching: it is not the case that this approach can be held to be the (environmental) origin of a complex reading difficulty.

1.2 *Dyslexia and Related Cognitive Processes*

It is widely argued that the dyslexic person can be differentiated from other poor readers on the basis of the presence of various deficient cognitive processes. The list of possible symptoms is very lengthy and includes difficulty in the areas of phonological awareness, rapid naming, working and short-term memory, processing speed, attention and concentration, organisation and self-regulation, sequencing, and physical ability including fine motor skills and balance. The reality is that difficulties in all of these areas are more common across a range of developmental difficulties, in which reading disability is but one manifestation. While phonological awareness problems are frequently (but not always) found in those described as dyslexic, there is no cognitive process, or set of processes, that are either necessary or sufficient to make a meaningful diagnosis of dyslexia. Diagnosing dyslexia on the basis of performance on cognitive tests is invalid (Elliott & Grigorenko, 2014) although this doesn't appear to stop such practices continuing.

Of course, the 'elephant in the room' here is the issue of intelligence. Advocates of the dyslexia construct frequently argue that the term is helpful for many struggling readers as it serves as a corrective against a perception that the child's literacy difficulties are a consequence of stupidity or laziness. Such attributions often served up as cruel barbs have left many poor readers feeling humiliated and doubting themselves. More than a century ago, Hinshelwood (1902) pointed out the powerful effect of these upon the child's wellbeing:

> It is a matter of the highest importance to recognise as early as possible the true nature of this defect, when it is met with in a child. It may prevent much waste of valuable time and may save the child from suffering and cruel treatment. When a child manifests great difficulty in learning to read and is unable to keep up in progress with its fellows, the cause is generally assigned to stupidity or laziness, and no systematised method is directed to the training of such a child ... The sooner the true nature of the defect is realised, the better are the chances of the child's improvement. (Hinshelwood, 1902, cited in Shaywitz, 2005, pp. 21–22)

For many years it was believed that there was a significant and meaningful difference between those poor readers with high IQs (identified on this basis as dyslexics) and others whose IQ appeared to match their level of reading skill. The attractions of this discrepancy model for struggling readers and their parents are all too obvious. Gaining a dyslexia diagnosis immediately undermines any inappropriate conclusions that the individual's problem stems from a lack of intelligence. The problem with this position was (and is) that such a distinction has been found to be groundless (Stuebing et al., 2002, 2009; Fletcher et al., 2007) for there is little relationship between IQ and decoding skill. Such findings have proven difficult for many to accept; Fletcher (personal communication, for example), described the "incredulous responses" of reviewers when his team (Stuebing et al., 2002) reported no significant differences between high and low IQ groups on a range of reading-related cognitive variables. IQ scores cannot help us predict who will be most responsive, or resistant, to intervention (Gresham & Vellutino, 2010; Flowers et al., 2001; Francis et al., 2001) nor help us select the most appropriate forms of intervention. Stuebing et al. (2009) found that IQ predicted only 1% to 3% of the variance of children's progress when given additional assistance. Such a figure cannot justify the use of a relatively expensive and time-consuming form of assessment, particularly when a simple baseline assessment of word reading skills has been shown to be a much stronger predictor (Vellutino et al., 2008).

To overcome the challenge to the use of IQ scores, some psychometricians have sought to focus upon performance on particular clusters of IQ subtests. Research has shown, however, that this approach is also not appropriate (British Psychological Society, 1999; Frederickson, 1999; Watkins, Kush, & Glutting, 1997; Moura, Simoes, & Pereira, 2014). Nevertheless, and despite the fact that the major dyslexia advocacy groups now accept that there is no relationship between IQ and decoding skill and that it is wholly inappropriate to use the discrepancy model, many practitioners continue to use and endorse this in schools (Machek & Nelson, 2007; O'Donnell & Miller, 2011) and universities (Elliott, 2014). Rather more savvy psychometricians have realised that such practices can no longer be justified and instead have sought to advocate the use of profiling of an individual's cognitive strengths and weaknesses. However, this approach has also been clearly shown to lack psychometric and clinical justification (Elliott & Resing, 2015; Fletcher & Miciak, 2017; Miciak et al., 2016; Taylor et al., 2017).

The reasons for the continuation of cognitive testing are many (Elliott & Grigorenko, 2014, pp. 22–24), although the most powerful reason for the resilience of the discrepancy model most likely lies in its obvious attractiveness for those who encounter reading difficulties. As noted above, those who struggle with reading disability have often been treated as if they are lacking in intelligence (Riddick, 2010) and the literature is replete with personal accounts detailing the humiliation and hurt that resulted. Parents of children with a reading disability may worry that teachers will attribute their child's difficulties to stupidity or laziness and fail to offer the sympathetic and supportive challenge that they will likely need. For the child who is struggling to read, such taunts, together with often unrewarding degrees of progress, may result in a sense of helplessness and a desire to protect oneself in the eyes of others

(Covington, 1992). In some cases, the child will visibly reduce their interest and effort in the hope that consequent failure will be attributed to this factor rather than to a lack of intellectual ability. A diagnosis by a clinician that the child is an intellectually able dyslexic individual who encounters a particular problem with decoding [and may also have a number of allied cognitive gifts (Davis, 1997)] will surely be grasped enthusiastically by family members. The diagnosis can also help the struggling reader gain a more positive sense of self. Thus, diagnosed dyslexic individuals often comment in their everyday lives, and frequently when interviewed in the media, that they had always thought that they were stupid but were delighted to discover that this was not actually true.

Given the issues raised above, surely it is possible that cognitive assessment has a helpful function? Here the problem is the conflation of cognitive assessment geared to assisting understanding of the level of intellectual demand that should be made of the child with its use to affect a categorical dyslexic/non-dyslexic distinction. No one could argue against the need for teachers to have an accurate understanding of the child's intellectual ability, in order that they might plan their lessons accordingly (although skilled educators hardly need an IQ score to assist them in this respect). Consider two children, both aged 10 years and reading at a level equivalent to an average six-year-old. One scores in the top 10% on measures of cognitive ability; the other is located in the lowest 10%. Clearly, while it is important that educational expectations are appropriately high for each child, the particular classroom tasks selected, the nature of the language used, and the complexity of the ideas and concepts that are presented should be very different for these two. However, this is not the case for reading intervention as there is no evidence that the nature of decoding instruction should vary significantly. Here there is no aptitude x treatment interaction. There is no justification for assuming that the prognosis is better for one than the other (Flowers et al., 2001; Francis et al., 1996) and no grounds to provide greater resources to one of these children.

What many advocates fail to grasp is that engaging in a labelling process often has negative ramifications (Arishi, Boyle, & Lauchlan, 2017). By arguing that a dyslexia diagnosis helps to overcome inappropriate attributions of stupidity or laziness, proponents are, in actuality, reinforcing such perceptions in respect of other poor readers who do not acquire the label. Thus, rather than challenging the false link between intelligence and decoding skill, they are maintaining this for so-called non-dyslexic poor readers. Unsurprisingly, members of this group are more likely to be those who suffer from economic and social disadvantage.

In their review of the scientific literature of reading disability/dyslexia, Vellutino et al. (2004) argued that intelligence tests have little value for diagnosing reading disability/dyslexia. Matching the conclusions of *The Dyslexia Debate,* these authors recommended that practitioners should:

> … shift the focus of their clinical activities away from emphasis on psychometric assessment to detect cognitive and biological causes of a child's reading difficulties for purposes of categorical labelling in favour of assessment that would eventuate in educational and remedial activities tailored to the child's individual needs. (p. 31)

Since this time, scientific research has further supported this position yet, as noted above, many assessors continue to use IQ tests to validate their dyslexia diagnoses.

1.3 *Theories of Dyslexia and Their Relevance for Educational Intervention*

In order to ensure that inclusion is effective, appropriate assessment should be employed to guide teachers in their work with children with special educational needs. It is widely held that to address the educational needs of those with decoding difficulties, underlying cognitive/sensory tests that can highlight deficient cognitive processes are required. Once particular areas of difficulty have been identified, specialised intervention can target these directly. As these underlying problems are remediated, the child's reading ability will increase. There is one problem with line of reasoning: it doesn't work in practice.

Table 7.2 lists the major cognitive/sensory theories currently employed to explain the underpinnings of reading disability/dyslexia. Detailed descriptions and evaluations of these are provided in Elliott and Grigorenko (2014) and, more briefly, in Elliott and Nicolson (2016) so will not be reproduced here. However, for the purposes of the current chapter, the key issue to be highlighted is whether these theories have a bearing upon educational practice. Interestingly, only one of the theoretical strands below (the phonological deficit hypothesis) has resulted in a related intervention that has (relatively) strong scientific report. While there have many claims for the effectiveness of interventions based upon the other theories (ranging from coloured lenses, physical exercises to computer-based working-memory training), these have not been supported by high quality research evidence. In relation to phonological awareness training for struggling readers, there is reasonably strong evidence that this can be effective as part of a broader structured educational programme involving phonics for young children but, even here, it is possible that initial gains may not be sustained over time (Olson, 2011).

TABLE 7.2 Theoretical explanations concerning the origins of dyslexia

a	Phonological deficit hypothesis
b	Rapid naming
c	Short term memory/working memory deficits
d	Auditory/speech processing
e	Visual processing/attention
f	Magnocellular problems
g	Scotopic sensitivity
h	Sluggish attentional shifting
i	Visual attention span deficit
j	Abnormal crowding
k	Anchoring deficits
l	Psychomotor processing

In terms of inclusion, reading disability, and the dyslexia debate, the fundamental issue, and one not sufficiently understood by many practitioners, is that there is only one form of intervention that currently has sufficient scientific support; that which involves systematic, phonics-based educational instruction. This is not to suggest, however, that utilising this approach will resolve all poor readers' difficulties. Sadly, there remains a small proportion of poor readers whose lack of progress, even given high-quality educational intervention over an extended period of time, continues to challenge scientific and practitioner communities. However, there is no evidence that this approach is differentially appropriate for so-called dyslexic and garden-variety poor reader groups. Identifying a poor reader as dyslexic, or not, cannot, at present, help to guide a teacher or clinician in developing an appropriate intervention; one that seeks to identify and build upon the particular mix of reading-related strengths and weaknesses, in conjunction with awareness of the dispositions, motivations and interests of the learner.

If only one effective approach to reading intervention has scientific support, and if this finding applies equally to poor decoders generally, one must question the value of distinguishing between the dyslexic and the non-dyslexic poor reader. Rather, we should simply identify all poor readers as early in their lives as possible and offer appropriate educational intervention. One might question why, when this point has been made, responses from many professional and lobby groups have ranged from the dismissive to the vituperative.

Answers to this question can be found in the many human stories that can be regularly found in the national press. The following case extract (Alex), taken from the internet, exemplifies many of the misunderstandings and misrepresentations that can proliferate. In various media reports, Alex's mother stated that she had paid around £2,000 on commissioning five independent reports showing how bright and intelligent he was despite his condition. She asserted that a local independent school for dyslexic children, with its specialist programmes and intensive teaching, was the perfect place for his secondary education. "Alex is not stupid; he is dyslexic", his mother is quoted as saying before adding:

> Every child is entitled to the education they need. This is clearly not being met in Alex's case. He needs specialist dyslexia tutoring before it is too late. My son is being let down severely by the school system.

This extract illustrates many of the problems that underpin the dyslexia debate. Firstly, there is a statement that several private assessments were needed before the desired result was obtained. One of the frequent criticisms of private dyslexia assessment, albeit, one that has not been systematically researched, is that a dyslexia diagnosis is almost a certainty where reading is poorer than average, and such an outcome is being actively sought. Secondly, there, is the conflation with intelligence and the notion of stupidity. In the quotation above, there is an implicit suggestion that poor readers with high IQs have a greater case for additional resources than those whose performance on cognitive tests is weaker. Here, it is important to repeat the point that IQ does not inform reading intervention or predict the reading progress that the child is likely to make. Thirdly, there is an appeal to provide for a child's educational needs. Here, of course, the provision sought takes the form of expensive private education. The justification for this is that only this can provide 'specialist dyslexia tutoring'. However, there is no secure research evidence that any such tutoring exists other than the sound, explicit, structured teaching that should be offered to all poor readers, whether considered to be dyslexic or not. The final statement that this child might be being let down by a school system that is failing to provide adequate intervention for poor reading may well be accurate – in too many cases, poor readers are not provided with the structured teaching they need. However, siphoning off a small number of children with learning difficulties into private schools, because mainstream school provision is inadequate, is surely not a sustainable solution for those seeking an effective inclusive educational system.

A complicating factor is that there is a significant proportion of poor readers for whom even the best available approaches appear relatively ineffective (Wanzek et al., 2013). This finding has challenged researchers and reading specialists who, to date, have been unable to offer little more advice beyond suggesting that existing educational interventions should be more intense (i.e. by increasing time and duration of specialised assistance) or by decreasing instructional group size. However, these steps may not prove sufficient, given these students' seeming inability to benefit from the support they have already received (Fuchs et al., 2013). Nevertheless, one can understand the anxieties and frustrations of parents and teachers in such circumstances and it is not surprising that they will be motivated to search for an alternative way forward. Given their understandable vulnerabilities, many will be susceptible to suggestions that the child will benefit from other non-educational forms of specialised dyslexia treatment (Snowling, 2010), such as the use of coloured lenses, food additives, and psychomotor exercises. Unfortunately, there is no strong scientific support that such interventions can assist those with complex reading difficulties (see Elliott & Grigorenko, 2014, pp. 152–160, for a detailed discussion of some popular schemes).

1.4 *Dyslexia and Inclusion*

So, what approach to reading difficulty is appropriate for use within an inclusive education system? Firstly, there needs to be a body of appropriately trained teachers who understand how to teach reading and know how to identify and intervene with those who appear to be making slow progress. At a broader, systemic level, there should be an allied programme of systematic screening that can identify any child who appears to be struggling with reading as early as possible. Where appropriate, medical assessment should first check for sensory difficulties that might be a significant factor. Irrespective of this outcome, attention needs to be given to the child's educational experience. Where class teacher action is proving insufficient, additional inputs should be offered in small group settings. The child's progress should be regularly monitored and this should inform future decision-making. Where problems continue, more intense, highly-structured individualised interventions should be provided. All forms of specialised intervention employed should have the support of rigorous scientific research. While it is important that screening identifies struggling children as early as possible, this should not be undertaken as a one-off event as the presence of reading disabilities can fluctuate through the child's lifespan (Etmanskie, Partanen, & Siegel, 2016; Torppa et al., 2015).

This approach already exists, and it is known as *Response to Intervention* (RTI). A detailed discussion of this multi-tiered approach, and some related challenges, can be found in Elliott and Grigorenko (2014). Despite these, meta-analytical reviews have concluded that such interventions generally result in meaningful gains (Scammacca et al., 2015, 2016; Wanzek et al., 2016). The beauty of RTI is that, where it operates effectively, all struggling readers are identified, all have their reading needs assessed, and, where appropriate, all receive scientifically validated intervention. The amount and degree of additional support provided is a function of the progress that is subsequently made; it is not based upon performance on psychological tests that have limited relationship to educational programming, or clinical assessments that disproportionately involve children from socially disadvantaged backgrounds. The child's response to the interventions:

> ... provide guidance as to his or her long-term instructional needs, regardless of the origin of his or her reading difficulties. (Vellutino et al., 2004, p. 35)

This approach has the benefit of ensuring that special provision is made available on the basis of need, rather than the persistence and persuasive abilities of those who are better placed to seek and obtain a dyslexia diagnosis.

The dyslexia 'industry', typically operating with unclear criteria and unhelpful tests, and advocating specialist dyslexia interventions that have no clear scientific support (above and beyond those which are appropriate for all poor readers) works against a truly inclusive approach. Despite its (often well-meaning) rhetoric of identifying struggling students and giving them the assistance they require, the processes that are currently endorsed and supported privilege one set of individuals at the expense of others. Funding is diverted from system-wide RTI-based schemes that could be designed to cater for all poor readers, as has been the case in some U.S. states.

There is no justifiable rationale for providing additional resourcing to dyslexic individuals at the expense of others whose literacy skills operate at a similar level. If we were to argue that dyslexia is a term that can be used by all struggling readers (i.e. all poor decoders), this criticism would no longer be valid. However, despite protestations to the contrary, it is highly unlikely that an approach that currently provides disproportionate funding, support and sympathetic understanding to those who are typically found in more favoured backgrounds will be amended at any time in the near future.

References

Arishi, L., Boyle, C., & Lauchlan, F. (2017). Inclusive education and the politics of difference: Considering the effectiveness of labelling in special education. *Educational and Child Psychology, 34*(4), 9–19.

Bowers, J. S. (2016). The practical and principled problems with educational neuroscience. *Psychological Review, 123*(5), 600–612.

British Psychological Society. (1999). *Dyslexia, literacy and psychological assessment: Report by a working party of the division of educational and child psychology of the British Psychological Society*. Author.

Calfee, R. C., & Drum, P. (1986). Research on teaching reading. In M. C. Whittock (Ed.), *Handbook of research on teaching* (pp. 804–849). Macmillan.

Chall, J. S. (1996). *Learning to read: The great debate* (3rd ed.). Harcourt Brace.

Covington, M. V. (1992). *Making the grade: A self-worth perspective on motivation and school reform*. Cambridge University Press.

Davis, R. D. (1997). *The gift of dyslexia*. Souvenir Press.

Elliott, J. G. (2014, March 6). Time to rethink dyslexia? *Times Higher Education, 2142*, p. 34.

Elliott, J. G. (2015a). The dyslexia debate: Actions, reactions, and over-reactions. *Psychology of Education Review, 39*(1), 6–16.

Elliott, J. G. (2015b). The Author's response to peer commentary. *Psychology of Education Review, 39*(1), 35–36.

Elliott, J. G., & Grigorenko, E. L. (2014). *The dyslexia debate*. Cambridge University Press.

Elliott, J. G., & Nicolson, R. (2016). *Dyslexia: Developing the debate*. Bloomsbury Publishing.

Elliott, J. G., & Resing, D. C. M. (2015). Can intelligence testing inform educational intervention for children with reading disability? *Journal of Intelligence, 3*(4), 137–157.

Etmanskie, J. M., Partanen, M., & Siegel, L. S. (2016). A longitudinal examination of the persistence of late emerging reading disabilities. *Journal of Learning Disabilities, 49*(1), 21–35.

Fletcher, J. M., Lyon, G. R., Fuchs, L. S., & Barnes, M. A. (2007). *Learning disabilities*. Guilford.

Fletcher, J. M., & Miciak, J. (2017). Comprehensive cognitive assessments are not necessary for the identification and treatment of learning disabilities. *Archives of Clinical Neuropsychology, 32*(1), 2–7.

Flowers, L., Meyer, M., Lovato, J., Wood, F., & Felton, R. (2001). Does third grade discrepancy status predict the course of reading development? *Annals of Dyslexia, 51*, 49–71.

Francis, D. J., Shaywitz, S. E., Stuebing, K. K., Shaywitz, B. A., & Fletcher, J. M. (1996). Developmental lag versus deficit models of reading disability: A longitudinal individual growth curves analysis. *Journal of Educational Psychology, 88*, 3–17.

Frederickson, N. (1999). The ACID test – Or is it? *Educational Psychology in Practice, 15*, 2–8.

Fuchs, D., McMaster, K. L., Fuchs, L. S., & Al Otaiba, S. (2013). Data-based individualization as a means of providing intensive instruction to students with serious learning disorders. In D. L. Swanson, K. R. Harris, & S. Graham (Eds.), *Handbook of learning disabilities* (pp. 526–544). Guilford Press.

Goodman, K. S. (1967). Reading: A psycholinguistic guessing game. *Journal of the Reading Specialist, 6*, 126–135.

Goodman, K. S. (1986). *What's whole in whole language?* Heinemann.

Gresham, F. M., & Vellutino, F. R. (2010). What is the role of intelligence in the identification of specific learning disabilities? Issues and clarifications. *Learning Disabilities Research & Practice, 25*(4), 194–206.

Hackman, D. A., Farah, M. J., & Meaney, M. J. (2010). Socioeconomic status and the brain: Mechanistic insights from human and animal research. *Nature Reviews Neuroscience, 11*, 651–659.

Hinshelwood, J. (1902). Congenital word-blindness, with reports of two cases. *Ophthalmology Review, 21*, 91–99.

Im, S. D., Varma, K., & Varma, S. (2017). Extending the seductive allure of neuroscience explanations effect to popular articles about educational topics. *British Journal of Educational Psychology, 87*(4), 518–534.

Jednoróg, K., Altarelli, I., Monzalvo, K., Fluss, J., Dubois, J., Billard, C., Dehaene-Lambertz, G., & Ramus, F. (2012). The influence of socioeconomic status on children's brain structure. *PLoS ONE, 7*(8), e42486.

Machek, G. R., & Nelson, J. M. (2007). How should reading disabilities be operationalized? A survey of practicing school psychologists. *Learning Disabilities Research & Practice, 22*, 147–157.

Miciak, J., Taylor, D. P., Stuebing, K. K., & Fletcher, J. M. (2016). Simulation of LD identification accuracy using a pattern of processing strengths and weaknesses method with multiple measures. *Journal of Psychoeducational Assessment.*

Moura, O., Simoes, M. R., & Pereira, M. (2014). WISC-III cognitive profile in children with developmental dyslexia: Specific cognitive disability and diagnostic utility. *Dyslexia, 20*, 19–37.

Nicolson, R. (2005). Dyslexia: Beyond the myth. *The Psychologist, 18*, 658–659.

O'Donnell, P. S., & Miller, D. N. (2011). Identifying students with specific learning disabilities: School psychologists' acceptability of the discrepancy model versus response to intervention. *Journal of Disability Policy Studies, 22*, 83–94.

Olson, R. K. (2011). Genetic and environmental influences on phonological abilities and reading achievement. In S. A. Brady, D. Braze, & C. A. Fowler (Eds.), *Explaining individual differences in reading: Theory and evidence* (pp. 197–216). Psychology Press.

Peterson, R. L., & Pennington, B. F. (2012). Developmental dyslexia. *The Lancet, 379*, 1997–2007.

Riddick, B. (2010). *Living with dyslexia: The social and emotional consequences of specific learning difficulties/disabilities*. Routledge.

Rutter, M. (1978). Prevalence and types of dyslexia. In A. Benton & D. Pearl (Eds.), *Dyslexia: An appraisal of current knowledge* (pp. 5–28). Oxford University Press.

Rutter, M., Kim-Cohen, J., & Maughan, B. (2006). Continuities and discontinuities in psychopathology between childhood and adult life. *Journal of Child Psychology and Psychiatry, 47*, 276–295.

Scammacca, N. K., Roberts, G. J., Cho, E., Williams, K. J., Roberts, G., Vaughn, S. R., & Carroll, M. (2016). A century of progress: Reading interventions for students in grades 4–12, 1914–2014. *Review of Educational Research, 86*(3), 756–800.

Scammacca, N. K., Roberts, G., Vaughn, S., & Stuebing, K. (2015). *A meta-analysis of interventions for struggling readers in Grades 4–12: 1980–2011. Journal of Learning Disabilities, 48*(4), 369–390.

Scarborough, D. S., & Brady, S. A. (2002). Toward a common terminology for talking about speech and reading: A glossary of the "phon" words and some related terms. *Journal of Literacy Research, 34*(3), 299–336.

Shaywitz, S. E. (2005). *Overcoming dyslexia*. Alfred Knopf.

Snow, C. E., & Juel, C. (2005). Teaching children to read: What do we know about how to do it? In M. J. Snowling & C. Hulme (Eds.), *The science of reading: A handbook* (pp. 501–520). Blackwell.

Snowling, M. J. (2010). Dyslexia. In C. L. Cooper, J. Field, U. Goswami, R. Jenkins, & B. J. Sahakian (Eds.), *Mental capital and mental wellbeing* (pp. 775–783). Oxford: Blackwell.

Stuebing, K. K., Barth, A. E., Molfese, P. J., Weiss, B., & Fletcher, J. M. (2009). IQ is not strongly related to response to reading instruction: A meta-analytic interpretation. *Exceptional Children, 76*, 31–51.

Stuebing, K. K., Fletcher, J. M., LeDoux, J. M., Lyon, R. G., Shaywitz, S. E., & Shaywitz, B. A. (2002). Validity of IQ-discrepancy classifications of reading disabilities: A meta-analysis. *American Educational Research Journal, 39*, 469–518.

Taylor, D. P., Miciak, J., Fletcher, J. M., & Francis, D. J. (2017). Cognitive discrepancy models for specific learning disabilities identification: Simulations of psychometric limitations. *Psychological Assessment, 29*(4), 446–457.

Torgesen, J. K. (2004). Lessons learned from research on interventions for students who have difficulty learning to read. In P. McCardle & V. Chhabra (Eds.), *The voice of evidence in reading research* (pp. 355–382). Brookes.

Torgerson, C. J., Brooks, G., & Hall, G. (2006). *A systematic review of the research literature on the use of systematic phonics in the teaching of reading and spelling*. Department for Education and Skills.

Torppa, M., Eklund, K., van Bergen, E., & Lyytinen, D. (2015). Late-emerging and resolving dyslexia: A follow-up study from age 3 to 14. *Journal of Abnormal Child Psychology, 43*(7), 1389–1401.

Vellutino, F. R., Fletcher, J. M., Snowling, M. J., & Scanlon, D. M. (2004). Specific reading disability (dyslexia): What have we learned in the past four decades? *Journal of Child Psychology & Psychiatry, 45*, 2–40.

Vellutino, F. R., Scanlon, D. M., Zhang, D., & Schatschneider, C. (2008). Using response to kindergarten and first grade intervention to identify children at-risk for long-term reading difficulties. *Reading and Writing, 21*, 437–480.

Wanzek, J., Vaughn, S., Scammacca, N. K., Gatlin, B., Walker, M. A., & Capin, P. (2016). Meta-analyses of the effects of tier 2 type reading interventions in grades K-3. *Educational Psychology Review, 28*(3), 551–576.

Wanzek, J., Vaughn, S., Scammacca, N. K., Metz, K., Murray, C. S., Roberts, G., & Danielson, L. (2013). Extensive reading interventions for students with reading difficulties after grade 3. *Review of Educational Research, 83*(2), 163–195.

Watkins, M. D., Kush, J. C., & Glutting, J. J. (1997). Discriminant and predictive validity of the WISC-III ACID profile among children with learning disabilities. *Psychology in the Schools, 34*, 309–319.

PART 3

School Level – Existing Practices & Future Needs

∵

CHAPTER 8

The Importance of Teacher Attitudes to Inclusive Education

Christopher Boyle, Joanna Anderson and Kelly-Ann Allen

1 Introduction

Recognising the importance of teacher attitudes to inclusion is crucial for understanding the effectiveness of inclusive education in the school and/or community. It has been reported that teachers who are more positive to inclusion have more controlled learning environments compared to teachers with more negative attitudes to inclusion (Monsen & Frederickson, 2004). The role of teachers is understated in many studies that have investigated inclusion and student experiences. It is important to understand the vital roles of teachers in fostering inclusive classrooms, and while inclusion in schools begins with the teachers, it is imperative that teachers themselves are supported by the education system through access to appropriate resources, and the provision of supportive leadership and effective policy.

2 Inclusion and the Importance of Values and Attitudes

Inclusion is considered to be a complex and dynamic process that responds to the diversity and needs of all learners within a classroom environment (UNESCO, 2005). The success of positive inclusion relies on what happens at the ground level, hence "… it must be remembered that the commitment to inclusion begins with each educator" (Boyle et al., 2011, p. 77). From a socioecological perspective, students' experience of inclusion is deeply related to the interactions they have with the broader social environment (Anderson, Boyle, & Deppeler, 2014; Boyle, 2007). Therefore, relationship factors, school climate, school and system policy and practice, as well as broad community contexts, culture, and legislation can influence the success of inclusionary approaches within a school. Of direct impact to students is their relationship with their teacher, and the role attitudes play here is significant. Attitudes stem from values, which are defined as being ones "enduring beliefs about what is right" (Loreman et al., 2011, p. 40), and whilst they exist internally, they externalise

 | DOI: 10.1163/9789004431171_008

themselves in how individuals behave, and influence their reaction to situations (Baloglu, 2012). This is illustrated in Figure 8.1.

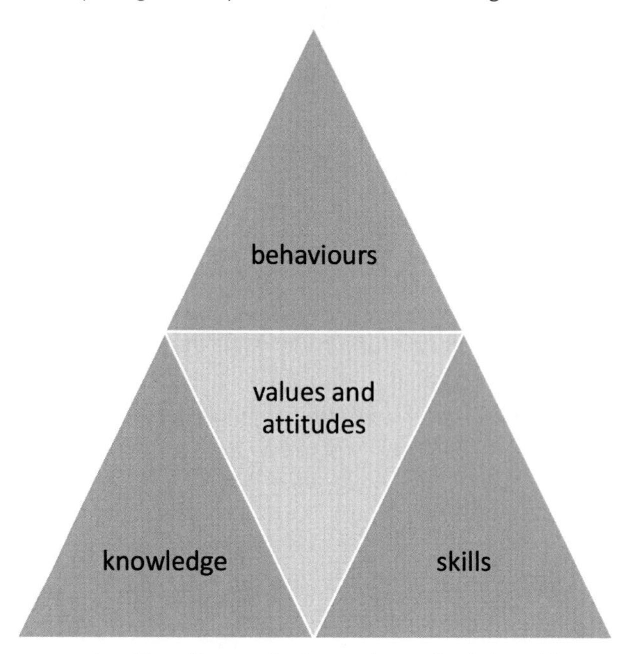

FIGURE 8.1 The influence of values and attitudes (adapted from Precey & Mazurkiewicz, 2013)

It follows that teacher values and attitudes will be pivotal to how inclusion is manifested both within individual classrooms, and collectively across the whole school.

Attitude towards working with students with Special Educational Needs (SEN) is clearly an important subject area and the large amount of research conducted into the area over past decades is testament to its significance (Saloviita, 2015). Beliefs of the individuals working in front-line services are an essential component for the success or failure of inclusion in mainstream classrooms. When integration hit the educational limelight in the 1980s, teacher attitudes were recognised as a potential barrier to the move towards students with SEN being placed into mainstream classrooms. A possible reason for this reluctance was described by Hannan and Pilner (1983); teachers' attitudes at the time reflected the attitude of the broader community towards people with disability.

> It appears that teachers, like the general public, are not overwhelmingly positive in their attitude toward the handicapped. Indeed, while there is

> some variation among conditions, in general teachers seem to have negative beliefs about and feelings toward these children as well as being somewhat reluctant to enter into teaching relationships with them. (p. 22)

Recent decades have seen the societal perception of disability shift in response to international declarations such as UNESCO's Salamanca Statement (1994) and the later UN Convention on the Rights of Persons with Disabilities (2006). While some gains have been made in the global effort to bring to the fore the rights, both educational and social, of people with a disability, quality of life outcomes for this group are still below that of people without a disability (see Anderson & Boyle, 2019, for a wider discussion). Nevertheless, things are moving, albeit slowly, in the right direction, including in education (Munyi, 2012). Despite the negative attitudes described by Hannan and Pilner in 1983, integration was challenged and the educational debate has become about inclusion, and teacher (both practising and pre-service) attitudes towards this ideal are the focus of much research in recent years. Yet measuring this accurately has presented its own challenges, not least because inclusion is a term that has proven difficult to define and therefore how the construct is understood differs between individuals. People may perceive questions and statements about inclusion in different ways based on their own belief systems. In a study by Ward, Center and Bochner (1994) among pre-school teachers in Australia, UK, and Canada, 80% of the respondents agreed with a positively worded statement about including all children in the mainstream classroom. When the data from that study was broken down it was discovered that some types of difficulty were regarded negatively and students with these needs were considered not suitable for inclusion in mainstream classes. Moderate intellectual disabilities were given a negative rating by all staff, including educational psychologists. It is important to note that there are different opinions about inclusion and based on the survey results, it might not always be clear what respondents agreed or disagreed on.

3 The Problem with Negative Attitudes

Attitudes, although drawn from cognitions, can pervasively impact teachers' affect and behavioural intentions. While teacher attitudes towards inclusion may be a product of their broader value system, as well as symptomatic of the societal and work environment that one is subjected to, negative attitudes can be unfavourable for the students in their educational charge. Negative attitudes may engender views such as: *some students do not have the capacity to learn, teachers do not need to teach students with varying needs, there is no time to individualise the curriculum,* and *students with additional needs are better educated outside mainstream schools.* Usually the latter is crouched under the 'choice' banner, and as being for the student's own benefit. It would be difficult to argue that any teacher who holds these types of views is able to provide a nurturing and engaging learning environment for all students with SEN in their classrooms. If negative attitudes to inclusion prevail, it can affect the perception of students with additional support needs' as being able to be educated within a mainstream environment, irrespective of whether this is evidentially accurate or not. According to UNICEF (2011), if children or young people with SEN are 'othered', they can become marginalised which can lead to bullying and ultimately, to being socially ostracised. Of course, the issue is self-fulfilling and cyclical, as represented in Figure 8.2.

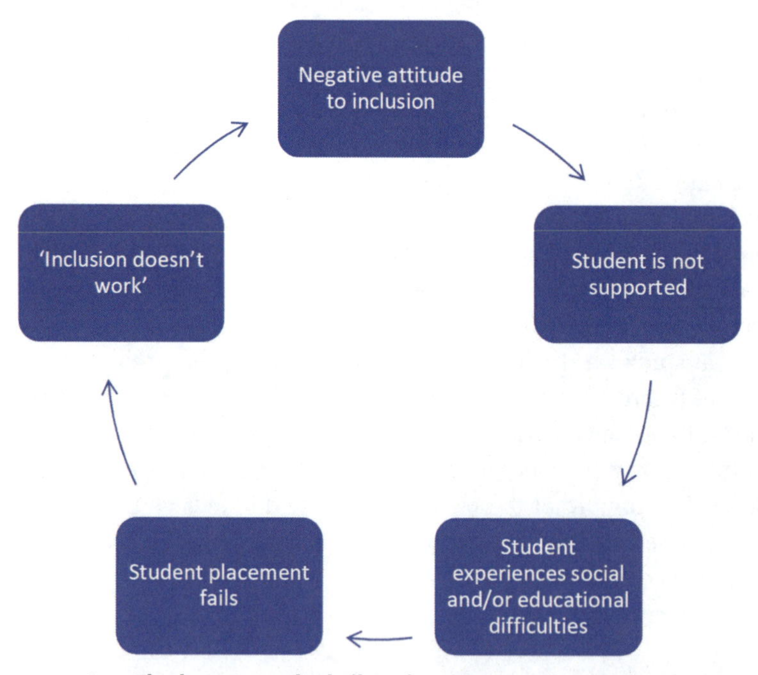

FIGURE 8.2 The damaging cyclical effect of negative attitudes to inclusion

Negative attitudes to inclusion are greatly influenced by prior exposure and may be the result of a lack of knowledge about, or experience in, inclusive processes. Teacher training is therefore key to ensuring that teachers have sufficient opportunities to both understand inclusive practices, and experience inclusive classrooms. Negative attitudes, after all, have been learnt and can therefore be similarly unlearned. Positively changing prospective teachers' attitudes to inclusion during university training is an important preventative way of fostering progressive teaching around inclusion. Boyle and colleagues have conducted several studies on the attitudes of pre-service teachers (e.g. Costello & Boyle, 2013; Hoskin, Boyle, & Anderson, 2015; Kraska & Boyle, 2014; Varcoe & Boyle, 2014) and this is discussed in more detail later in this chapter. It should be noted here that while attitudes can be 'unlearned' or altered reasonably easily, changing underlying value systems is more difficult (Rochon, 1998). For this reason, there are some who argue for educators to be selected on the basis of having a value system that aligns to the ideal of inclusion (Dyson, Howes, & Roberts, 2002). Negative attitudes towards inclusion by teachers can create a self-fulfilling prophecy and it is reasonable to assume that unfavourable attitudes and a lack of understanding about inclusive practices may inhibit its application by teachers in school settings. Subsequently, understanding teacher attitudes towards inclusion is an important component of progressing inclusion within schools.

4 Pre-Service Teacher Attitudes

Pre-service teacher attitudes to inclusion have been studied at length, with some concerning trends beginning to emerge. Students, as they progress through their degrees, become less positive towards inclusion as they move through their teacher training. Research conducted by Costello and Boyle (2013) reported more positive attitudes towards inclusion from students in their first year than in the following years. Another study by Saloviita (2015) found similar findings; students in their first year of study held positive attitudes towards inclusion (though expressed concern at the perceived workload related to it), however students who were further through their degrees began to show more negative attitudes towards 'the desirability of inclusive education' (p. 71). Hoskin, Boyle, and Anderson (2015) found that pre-service pre-school teachers' attitudes also declined during the duration of their study, however the shift was not in how they perceived inclusion, but rather in their capacity to effectively implement inclusive practices. A recent study looking at pre-service primary school students in Australia found that while attitudes towards inclusion decreased after the first year, by the final year of study students felt more positive about the inclusion of students with additional dialects, however still held concerns about students with disabilities being educated in inclusive classrooms (Goddard & Evans, 2018). Not all research has found this negative trend of declining attitudes across the course of a teaching degree. Kraska and Boyle's study (2014) found that the majority of preschool and primary school preservice teachers they surveyed were positive about inclusive education, regardless of how far through their degrees they were. There is a myriad of reasons to explain the different results. Studies were conducted across different countries, within different universities, and across different groups of student cohorts. Saloviita (2015) also explains that the use of different survey tools can produce very different results, given the complexity of the construct – inclusion – being researched. Despite these issues, the undeniable trend of declining attitudes towards inclusion across the duration of a teacher training programme cannot be discounted as being of concern. The attitudes that pre-service teachers leave their studies with, will dictate the practices they take with them into their classrooms (Goddard & Evans, 2018).

The solutions here are not simple. Gigante and Gilmore (2018) found that merely gaining knowledge (through a module or unit of work) on disability and/or special education did not improve teachers' self-efficacy for, and therefore their attitude towards, teaching in inclusive classrooms. Rather, what has been shown to improve pre-service teacher attitudes is access to a program of study pertaining to inclusive practices (Civitillo, de Moor, & Vervloed, 2016). An interesting study by Lambe (2007) provided details on the attempts that were made in a Northern Irish university towards changing pre-service teacher attitudes towards inclusive education. Participants of the study included 108 student teachers (response rate of 86.4%), who were asked to complete a questionnaire on their attitude towards inclusion at three different points in their training (at the beginning of the course, after the second phase of teaching and at the end of the course). Results showed that:

> … it is in the pre-service period that offers significant potential to influence positive attitudes. Increased concentration on this phase of teacher education might in fact provide the best means to create a new generation of teachers who will ensure the successful implementation of inclusive policies and practices in Northern Ireland. (Lambe, 2007, p. 62)

Lambe's study supports the importance of proper guidance on teaching strategies and acceptable attitudes for the teachers of the next generation, rather than just the delivery of isolated modules or units. By the end of the second phase of this study, respondents indicated that they felt that it was imperative for all teachers to work with children who have special educational needs.

Clearly, there is work to be done in Northern Ireland, and globally, vis-à-vis the attitudes and perception of pre-service teachers towards the practice of inclusion. The important point here is to recognise and accept that these negative attitudes exist, and to know that proper re-education programmes need be initiated to change these points of view.

5 In-Service Teacher Attitudes

As for pre-service teachers, much research has been conducted on the attitudes towards inclusion of in-service teachers. A study in Ireland found that while teachers held positive attitudes towards the construct of inclusion, the actuality of practice was closer to that of integration, with students having to 'fit in' (Young, McNamara, & Coughlan, 2017). These findings are similar to those of teachers in Malaysia, where Bailey, Nomanbhoy, and Tubpun (2015) found that while teachers held a generally positive attitude towards inclusion as an idea, their self-efficacy to implement inclusive practices successfully was lacking and therefore their attitude towards it being possible was less positive. This link between self-efficacy and attitude was also highlighted in a comparative study between teachers in Japan and Finland. Yada, Tolvanen, and Savolainen (2018) found that teachers who held a stronger belief in their capacity to enact inclusive practices successfully in their classrooms, held a more positive attitude about the construct. In a study looking at attitudes towards inclusion in India, there was a notable difference between teachers attitudes towards inclusion as a policy idea, and their ability to be able to enact that successfully within schools (Tiwari, Das, & Sharma, 2015). Subban and Sharma (2006) studied the attitudes towards inclusion of students with disabilities in Victoria, Australia, and the main finding was that, '... while teachers appear accepting and positive of inclusionary programs, there remains some concern about implementing inclusive education in the mainstream classroom' (p. 51). It is interesting to note that in all of these studies there seems to be a similar thread. Teachers hold positive attitudes towards inclusion as an idea, but feel less positive about their capacity to implement inclusive practices in their classrooms. This 'theory' to 'practice' gap is of concern if inclusion is something to be pursued.

Considering aspects from a different viewpoint, Boyle et al. (2013) examined teachers' attitudes to inclusion through a number of lenses, including that of teaching experience. The main finding from this study was that teachers became more negative about inclusion after the first year of teaching, however once at this level of attitude, it did not change significantly over the ensuing years of experience, as can be seen in Figure 8.3.

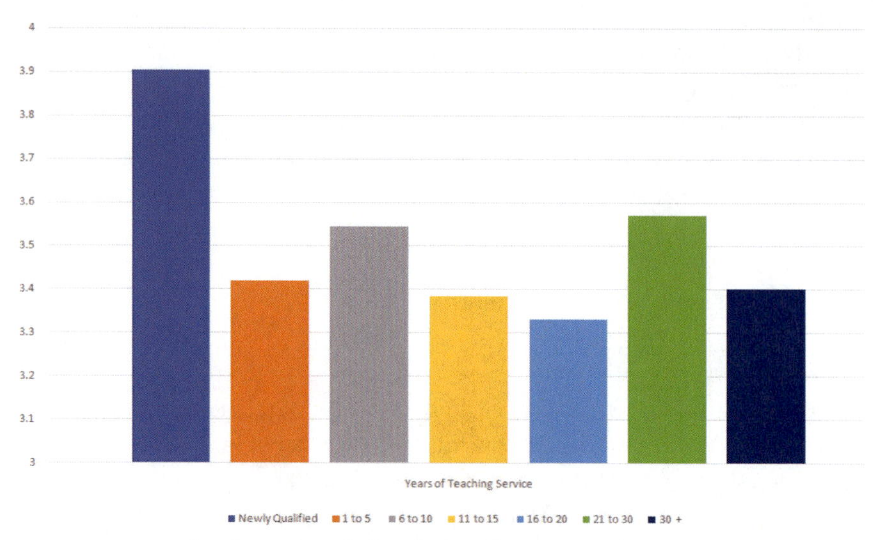

FIGURE 8.3 Overall inclusion score by length of teaching service (Boyle et al., 2013)

This significant decline in attitude from university graduate to in-service teacher was likely to have been heavily influenced by the developing understanding of the complex requirements of the teaching role. This finding sits comfortably with the common theme taken from much of the research about teacher attitudes to inclusion – in theory inclusion makes sense, but the practice of successful implementation is proving itself to be much more challenging (Boyle & Anderson, in press) and this is reflected in the shifting attitudes of teachers from the beginning of the teacher training degrees through to the first few years of their service.

There are clear implications for policies that attempt to bring students into the mainstream if teachers hold a negative view towards inclusion and believe that they should not be there, or that they are somebody else's responsibility. Contrastingly, teachers who exhibit a more positive attitude to inclusion are more likely to modify their teaching approaches to help students with additional support needs (Lüke & Grosche, 2018; Subban & Mahlo, 2017).

6 Inclusion and Teacher Efficacy

An issue that was been alluded to earlier, albeit briefly, is that of the effect of teacher efficacy and its subsequent relationship to attitudes towards inclusion. A study by Parker, Hannah, and Topping (2006) considered the views of 66 teachers (response rate of 50.5%) in 15 primary schools in a small Scottish local authority vis-a-vis the subject of teacher efficacy. The results of the study are summarised below:

> … despite great concern about socio-economic deprivation, behavioural problems and low parental expectations, which led to teacher stress, these teachers saw respect for and good relations with their pupils and a positive ethos in the school as key to high attainment, sustained by teacher motivation to learn, peer support and high quality in-service training. (p. 9)

Although the aforementioned study was not specifically related to teacher attitudes towards inclusion, it emphasised that good relationships with peers (also a significant finding in Boyle et al., 2012), a positive school ethos, and high-quality in-service training are essential for teachers to feel that they are competent and confident in their teaching abilities. Pre-service teacher training and plentiful resources are also areas that the research has identified as being a predictor of positive self-efficacy and therefore attitudes to inclusion.

6.1 *The Importance of Peer Support*

Peer support is one key to helping teachers put inclusive strategies into place in their classrooms. While different educational stakeholders may hold different opinions about inclusion, other teachers, school leaders and support staff (such as educational psychologists) are in a position to provide teachers with the support they need to implement inclusive practices. Although inclusion policies may exist, teachers play an instrumental role in the success or failure of the aims of such policy. Boyle and colleagues (2012) reported that informal and formal teacher peer support was one of the most effective resources available to teachers to ensure effective inclusive education. Support and involvement from other members of staff can have a positive influence on the outcome of inclusive contexts in the classroom (Mulholland & O'Connor, 2016; Scruggs & Mastropieri, 2017). The value of peer support cannot be understated (Boyle et al., 2012).

It is reasonable to assume that if teachers, who are absolutely the key to the success or failure of inclusion policy, are not supportive of the main aims of the inclusion process there will be lower likelihood of success. Past research (Ainscow, 2015) has demonstrated that the involvement of teachers and other members of staff who will, effectively, be highly influential as to the outcome of the policy, is crucial.

6.2 *Positive School Culture*

School culture, described as the 'values, beliefs, attitudes, ways of thinking, customs and rituals' (Berzina, 2010, p. 76) of each individual setting, has been depicted as a significant determinant of the success, or not, of inclusive practices (Berzina, 2010). If the school culture is one that promotes inclusion through enshrining its principles in school policy, processes and practices, teachers are more likely to feel supported to engage in inclusive practices in their classrooms (Parker, Hannah, & Topping, 2006), and to experience success when they do this (Osiname, 2018). As noted previously, success leads to improved perceptions of teacher self-efficacy, which in turn improves their attitudes towards inclusion. School leaders, and in particular the principal, are key determinants of school culture, and the drivers of any necessary change. What this link between a positive school and teacher attitudes means for their work will be explored in more detail later.

6.3 *Pre-Service and In-Service Teacher Training, and Links to Perceptions*

A seminal review of the literature on teacher attitudes conducted by Avramidis and Norwich (2002) recommended future research to investigate the reasons for the teachers' perceptions on inclusion, as well as the quality of training, both before and after teacher training. In another study, many teachers were found to have positive attitudes towards inclusion, but still have concerns regarding adapting and modifying classroom arrangements, in part because of a lack of relevant training (Boyle et al., 2013).

An attempt was made at a teacher training institution in the UK to provide trainee teachers with the skills to effectively modify their teaching methods to work with a wide spectrum of students including those with additional support needs (Golder, Norwich, & Bayliss, 2005). A course was integrated into a professional PGCE course and trainee teachers were provided with resources such as a mentor, access to the Special Educational Needs Co-ordinator (SENCO) for the school and strategic online support. Trainees were allocated one pupil to work with and they planned appropriate support through consultation with the SENCO and class teachers, thus gaining appropriate information on the pupil's strengths, weaknesses, and additional support needs amongst others. It was reported by the trainee teachers to be:

> … a valuable exercise, particularly with reference to improving knowledge, understanding and awareness of issues such as the identification of pupils with special educational needs, differentiation, understanding individual needs and planning for pupils with special educational needs. (Golder et al., 2005, p. 98)

The importance of providing support for teacher training and positive attitude towards teaching students with special educational needs is again highlighted in a study of teacher attitudes in one high school in San Antonio, Texas by Van Reusen, Shoho, and Barker (2001). Findings of the study are summarised by the authors in this paragraph:

> The results of this study support earlier findings that positive teacher attitudes about including and teaching students with disabilities in general education classrooms appear related to the levels of special education training, knowledge, and experience in working with or teaching students with disabilities. (p. 11)

Support is again given to the importance of not just pre-service training but, and arguably more so, good quality ongoing training that involves the appropriate input of teaching staff so that they feel that they can adequately make a difference to their teaching practice. This could respond to concerns that teachers are leaving the profession because they are not getting enough SEN training post qualifying (Bennett, 2008).

Administrators and high school principals should take into consideration the attitudes to inclusion of teachers prior to the development and implementation of any professional development in this area. Van Reusen et al. (2001) suggest that one day workshops and orientations are useless, and proper ongoing training and instructional support to assist with inclusion programmes is necessary. Instead, quite often, it is the response 'the teacher should be differentiating' that is given when questions are raised about a teacher's ability to work with children who require additional support, however this can be unrealistic without proper support. It follows that before a programme of inclusion is implemented, a full survey of teacher attitudes and level of experience should be conducted, to better understand what teachers need. Teachers with no background or training in SEN should be targeted even before the inclusion programme begins. Van Reusen et al. (2001) also suggested that time should be given to allow teachers to learn skills such as team teaching, in-school networking and behavioural management strategies.

Based on the results of previous studies of pre-service training, it could be postulated that education establishments must include a curriculum that will challenge negative attitudes towards inclusion and just as importantly to promote teacher competence in this area (for further discussion of this area see Carrington & Brownlee, 2001; Sharma, Forlin, Loreman, & Earle, 2006). The importance of clear inclusion components and curricular subject content has been highlighted in three previous studies of pre-service teacher education (Costello & Boyle, 2013; Kraska & Boyle, 2014; Varcoe & Boyle, 2015). Taking this point to an extreme would suggest that teachers who continually fail the 'inclusiveness component' should not be allowed to pass the course. Appropriate attitudes towards including students in mainstream classes are fundamental to the teaching profession and should be integral to a person qualifying as a teacher. For inclusion to be successful, universities and teaching professionals must be prepared to work together to '… formulate and integrate new knowledge about inclusive learning management, particularly in the hearts and minds of those entering the profession' (Bradshaw & Mundia, 2006, p. 39). Teachers are the key to change in education, therefore if their beliefs are negative or if they feel that they do not have the skills and resources then this could be a barrier to inclusive education.

6.4 *Educational Resources vs. Attitudes*

While a teacher's attitude towards inclusion is central to guiding successful inclusive practices, teachers also require systemic support through access to appropriate resources in order to foster inclusive climates. Educational resourcing is always flagged as a perennial issue in schools, but this is even more prevalent when support for students with SEN is factored in (Boyle & Anderson, in press; Boyle, Topping, Jindal-Snape, & Norwich, 2012; Myles, Boyle, & Richards, 2019). There are always demands on finite resources and with many governments attempting to be more inclusive, issues concerned with resourcing (such as a lack of specialised equipment and/or staffing) can become a barrier (whether perceived or actual) to inclusion. Attitudes and resources become central to how effective (or ineffective) inclusive practices are. Figure 8.4 demonstrates the notion that neither positive attitudes or plentiful resources alone can facilitate effective inclusionary practices in the classroom. In fact, in order for inclusion to work optimally, schools need both positive attitudes from teachers and plentiful classroom/school resources simultaneously. For example, a school with adequate facilities, equipment and tools for creating a climate of inclusion for all children will not be effective if the teachers that work there hold negative attitudes. Likewise, if teachers hold positive attitudes, but are affected from under resourcing, inclusionary approaches are hindered.

The duality of attitudes and resources towards the success of inclusion is not new and the idea that positive attitudes towards working with students with SEN is a necessary component for positive inclusion has been around for a long period of time, particularly in the post-Warnock era (in the UK). Empirical research supporting this notion has been around for decades, and findings do not differ greatly between studies of the 1980s and those undertaken more recently (e.g. Hannah & Pilner, 1983; Center, Ward, Parmenter, &

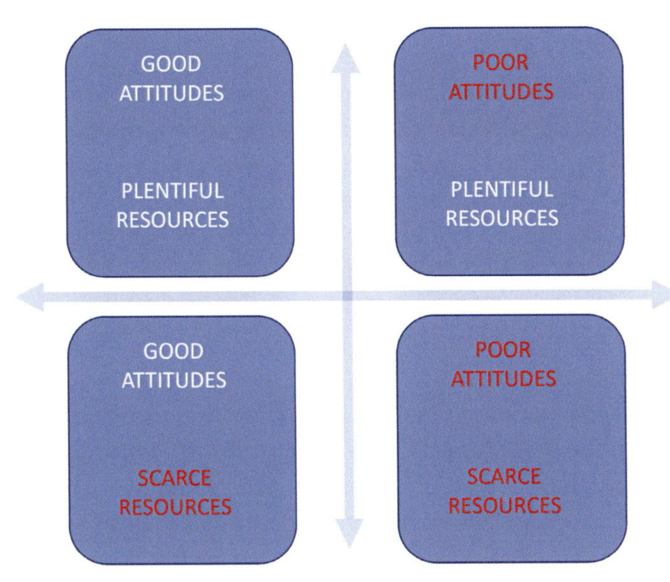

FIGURE 8.4 Attitudes vs. resources (Boyle et al., 2012)

Nash, 1985; Parkins, 2002; Mitchell, 2008; Warnock, 2010; Subban & Mahlo, 2017; Page, Boyle, McKay, & Mavropoulou, 2019).

7 Towards a Positive Profession

Regardless of the personal opinions and attitudes of others towards inclusion, teachers have an obligation – professional, moral and in some cases legal – to recognise and implement effective inclusive strategies. The evidence suggests that this will happen more effectively if teachers hold a positive attitude to the construct (Boyle et al., 2011).

Positive attitudes for inclusion begin with the teacher, who has the power to shape and influence how inclusion is viewed and applied within a school (Boyle et al., 2011). However, this cannot be the work of the teacher alone. Leaders within the school – those responsible for delivering school policies and processes, and driving effective practices, including the school principal – must also hold a positive attitude towards inclusion to ensure the school has a culture that embraces and celebrates diversity, or are at least open to this notion. If teachers are not supported through a positive school culture and inclusive schoolwide processes, resources, materials and/or tools for inclusion will not be enough. Even professional development in isolation is likely to be of no use unless inclusion is nurtured and supported at the school level, and teachers hold positive attitudes towards its implementation.

If one considers teachers as the public face of education, and within the particular parameters of this chapter, as that of the face of inclusion, then it follows that these 'street level workers' in any system (to borrow from Lipsky, 1980, 2010) are the teachers. The success or failure of government policy rests on their ability or, indeed, willingness to implement the policy objectives. Teacher attitudes to inclusion are highly influential in shaping their level of motivation to effectively implement inclusion at the school and class level (Boyle et al., 2013; Hoskin et al., 2015).

7.1 *Policy for Inclusion*

Policy makers around the world continue to include the terms inclusion or inclusive education in the work they do. Regrettably, this has not translated into successful inclusive practices within systems and individual schools, and as a result Slee (2018) describes the current rhetoric in policy as 'an empty language' (p. 20). There are many reasons for this. One such reason is that inclusion policy has been enacted alongside other reform agendas, such as standardisation and competition (Schlessinger, 2018), which run counterintuitively to the philosophical underpinnings of inclusive education (Artiles & Kozleski, 2016). This type of paradoxical policy implementation is challenging for practitioners (Ekins, 2013); when there are competing discourses from different sectors within an educational organisation, which are they to adhere to? Another reason is that '... policymakers often advocate inclusive education without an understanding of the pedagogical approaches that teachers can use to operationalise the policy' (Nind & Wearmouth, 2006, p. 122). Without an understanding of how to enact inclusion and the supports required for its implementation, school leaders and teachers are not going to have the systemic supports they need to deliver the outcomes of the policy.

Further examination of why inclusion policies have not had the intended outcomes is beyond the scope of this chapter, however from the two reasons explored above, it is evident that policies have not made the inroads to inclusive reform that perhaps they could. For this to change, policy makers need to acknowledge and understand the barriers and challenges that are getting in the way of inclusive reform. Part of this is recognising the role teacher attitudes play in the reform process. Until this time, inclusive reform remains the responsibility of the schools, and it is up to school leaders to ensure school policies and processes are meeting the needs of all students who pass through the school gate.

7.2 *Implications for School Leadership*

Research has consistently reflected the importance of school leadership as a predictor of school culture (Piotrowsky, 2016; Fullan, 2014). Principals and school leaders have a far-reaching level of influence on students, teachers, parents and the wider school community; on the 'values, ideals, aspirations, emotions and identities' of these different groups (Alvesson & Spicer, 2012, p. 384). The way this influence presents itself is determined by the leadership practices adopted and applied by the principal (Leithwood, Harris, & Hopkins, 2008). This dictates that principals are the key participant in directing school change and creating schools that support teachers to meet the needs of all students (Macmillan & Edmunds, 2010), and they are identified as being even more important in schools with heterogenous populations (Hoppey & McLeskey, 2013). Principals must work to create a culture where the school takes responsibility for overcoming 'socially constructed barriers to learning' for all students (Ekins, 2013, p. 30); a school with a focus on inclusive education practices (Carter & Abawi, 2018). When school leaders set an expectation for inclusion, and provide the supports to do so, teachers are more likely to hold a positive attitude towards it. As such, research has found that it is essential that teaching staff are involved in the implementation of school inclusion policy if it is to be fully accepted and applied at school (Boyle et al., 2013). Supportive leadership is needed to ensure positive, proactive school policies are in place, professional development and training is implemented, and the overall school culture is providing a nurturing and inclusive environment for all students.

8 Conclusion

While discussions of inclusive practices can be stuck at a policy and practice level, using a socio-ecological lens to view inclusion can guide schools towards acknowledging a whole-school approach to creating a culture of inclusion. Within this framework is the importance of student-teacher relationships, and teacher attitudes and beliefs. However, teacher attitudes alone are not sufficient to influence inclusion within a school setting. It is essential that teachers are supported by proactive leadership, supportive peers and policy that is cohesive and consistent with their beliefs toward inclusion. Some of this is the responsibility of the schools, and some of the systems they operate within.

Research showed that current practices are not consistently meeting school goals, expectations or legislator requirements towards inclusion (Anderson & Boyle, 2019). Understanding whether inclusion is successful in the various spheres of education is problematic (Forlin et al., 2013), and this is confounded by the complexity of the construct itself. Slee (2018) argues that rather than debating the nuances of what inclusion is, work should be considered in terms of eliminating exclusionary practices. To do this, those working with students at the coal face – the teachers – need to feel positively about their capacity to support and nurture all students through the utilisation of inclusive strategies and practices in their classrooms. While approaches to inclusion may (and in fact should) vary from individual to individual, school to school, and country to country, there is much work to be done to continue ensuring that all schools, and teachers, are meeting the needs of all students (Boyle & Sharma, 2015). Understanding teachers' attitudes towards inclusion and how this can be improved, is an important step forward.

References

Ainscow, M. (2015). *Towards self-improving school systems. Lessons from a city challenger*. Routledge.

Anderson, J., & Boyle, C. (2019). Looking in the mirror: Reflecting on 25 years of inclusive education in Australia. *The International Journal of Inclusive Education, 23*(7–8), 796–810. doi:10.1080/13603116.2019.1622802

Anderson, J., Boyle, C., & Deppeler, J. (2014). The ecology of inclusive education: Reconceptualising Bronfenbrenner. In Z. Zhang, P. D. K. Chan, & C. Boyle (Eds.), *Equality in education: Fairness and inclusion* (pp. 23–34). Sense Publishers.

Avramidis, E., & Norwich, B. (2002). Teachers' attitudes towards integration/inclusion: A review of the literature. *European Journal of Special Needs Education, 17*(2), 129–147.

Bailey, L., Nomanbhoy, A., & Tubpun, T. (2015). Inclusive education: Teacher perspectives from Malaysia. *International Journal of Inclusive Education, 19*(5), 547–559. doi:10.1080/13603116.2014.957739

Bennett, A. (2008). Teachers forced from profession by lack of SEN training. *Children and Young People Now – Daily Bulletin.* Retrieved from http://doi.cypnow.co.uk/bulletins

Berzina, Ž. (2010). Teachers' perceptions on what inclusion is. *Journal of Teacher Education for Sustainability, 12*(1), 75–84. doi:10.2478/v10099-009-0048-8

Boyle, C., & Anderson, J. (in press). Inclusive education and the progressive inclusionists. In U. Sharma & S. Salend (Eds.), *The Oxford research encyclopedia of education.* Oxford University Press.

Boyle, C., Scriven, B., Durning, S., & Downes, C. (2011). Facilitating the learning of all students: The 'professional positive' of inclusive practice in Australian primary schools. *Support for Learning, 26*(2), 72–78. doi:10.1111/j.1467-9604.2011.01480.x

Boyle C., Topping, K., & Jindal-Snape, D. (2013). Teachers' attitudes towards inclusion in high schools. *Teachers and Teaching: Theory and Practice, 19*(5), 527–542. doi:10.1080/13540602.2013.827361

Boyle, C., Topping, K., Jindal-Snape, D., & Norwich, B. (2012). The importance of peer-support for teaching staff when including children with special educational needs. *School Psychology International, 33*(2), 167–184. doi:10.1177/0143034311415783

Boyle, C., & Sharma, U. (2015). Inclusive Education – Worldly views? *British Journal of Support for Learning, 30*(1), 2–3. doi:10.1111/1467-9604.12077

Bradshaw, L., & Mundia, L. (2006). Attitudes to and concerns about inclusive education: Bruneian inservice and preservice teachers. *International Journal of Special Education, 21*(1), 35–41.

Carrington, S., & Brownlee, J. (2001). Preparing teachers to support inclusion: The benefits of interaction between a group of pre-service teachers and a teaching assistant who is disabled. *Teaching Education, 12*(3), 347–357.

Center, D., Ward, J., Parmenter, T., & Nash, R. (1985). Principals' attitudes toward the integration of disabled children into regular schools. *The Exceptional Child, 32*, 149–161.

Civitillo, S., de Moor, J., & Vervloed, M. (2016). Pre-service teachers' beliefs about inclusive education in the Netherlands: In exploratory study. *Support for Learning, 31*(2), 104–121. doi:10.1111/1467-9604.12119

Costello, S., & Boyle, C. (2013). Pre-service secondary teachers' attitudes towards inclusive education. *Australian Journal of Teacher Education, 38*(4), 129–143. doi:10.14221/ajte.2013v38n4.8

Dyson, A., Howes, A., & Roberts, B. (2002). *A systemic review of the effectiveness of school-level actions for promoting participation by all students*. Institute of Education.

Ekins, A. (2013). Special education within the context of an inclusive school. In G. Mac Ruairc, E. Ottenson, & R. Precey (Eds.), *Leadership for inclusive education* (pp. 19–34). Sense Publishers.

Forlin, C., Chambers, D., Loreman, T., Deppeler, J., & Sharma, U. (2013). *Inclusive education for students with disability: A review of the best evidence in relation to theory and practice.* Australian Research Alliance for Children and Youth.

Gigante, J., & Gilmore, L. (2018). Australian preservice teachers' attitudes and perceived efficacy for teaching in inclusive classrooms. *International Journal of Inclusive Education* (Published online first). doi:10.1080/13603116.2018.1545875

Goddard, C., & Evans, D. (2018). Primary pre-service teachers' attitudes towards inclusion across the training years. *Australian Journal of Teacher Education, 43*(6), 122–142. doi:10.14221/ajte.2018v43n6.8

Golder, G., Norwich, B., & Bayliss, P. (2005). Preparing teachers to teach pupils with special educational needs in more inclusive schools. *Journal of Special Education, 32*(2), 92–99.

Hannah, M. E., & Pilner, S. (1983) Teacher attitudes toward handicapped children: A review and syntheses. *School Psychology Review, 12*(1), 12–25.

Hoskin, J., Boyle, C., & Anderson, J. (2015). Inclusive education in pre-schools: Predictors of pre-service teacher attitudes in Australia. *Teachers and Teaching: Theory and Practice, 21*(8), 974–989. doi:10.1080/13540602.2015.1005867

Kraska, J., & Boyle, C. (2014). Attitudes of pre-school and primary school pre-service teachers towards inclusive education. *Asia-Pacific Journal of Teacher Education, 42*(3), 228–246. doi:10.1080/1359866X.2014.926307

Lambe, J. (2007). Northern Ireland student teachers' changing attitudes towards inclusive education during initial teacher training. *International Journal of Special Education, 22*(1), 59–71.

Lipsky, M. (1980). *Dilemma of the individual in public services.* Russell Sage Foundation.

Lipsky, M. (2010). *Street-level bureaucracy: Dilemmas of the individual in public services* (30th anniversary expanded ed.). Russell Sage Foundation.

Lüke, T., & Grosche, M. (2018). What do I think about inclusive education? It depends on who is asking. Experimental evidence for a social desirability bias in attitudes towards inclusion. *International Journal of Inclusive Education, 22*(1), 38–53. doi:10.1080/13603116.2017.1348548

Macmillan, R., & Edmunds, A. (2010). Leadership for inclusion: Questions and dilemmas. In A. Edmunds & R. MacMillan (Eds.), *Leadership for inclusion: A Practical guide* (pp. 1–7). Sense Publishers.

Munyi, C. (2012). Past and present perceptions towards disability: A historical perspective. *Disability Studies Quarterly, 32*(2). doi:10.18061/dsq.v32i2.3197

Myles, O., Boyle, C., & Richards, A. (2019). The social experiences and sense of belonging in adolescent females with Autism in mainstream school. *Educational and Child Psychology, 36*(4), 8–21.

Mitchell, D. (2008). *What really works in special and inclusive education: Using evidence-based teaching strategies.* Routledge.

Monsen, J., & Frederickson, N. (2004). Teachers' attitudes towards mainstreaming and their pupils' perceptions of their classroom learning environment. *Learning Environments Research, 7*(1), 129–142.

Mulholland, M., & O'Connor, U. (2016). Collaborative classroom practice for inclusion: Perspectives of classroom teachers and learning support/resource teachers. *International Journal of Inclusive Education, 20*(10), 1070–1083. doi:10.1080/13603116.2016.1145266

Nind, M., & Wearmouth, J. (2006). Including children with special educational needs in the mainstream classrooms: Implications for pedagogy from a systematic review. *Journal of Research in Special Educational Needs, 6*(3), 116–124.

Osiname, A. (2018). Utilizing the critical inclusive praxis: The voyage of five selected school principals in building inclusive school cultures. *Improving Schools, 21*(1), 63–83. doi:10.1177/1365480217717529

Page, A., Boyle, C., McKay, K., & Mavropoulou, S. (2019). Teacher perceptions of inclusive education in the Cook Islands. *Asia-Pacific Journal of Teacher Education, 47*(1), 81–94. doi:10.1080/1359866X.2018.1437119

Parker, K., Hannah, E., & Topping, K. J. (2006). Collective teacher efficacy, pupil attainment and socio-economic status in primary school. *Improving Skills, 9*(2), 111–129.

Parkins, D. (2002). *Review of low support needs students – Integration.* New South Wales Department of Education & Training.

Piotrowsky, M. J. (2016). *The impact of leadership on school culture and student achievement.* Unpublished thesis. Clemson University.

Rochon, R. (1998). *Culture moves: Ideas, activism, and changing values.* Princeton University Press.

Saloviito, T. (2015). Measuring pre-service teachers' attitudes towards inclusive education: Psychometric properties of the TAIS scale. *Teaching and Teacher Education, 52*(1), 66–72. doi:10.1016/j.tate.2015.09.003

Scruggs, T. E., & Mastropieri, M. A. (2017). Making inclusion work with co-teaching. *Teaching Exceptional Children, 49*(4), 284–293. doi:10.1177/0040059916685065

Sharma, U., Forlin, C., Loreman, T., & Earle, C. (2006). Pre-service teachers' attitudes, concerns and sentiments about inclusive education: An international comparison of the novice pre-service teachers. *International Journal of Special Education, 21*(2), 80–93.

Slee, R. (2018). *Inclusive education isn't dead, it just smells funny.* Routledge.

Specht, J., McGhie-Richmond, D., Loreman, T., Mirenda, P., Bennett, S., Gallagher, T., Young, G., Metsala, J., Aylward, L., Katz, J., Lyons, D., Thompson, S., & Cloutier, S. (2016). Teaching in inclusive classrooms: Efficacy and beliefs of Canadian preservice teachers. *International Journal of Inclusive Education, 20*(1), 1–15. doi:10.1080/13603116.2015.1059501

Subban, P., & Mahlo, D. (2017). 'My attitude, my responsibility' Investigating the attitudes and intentions of pre-service teachers toward inclusive education between teacher preparation cohorts in Melbourne and Pretoria. *International Journal of Inclusive Education, 21*(4), 441–461. doi:10.1080/13603116.2016.1197322

Subban, P., & Sharma, U. (2006) Primary school teachers' perceptions of inclusive education in Victoria, Australia. *International Journal of Special Education, 21*(1), 42–52.

Tiwari, A., Das, A., & Sharma, M. (2015). Inclusive education a "rhetoric" or "reality"? Teachers' perspectives and beliefs. *Teaching and Teacher Education, 52*(1), 128–136. doi:10.1016/j.tate.2015.09.002

UNESCO. (1994). *The Salamanca statement and framework for action on special needs education.* United Nations Educational, Scientific, and Cultural Organisation.

UNESCO. (2005). *Guidelines for inclusion: Ensuring access to education for all.* United Nations Educational, Scientific and Cultural Organization.

UNICEF. (2011). *The right of children with disabilities to education: A rights-based approach to inclusive education.* UNICEF Regional Office for Central and Eastern Europe and the Commonwealth of Independent States.

Van Reusen, A. K., Shoho, A. R., & Barker, K. S. (2001). High school teacher attitudes toward inclusion. *High School Journal, 84*(2), 7–21.

Varcoe, L., & Boyle, C. (2014). Primary pre-service teachers' attitudes towards inclusive education. *Educational Psychology, 34*(3), 323–337. doi:10.1080/01443410.2013.785061

Ward, J., Center, D., & Bochner, S. (1994). A question of attitudes: Integrating children with disabilities into regular classrooms? *British Journal of Special Education, 21*(1), 34–39.

Warnock, M. (2010). Special educational needs: A new look. In L. Terzi (Ed.), *Special educational needs: Key debates in educational policy* (pp. 11–45). Continuum.

Yada, A., Tolvanen, A., & Savolainen, D. (2018). Teachers' attitudes and self-efficacy on implementing inclusive education in Japan and Finland: A comparative study using multi-group structural equation modelling. *Teaching and Teacher Education, 75*(1), 343–355. doi:10.1016/j.tate.2018.07.011

Young, K., McNamara, P., & Coughlan, B. (2017). Authentic inclusion-utopian thinking? Irish post-primary teachers' perspectives of inclusive education. *Teaching and Teacher Education, 68*(1), 1–11. doi:10.1016/j.tate.2017.07.017

CHAPTER 9

Transforming Teacher Education Classroom Management to Provoke Philosophies and Engender Practices of Inclusivity

Angela Page and Marguerite Jones

1 Introduction

Reports on poor classroom behaviour that subsequently hinders student learning has been a topic of media attention in Australia since the release of the 2018 PISA (Programme for International Student Assessment) results (OECD, 2018). Interrogations of the PISA report echo concerns from the 2015 report (Thomson, De Bortoli, & Underwood, 2017) regarding the relationship between student disengagement and disruption, and levels of academic achievement (Black & Fernando, 2014; Peters, 2012; Rivkin & Schiman, 2015). Likewise, Hamilton (2015) and Millei and Petersen (2014) express similar concerns for teachers who struggle to manage student behaviours and maintain classroom 'discipline'.

This chapter problematises prevailing Australian narratives of student (mis)behaviour, and teacher 'discipline' of such perpetrators (McDonald, 2010). It also critiques current teacher education programme delivery of classroom management in Australia, and the implications of these for practices in schools. Finally, an alternative model for conceptualising and teaching classroom management is presented that incorporates philosophies, principles and practices of inclusive classroom management.

1.1 *Problematising Existing Approaches to Classroom Management*

Classroom management, in its traditional sense, has been defined as behaviour management, focussing on teachers containing low-level behaviours, including disruptive, disengaged, aggressive, and anti-social behaviours. For many years, teachers have relied on reward and punishment strategies to curb unproductive behaviour and to promote compliance. These have involved the implementation of increasingly punitive strategies, from giving warnings, in-class time-out, out-of-class time-out, referrals, suspension, and finally, school expulsion. The exclusion of students may provide an opportunity for a teacher to

 | DOI: 10.1163/9789004431171_009

regain a sense of control, but it also isolates the 'offending' student. Although, as Sullivan, Johnson, Conway, Owens, and Taddeo (2012) report, 85% of teachers indicate that they use such a tiered system to address student behaviours, only 33.3% reported this approach to be effective. The approach clearly creates a binary of an 'in-group' and an 'out-group' of students, as attempts are made to change the individual, rather than the context within which the student operates. Typologising the student as the problem brings into question external variables of power, and complex discourses of inclusion and exclusion (Ringrose & Rawlings, 2015). 'Inclusion' and 'exclusion' can be even more complex to define when the additional complexity of situating students who require teacher assistant support at the back of a classroom and naming it inclusive practice (Slee, 2013).

The construction of children and childhood continues to permeate the way we respond to behaviours that are challenging (Michail, 2011). When prevailing psychological theories conceptualise student behaviour in terms of control, teacher management strategies are concerned with regimes of compliance. Student behaviour can be equated with problem behaviour, and is often defined as disruptive and defiant, being pathologically located within the child (Millei & Petersen, 2014). The theoretical positioning of students and their behaviour in this manner has informed the popular term 'classroom behaviour management'.

Such theorising is perpetuated in international testing such as PISA, 2015 (Thomson et al., 2017), in which the very questions asked appear to be philosophically underpinned by a deficit view of the student. For example, in the 2015 PISA study, students were asked about disruptions in their science classrooms (Thomson et al., 2017). Findings reported by Australian students included perceptions that: their peers do not listen to the teacher (32%), there is noise and disorder in the classroom (33%), the teacher waits too long for students to quieten down (29%), they could not work well (22%), and that they don't start working for a long time after the lesson begins (26%).

Furthermore, it is troubling to see that Australia's poor PISA results were reported in the popular news media as being a consequence of 'chaos in the classroom' (Balogh, 2017) and repeated again in 2018, where students from Australia are the 'least disciplined in the world' (Carey, 2019). Highly emotive descriptions of Australian student behaviour and performance such as reflecting 'grave concerns' (Thomson et al., 2017), and the Federal Education minister, Simon Birmingham call for 'zero tolerance' of disruptive behaviours that 'infect' entire classrooms (Henebery, 2017) ensued. Likewise, Krskova and Baumann (2017), in response to poor Australian PISA results, advocated that teachers engage in strict, high discipline to ensure students successfully complete their schooling and 'ultimately contribute to a more competitive workforce and economy' (p. 306).

It should be noted, however, that the PISA statistics in Australia relating to classroom discipline were found to be similar to those of Canada, the United States of America, New Zealand, and the United Kingdom (Reid, 2017). The country that stood above the rest in all measures of student-related behaviours that positively impacted upon their engagement and learning, was Finland. It is opportune to ponder the philosophy, principles and practices embraced in Finnish education that have contributed to consistent results across time (Organisation for Economic Co-operation and Development, 2010). While any explanation of successful educational models is always complex and cannot be isolated, nor plucked out and easily replicated, perhaps there is much to learn from the accomplishments of the Finnish education system rather than recoil at our own shortcomings.

Lopez (2012) reports that pedagogical approaches in Finnish schools promote participation rather than teacher generated instruction methods. Likewise, professional learning communities amongst teachers are integral to sharing good practice. The education system is based on the philosophy of inclusion and an ethos of equity and equality (Finnish National Agency for Education, n.d.; Järvinen, 2007). The teacher-learner relationship is evidenced within an ecological approach in which student wellbeing is central (Vukovic, 2016). Finnish education is provided in a way that encourages student agency and allows for individuals to be accountable for their behaviour. General education is available for all students and supports all learning needs. Intensified support is offered on the basis of specialist assessment (Finnish National Agency for Education, n.d.). Classroom management in the Finnish education system provides a significant contrast to traditional behaviour management pedagogy presented in Australian teacher education.

Clearly, it is timely to critique the philosophy, principles and practices of current classroom management and pedagogy within teacher education in Australian universities. The inclusive and highly effective approaches of the Finnish educational context provide a direction for Australian teacher education coursework.

2 Critique of Current Classroom Management in Teacher Education

As recently as 2011, classroom management courses in Australian teacher education programmes were predominantly characterised by the delivery of isolated topics of psychological theory. The practice of teaching one theory a week, although common, is problematic (O'Neill & Stephenson, 2011). There is a lack of evidence to support many of the largely psychotherapeutic approaches favoured in current classroom management coursework in Australian teacher education. Only 18 out of the 55 teacher education courses in Australia in 2014 delivered evidence-based classroom management strategies to teacher education students (O'Neill & Stephenson, 2014).

Page and Jones (2018) conceptualise traditional theories and practices of classroom management in teacher education as constituted by disparate components of theory, professional experience and observation. There are considerable limitations to this approach since opportunities to create a cohesive understanding are restricted during professional experience in classrooms.

As Figure 9.1 shows, the three areas of delivery illustrate the disconnect that contributes towards graduate teachers feeling ill-prepared to enter the teaching profession with the necessary confidence, knowledge, skills and beliefs in their ability to manage classrooms effectively (Hamilton, 2015; Jackson, Simoncini, & Davidson, 2013; Reupert & Woodcock, 2010). When prevailing psychological theories conceptualise student behaviour in terms of control, teacher management strategies are concerned with regimes of compliance. A paradigm shift from this narrative is long overdue. The emphasis on 'behaviour' implies a sole focus on '(mis)behaviour' (Jackson et al., 2013, p. 30) and negates the necessity for understanding that behaviours do not occur in isolation, but rather within the complexities of classroom contexts. Teacher education in

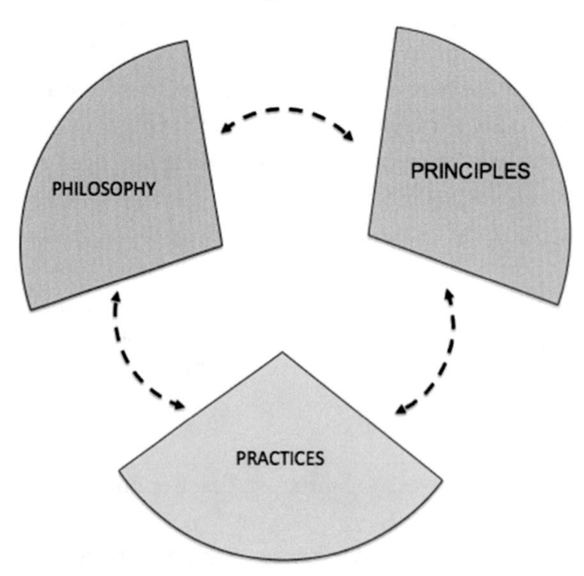

FIGURE 9.1
Non-synthesis of philosophies, principles and practices

classroom management needs to embrace this shift, in particular by challenging the dominant philosophy, principles and practices and interrogating new directions.

For teacher education students a dichotomy may arise when on professional experience, if they encounter an emphasis on compliance and control strategies. These prevailing strategies are at odds with educational theory, curriculum and pedagogy that promote 'problem-solving, independence, negotiation, active participation and personal accountability' (McDonald, 2010, p. 18). Professional placement in school classrooms for teacher education students can be fraught with a range of concerns that can impact on an optimal practicum experience. Firstly, there is the potential danger of supervising teachers modelling poor teaching practices (Hamilton, 2015). Secondly, students may receive inadequate supervision due to time constraints (Levine, 2011). Furthermore, observation frameworks can be problematic in that they are generalist in nature. Bradfield and Hudson (2012) report that often there is a lack of adequate scaffolds for collecting data during classroom observation exercises, leaving students bewildered about what and how to observe. Likewise, students may be unfamiliar with processes of data analysis, reporting, and responding to affect improvements in their understandings and implementation of informed and ethical classroom management practice (Bradfield & Hudson, 2012), and rather, rely on a 'bag of tricks' as a quick fix to manage student behaviour (Lyons, Ford, & Slee, 2014). It is argued in this chapter that teacher education students need to be equipped with a more holistic view of classroom management, in terms of their own philosophy, principles and practices.

3 Reconceptualising Classroom Management Practice

In recent years, a reconceptualisation of classroom *behaviour* management has begun, removing the emphasis on 'behaviour'. This shift in thinking encompasses a broader understanding that moves the focus from student behaviour to classroom ecologies. Factors of the physical environment, the social and the pedagogic practices, and the procedures that support student engagement and learning are now encompassed. Thus, the term 'classroom management' is preferred to signify the belief that 'teachers' professional reflections should holistically focus on the classroom environment inclusive of teacher strategies and student behaviour' (Jackson et al., 2013, p. 30). The approach characterises an alternative view of children and young people as knowledgeable, interactive and competent individuals who contribute to their own learning. The reconceptualisation also 'presents a very different frame in which to address challenging behaviour and allows the student to be intimately involved in addressing their own behaviour by taking responsibility for their actions (Michail, 2011, p. 16).

Accordingly, an alternative model for understanding and teaching classroom management was conceptualised and implemented in a regional Australian teacher education course. The intention was to bridge the gap between the philosophy, principles and practices of a classroom management course underpinned by inclusive methodologies. In order to meet this end, we have developed a new framework for teaching classroom management that advances these key concepts. Our innovative approach was the product of research undertaken that confirmed the need to prioritise ecological theory, replacing in-school professional experience with video recordings of classroom practice to enable greater control over the quality of teaching, iteratively developing observation and reporting skills, and synthesising the knowledge and skills through critical reflection. Through this interlinked approach, beliefs (philosophy), theories (principles), and knowledge, understanding and observation skills (practices), and can be integrated to form a holistic and inclusive conceptualisation of classroom management.

At the outset it was essential to articulate the philosophies that underpin inclusive classroom management, and to understand the imperative of ensuring these were consistent with the ethos of equity and equality in the education system (Järvinen, 2007). Secondly, it was deemed essential to embrace the principles of inclusive education when making decisions about the theories that the teacher education students would be introduced to in the classroom management unit. A wonderful opportunity arose to integrate theory and practice through an online professional experience rather than one traditionally undertaken face-to-face in schools and classrooms. The following sections of this chapter discuss the philosophy of classroom management deemed foundational to the unit, the principles of classroom management that were prioritised, and the practices in which the teacher education students used to observe, analyse and critique.

3.1 *Philosophy*

It is particularly significant to note that teacher education students bring to their learning and teaching uncritically assimilated habits of mind and points of view (Mezirow, 1997) from their experiences as students. This can be problematic since, as Eisner (1992) wrote some 25 years ago, the possibilities of any educational reform are likely to be difficult because 'familiar practices are not threatening; the past almost always has a rosy glow' (p. 140). It comes as no surprise therefore, that first year teacher education students are found to hold beliefs, which align with corrective behaviourist classroom management strategies (Peters, 2012).

The epistemology taken in the classroom management unit considered an ethical alternative to current philosophies of classroom management driven by psychological medical models (Sullivan et al., 2016). In doing so, teacher education students were scaffolded to articulate their beliefs. Often these placed the onus of behaviour within the individual student, and reflected a political ideology of control. Challenging this misalignment with an ethos of equity and equality was believed to circumvent the misfire of traditional classroom management, and instead inform inclusive principles and practices (Page & Jones, 2018). Additionally, the classroom management unit sought to create a state of tension in order to challenge existing beliefs that teacher education students may hold about teaching and learning that are derived from personal motivations and experiences (Borg, 2018; Phipps & Borg, 2009).

Current inclusive education philosophy, spearheaded by the disability community, advocates an approach that regards difference as a shortcoming of societal organisation. A disabling society creates attitudinal, environmental and institutional barriers that prevent people taking control of their lives. Additionally, the inclusive education movement advocates for a rights-based model, which pursues an aim to ensure equality of participation (Harris & Enfield, 2003). Building on inclusive education perspectives, we have presented within the unit a philosophy of participation in the classroom as a basic human right. The cornerstone of this position is that all students are cared for, respected and valued (Graham, Truscott, Powell, & Anderson, 2016).

The philosophy of participation, more recently expanded on by Terzi (2010), goes further, and advocates an understanding of individual difference beyond what is possible under 'one roof'. Terzi states that under a 'capabilities approach', the focus instead is on maximising individual potential. This is in contrast to emphasising sameness and providing one approach for all, regardless of its relevance. A capability approach moves to a relational perspective that considers the individual and educational arrangements. It considers the specificity of the situation, as well as each student's agency, as a matter of social justice and well-being. Social justice in this sense refers to full participation to meet individual needs in an appropriate learning environment.

This philosophy further reflects a perspective that classroom management is addressed from an ecological standpoint that places the responsibility for its organisation and adaptation on the teacher. Adaptations to the environment are made in accordance to the needs of the students who interact within that ecology. Primarily this takes place within the mainstream classroom, although other environments are recognised as potentially relevant. Caution however is required at this point to address tensions between individual choice and public policy (Foreman & Arthur-Kelly, 2016; Norwich, 2014).

By replacing the language of deficit and difficulty, and embracing an alternative paradigm of classroom management, the next challenge was to align these core beliefs with appropriate principles. The Quality Teaching framework was introduced to facilitate this goal, as it provided a context for teaching that was underpinned by an ideology of inclusion and social justice.

3.2 *Principles*

The Quality Teaching (QT) framework in New South Wales (NSW DET, 2003) provided the principles and practices informing the classroom management unit. It was envisaged as a means of enabling the teacher education students to develop a more holistic and inclusive set of beliefs and principles that would go on to inform their practice. The QT framework, with its three dimensions of pedagogy: 'Intellectual Quality', 'Quality Learning Environment', and 'Significance', provided a conceptualisation of classroom management that was far removed from the pathologising of student behaviours. Classroom management, teaching and learning described by Page and Jones (2018) after the work by Bowe and Gore (2017), with the framework embraces:

- curriculum (such as depth of knowledge, knowledge integration, treatment of knowledge as fact or socially constructed),
- student engagement (such as investment in the work, self-regulation, and control over aspects of learning),
- social justice (such as inclusive classrooms and inclusion of non-dominant cultural knowledge), and
- pedagogical practices (such as providing explicit criteria for the quality of work and opportunities for elaborated communication).

The Wellbeing Framework for Schools (NSW DET, 2015) was also introduced into the unit. The framework was considered invaluable since it embraced the philosophy and principles that were guiding the policies and practices of inclusive classroom management to support student wellbeing and enable engagement and learning for all, in NSW schools. The importance of addressing wellbeing is widely recognised in terms of its impact on classroom behaviour. Student learning, behaviour and wellbeing are inseparable and a strong relationship has been identified between managing classrooms in ways that encourage students to develop self-management strategies and subsequent positive behaviour outcomes (New Zealand Ministry of Education, 2017). In New South Wales, many schools have embedded the Wellbeing framework to address classroom management from an ecological positive learning perspective (McDonald, 2010).

In reconceptualising classroom management, the challenge was to understand the principles that facilitated inclusivity underpinned by a philosophy of emotional, social and academic wellbeing. *Positive Behaviour for Learning* (PBL) was embraced within the unit since the model has undergone changes to meet the Australian context. Initially, PBL originated from a school-wide approach to classroom and behaviour management that was developed in the United States and known as School-wide Positive Behavioural Interventions and Support (SWPBIS) (Simonsen, Fairbanks, Briesch, Myers, & Sugai, 2008; Sugai & Horner, 2002). The shift in emphasis within NSW schools from student behaviour to students' behaviour *for learning* reflected the inclusion of Australian language and schooling expectations (Mooney, Dobia, Barker, Power, & Watson, 2008). An additional feature of PBL is the emphasis on embracing strategies that are evidence-based (Parsonson, 2012). The inclusion of practices proven to be effective in classroom management enable teacher educators to make decisions that are more informed by empirical research about classroom behaviour (O'Neill & Stephenson, 2014).

3.3 *Practices*

Evidence-based literature informed understandings of ecological approaches to classroom management. A key priority for the teacher education students was to understand the fundamental goal of pupil engagement and learning (Lyons, Arthur-Kelly, & Ford, 2015), hence PBL practices (Kern & Clemens, 2007) were integrated. PBL is an effective strategy for low-level behaviour in the first instance, where 80% of classroom behaviour issues are considered to lie (Michail, 2011). These are regarded as preventative measures intended to moderate student behaviour before it escalates.

Effective classroom management requires consistent implementation of antecedent strategies that include: clear, simple rules and expectations, establishing routines, specific and descriptive praise, differentiation to ensure engagement, opportunities to respond, seating arrangements, effective instructions, pace of instruction, and choice (Parsonson, 2012).

3.4 *Observation and Critique*

The teacher education students were equipped to articulate their evolving philosophy (beliefs), principles (theories) and teaching intentions (practices) regarding inclusive classroom management, through observation of videos of classroom practice, scaffolding of observation, data collection, analysis and evidence-informed critique. This approach endeavoured to address calls by the Teacher Education Ministerial Advisory Group (TEMAG) (Craven et al., 2014) that teacher education students' knowledge and skills in observation, data collection, analysis and reporting requires more attention in courses. While observation methods are open to subjectivity, they were understood to be useful in collecting purposeful and evidence-based data that contributes to decision making (Renninger & Bachrach, 2015). Moreover, there is a growing field of research contributing to support the use of video observation rather than face-to-face-classroom observation (Santagata & Yeh, 2016; Schlesinger & Jentsch, 2016), in teacher education.

'Lesson observation is vital to best practice' (Subban & Round, 2015, p. 129). However, in traditional face-to-face observation professional experience placements, inadequate scaffolds for collecting data are provided to teacher education students (Bradfield & Hudson, 2012). Suitable scaffolds were therefore iteratively introduced to enable teacher education students to collect data and link theory to subsequent analysis, evaluation and reflection (Jackson et al., 2013).

Teacher education courses and the professional standards framework (Australian Institute of Teaching and School Leadership, 2011) prioritise the skill of reflective practice, and the importance of critically reflective teachers. The judgements teacher education students make based on their observations during professional experience can be used most powerfully to inform critical reflection and transformative learning (Mezirow, 1997). The development of critically reflective practices requires explicit modelling within coursework (Sempowicz & Hudson, 2012). When reflective practice is confined to the non-critical, in the form of content and process reflection (Cranton, 1994) characterised by asking the superficial questions, 'What worked?', 'What did not work?', and 'What will I do differently next time?', serve as little more than 'a coffee break' (Korhonen, Heikkinen, Kiviniemi, & Tynjälä, 2017, p. 1). To enable critical reflection, Learning Community forums of eight students were created within the learning platform to provoke the articulation of their evolving philosophy (beliefs), principles (theories) and teaching intentions (practices) regarding inclusive classroom management. Figure 9.2 provides a visual representation of the three parts.

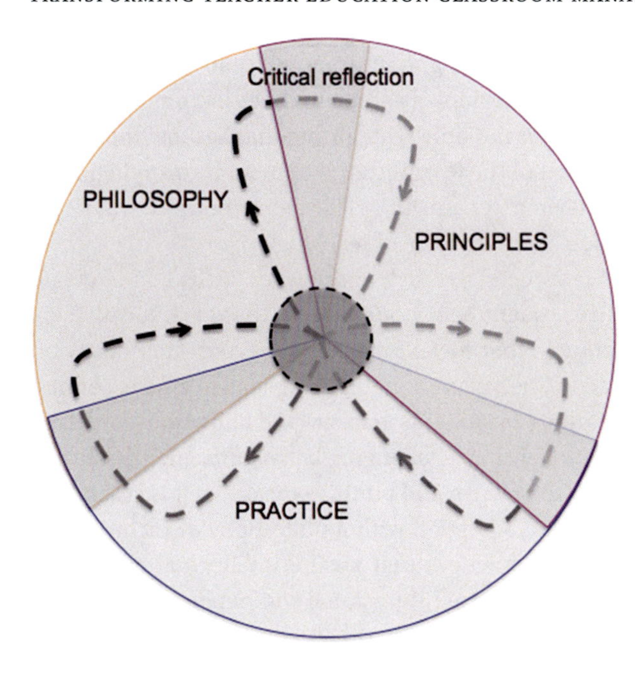

FIGURE 9.2
Synthesis of philosophies, principles and practices

4 Conclusion

Sullivan et al. (2016) called for teacher educators to challenge current discourses of classroom 'student (mis)behaviour' and instead, 'consider ethical alternatives' (p. 2). We believe we have responded to that challenge by providing a framework offering a social justice approach that allows for student agency to be recognised and valued. This narrative of the student positions them as full participants in their education community, which acknowledges and responds to their individual differences. The shift from the traditional story relies on changes in the student-teacher power relationship. The new narrative is made possible only if teachers can accept responsibility for the role they play in creating and maintaining effective learning environments.

Our approach is also consistent with, and reflective of, current reviews in Australian teacher education. Firstly, the national review of the Australian Curriculum in 2014 called for the reconceptualisation of the curriculum to value student wellbeing, and include holistic and systematic approaches, particularly in relation to quality teaching. To prepare for this, the review recommended that planning take better account of the context of teaching and the learning environment (Donnelly & Wiltshire, 2014). Secondly, the TEMAG (Craven et al., 2014) highlights that teacher education students' need to ensure the physical, cultural, social, linguistic and intellectual wellbeing of their students and create positive relationships in order to meet learning goals. The model presented in this chapter not only strongly emphasises the importance of teaching within the context of the learning environment by introducing the principles of positive behaviour for *learning*, it also promotes a philosophy that places student wellbeing at the centre of teaching.

Teacher education courses need to teach approaches, skills and strategies for handling unproductive student behaviour in ways that are educative and caring, but, most importantly, that focus on how to prevent such behaviour occurring in the first place. When classroom teaching fails to take account of the significance of the learning to students' background knowledge and experience disengagement from learning, challenging behaviours and apathy may arise. Rather than resorting to reactive and punitive measures it is crucial that teacher education students are equipped with a philosophy of inclusion and a range of evidence-informed practices that ensure intellectual quality and learning environments. Through these professional competencies and intrapersonal qualities teacher education students will be better equipped to address the social, emotional, psychological and academic factors that contribute to positive learning environments for all.

References

Australian Institute of Teaching and School Leadership. (2011). *Australian professional standards for teachers.* Retrieved from https://www.aitsl.edu.au/docs/default-source/national-policy-framework/australian-professional-standards-for-teachers.pdf?sfvrsn=5800f33c_64

Balogh, S. (2017, March 15). Australian students among worst behaved in the developed world. *The Australian.* Retrieved from https://www.theaustralian.com.au/nation/education/australian-students-among-worst-behaved-in-the-developed-world/news-story/73a493b8f105feb672482eb0d17b1b5f

Black, D. S., & Fernando, R. (2014). Mindfulness training and classroom behavior among lower-income and ethnic minority elementary school children. *Journal of Child and Family Studies, 23*(7), 1242–1246. doi:10.1007/s10826-013-9784-4

Bowe, J., & Gore, J. (2017). Reassembling teacher professional development: The case for quality teaching rounds. *Teachers and Teaching, 23*(3), 352–366. doi:10.1080/13540602.2016.1206522

Bradfield, K., & Hudson, P. (2012). *Examining teaching strategies within pre-service teachers' practicum experiences.* Paper presented at the 19th International Conference on Learning, London.

Cranton, P. (1994). *Understanding and promoting transformative learning: A guide for educators of adults.* Jossey-Bass.

Craven, G., Beswick, K., Fleming, J., Fletcher, T., Green, M., Jensen, B., ... Rickards, F. (2014). *TEMAG report action now: Classroom ready teachers.* Retrieved from https://docs.education.gov.au/system/files/doc/other/action_now_classroom_ready_teachers_accessible.pdf

Donnelly, K., & Wiltshire, K. (2014). *Review of the Australian curriculum final report.* Retrieved from https://docs.education.gov.au/system/files/doc/other/review_of_the_national_curriculum_final_report.pdf

Eisner, E. D. (1992). Educational reform and the ecology of schooling. *Teachers College Record, 93*(4), 610–627.

Finnish National Agency for Education. (n.d.). *Support in basic education.* Retrieved from https://www.oph.fi/en/education-system/basic-education

Foreman, P., & Arthur-Kelly, M. (2016). *Social justice principles, the law, and research, as bases for inclusion: An update.* Department of Education & Training Victoria.

Graham, A., Truscott, J., Powell, M. A., & Anderson, D. (2016). Reframing 'behaviour' in schools: The role of recognition in improving student wellbeing. In A. Sullivan, B. Johnson, & B. Lucas (Eds.), *Challenging dominant views on student behaviour at school* (pp. 97–113). Springer.

Hamilton, L. (2015). Early professional development in the Scottish context: Pre-service high school teachers and the management of behaviour in classrooms. *Teacher Development, 19*(3), 328–343. doi:10.1080/13664530.2015.1032338

Harris, A., & Enfield, S. (2003). *Disability, equality and human rights. A training manual for development and humanitarian organisations.* Oxfam Publishing.

Henebery, B. (2017, March 15). PISA, TIMMS results revealed. *The Educator.* Retrieved from http://doi.educatoronline.com.au/breaking-news/pisa-timms-results-revealed-234077.aspx

Jackson, C., Simoncini, K., & Davidson, M. (2013). Classroom profiling training: Increasing preservice teachers' confidence and knowledge of classroom management skills. *Australian Journal of Teacher Education, 38*(8), 30–45. doi:10.14221/ajte.2013v38n8.2

Järvinen, R. (2007). *Current trends in inclusive education in Finland.* Retrieved from http://www.ibe.unesco.org/fileadmin/user_upload/Inclusive_Education/Reports/sinaia_07/finland_inclusion_07.pdf

Kern, L., & Clemens, N. D. (2007). Antecedent strategies to promote appropriate classroom behavior. *Psychology in the Schools, 44*(1), 65–75. doi:10.1002/pits.20206

Korhonen, D., Heikkinen, D. L., Kiviniemi, U., & Tynjälä, P. (2017). Student teachers' experiences of participating in mixed peer mentoring groups of in-service and pre-service teachers in Finland. *Teaching and Teacher Education, 61*, 153–163. doi:10.1016/j.tate.2016.10.011

Krskova, D., & Baumann, C. (2017). School discipline, investment, competitiveness and mediating educational performance. *International Journal of Educational Management, 31*(3), 293–319. doi:10.1108/IJEM-05-2016-0099

Levine, T. D. (2011). Features and strategies of supervisor professional community as a means of improving the supervision of preservice teachers. *Teaching and Teacher Education, 27*(5), 930–941. doi:10.1016/j.tate.2011.03.004

Lopez, A. (2012, April 9). How Finnish schools shine. *The Guardian.* Retrieved from https://www.theguardian.com/teacher-network/teacher-blog/2012/apr/09/finish-school-system

Lyons, G. L., Ford, M., & Slee, J. (2014). *Classroom management: Creating positive learning environments.* Cengage Learning.

McDonald, T. (2010). Positive learning framework: Creating learning environments in which all children thrive. *Reclaiming Children and Youth, 19*(2), 16–20.

Mezirow, J. (1997). Transformative learning: Theory to practice. *New Directions for Adult and Continuing Education, 74*, 5–12.

Michail, S. (2011). Understanding school responses to students' challenging behaviour: A review of literature. *Improving Schools, 14*(2), 156–171.

Millei, Z., & Petersen, E. B. (2014). Complicating 'student behaviour': Exploring the discursive constitution of 'learner subjectivities'. *Emotional and Behavioural Difficulties, 20*(1), 20–34. doi:10.1080/13632752.2014.947097

Mooney, M., Dobia, B., Barker, K., Power, A., & Watson, K. (2008). Positive behaviour for learning: Investigating the transfer of a United States system into the NSW Department of Education and Training Western Sydney Region schools. *Curriculum Leadership Journal (Online), 6*(20).

New Zealand Ministry of Education. (2017). *Inclusive education guide for schools.* Retrieved from http://inclusive.tki.org.nz/guides/behaviour-and-learning/

Norwich, B. (2014). How does the capability approach address current issues in special educational needs, disability and inclusive education field? *Journal of Research in Special Educational Needs, 14*(1), 16–21. doi:10.1111/1471-3802.12012

NSW Department of Education and Training (NSW DET). (2003). *Quality teaching in NSW public schools.* NSW Government.

NSW Department of Education and Training (NSW DET). (2015). *The wellbeing framework for schools.* NSW Government.

O'Neill, S., & Stephenson, J. (2011). Classroom behaviour management preparation in undergraduate primary teacher education in Australia: A web-based investigation. *Australian Journal of Teacher Education, 36*(10), 35–52. doi:10.14221/ajte.2011v36n10.3

O'Neill, S., & Stephenson, J. (2014). Evidence-based classroom and behaviour management content in Australian pre-service primary teachers' coursework: Wherefore art thou? *Australian Journal of Teacher Education, 39*(4), 1–22. doi:10.14221/ajte.2014v39n4.4

Organisation for Economic Co-operation and Development (OECD). (2010). *Finland: Slow and steady reform for consistently high results.* Retrieved from https://www.oecd.org/pisa/pisaproducts/46581035.pdf

Page, A., & Jones, M. (2018). Rethinking teacher education for classroom behaviour management: Investigation of an alternative model using an online professional experience in an Australian university. *Australian Journal of Teacher Education, 43*(11), 84–104.

Parsonson, B. (2012). Evidence-based classroom behaviour management strategies. *Kairaranga, 13*(1), 16–23.

Peters, J. D. (2012). Are they ready? Final year pre-service teachers' learning about managing student behaviour. *Australian Journal of Teacher Education, 37*(9), 18–42.

Reid, A. (2017). *Serious flaws in how PISA measured student behaviour and how Australian media reported the results.* EduResearch Matters website. Retrieved from https://www.aare.edu.au/blog/?p=2455

Renninger, K. A., & Bachrach, J. E. (2015). Studying triggers for interest and engagement using observational methods. *Educational Psychologist, 50*(1), 58–69. doi:10.1080/00461520.2014.999920

Reupert, A., & Woodcock, S. (2010). Success and near misses: Pre-service teachers' use, confidence and success in various classroom management strategies. *Teaching and Teacher Education, 26*(6), 1261–1268. doi:10.1016/j.tate.2010.03.003

Ringrose, J., & Rawlings, V. (2015). Posthuman performativity, gender and "school bullying": Exploring the material-discursive intra-actions of skirts, hair, sluts, and poofs. *Confero: Essays on Education, Philosophy and Politics, 3*(2), 80–119. doi:10.3384/confero.2001-4562.150626

Rivkin, S. G., & Schiman, J. C. (2015). Instruction time, classroom quality, and academic achievement. *The Economic Journal, 125*(588), 425–448. doi:10.1111/ecoj.12315

Santagata, R., & Yeh, C. (2016). The role of perception, interpretation, and decision making in the development of beginning teachers' competence. *ZDM Mathematics Education, 48*, 153–165. doi:10.1007/s11858-015-0737-9

Schlesinger, L., & Jentsch, A. (2016). Theoretical and methodological challenges in measuring instructional quality in mathematics education using classroom observations. *ZDM Mathematics Education, 48*, 29–40. doi:10.1007/s11858-016-0765-00

Sempowicz, T., & Hudson, P. B. (2012). Mentoring preservice teachers' reflective practices towards producing teaching outcomes. *International Journal of Evidence Based Coaching and Mentoring, 10*(2), 52–64.

Simonsen, B., Fairbanks, S., Briesch, A., Myers, D., & Sugai, G. (2008). Evidence-based practices in classroom management: Considerations for research to practice. *Education and Treatment of Children, 31*(3), 351–380.

Slee, R. (2013). How do we make inclusion happen when exclusion is a political predisposition? *International Journal of Inclusive Education, 17*, 895–907. doi:10.1080/13603116.2011.602534

Subban, P. K., & Round, P. N. (2015). Differentiated instruction at work. Reinforcing the art of classroom observation through the creation of a checklist for beginning and pre-service teachers. *Australian Journal of Teacher Education, 40*(5), 117–131. doi:10.14221/ajte.2015v40n5.7

Sugai, G., & Horner, R. (2002). The evolution of discipline practices: School-wide positive behavior supports. *Child and Family Behavior Therapy, 24*(1–2), 23–50. doi:10.1300/J019v24n01_03

Sullivan, A., Johnson, B., Conway, R., Owens, L., & Taddeo, C. (2012). Punish them or engage them? Teachers' views on student behaviours around the school. *Behaviour at school study: Technical Report 2.* Retrieved from https://core.ac.uk/download/pdf/51343305.pdf

Terzi, L. (2014). Reframing inclusive education: Educational equality as capability equality. *Cambridge Journal of Education, 44*(4), 479–493. doi:10.1080/0305764X.2014.960911

Thomson, S., De Bortoli, L., & Underwood, C. (2017). *Programme for International Student Assessment (PISA) 2015. Reporting Australia's results.* Retrieved from http://research.acer.edu.au/ozpisa/22/

Vukovic, R. (2016, May 10). Race to the Finnish: Why Finland is leading the way in education. *Education HQ.* Retrieved from http://au.educationhq.com/news/34646/race-to-the-finnish-why-finland-is-leading-the-way-in-education/

CHAPTER 10

Transitions of Children with Additional Support Needs across Stages

Daniel Mays, Divya Jindal-Snape and Christopher Boyle

1 Introduction

Educational transition is a dynamic and ongoing process of adaptation due to a move from one educational context and set of interpersonal relationships to another (Jindal-Snape, 2010). The educational context can involve a change in educational systems or moving across different stages of education, such as moving from one class to another, moving from primary school to secondary school, or from a special school to a mainstream primary or secondary school. The changes in interpersonal relationships involve leaving old peers and staff behind and forming relationships with the people in the new environment. Further, transition also involves a change in identity, for example from a primary to a secondary school student, with subtle and hidden changes in expectations and rules in the new educational context (Bronfenbrenner, 2009). Transitions trigger fundamental changes in personal circumstances and can be a period of intensive learning, with the individual experiencing multiple, and in some cases, simultaneous phases of accelerated change (Griebel & Niesel, 2004; Mays, 2014). The child's educational transitions are therefore embedded in other simultaneous, multiple transitions. Their transitions trigger transitions for significant others, such as their family and professionals, and vice versa. Therefore, transitions are multiple and multi-dimensional (see Multiple and Multi-dimensional Transitions Theory, Jindal-Snape, 2016).

Research suggests that most children navigate transitions successfully and that for some, they involve adaptation and adjustment over a longer period of time (Jindal-Snape & Foggie, 2008; Lucey & Reay, 2000). The same child can find educational transitions to be positive at one time point but challenging and stressful at another. Positive transitions can stimulate a child's development, while negative transitions can lead to difficulties with their social and emotional wellbeing as well as to a dip in their academic attainment and academic motivation (Galton & Hargreaves, 2002; Jindal-Snape, 2016). The stress is sometimes triggered if the environment and staff are unknown, there is a loss of friendship groups without ongoing networks outside the school, by the

 | DOI: 10.1163/9789004431171_010

need to form new relationships, by navigating the new physical, academic and social environment, and/or due to the high Need for Cognitive Closure (NCC) that some children might have (Jindal-Snape, 2016). Children and young people with high NCC find it important to have all the relevant information before going into a new situation or environment in order to reduce their sense of confusion, uncertainty and ambiguity (Kashima & Sadewo, 2016). This kind of information, however, is not always available to them if there is a lack of effective transition practice that familiarises them with the new environment and context over a period of time (Jindal-Snape, 2016).

These transitions can be even more complex for those with *additional support needs* or *special educational needs*. For example, for children who are migrants or refugees, a transition might involve learning to study in a new language, living in a new country and studying in a new educational system (Gunasekera Houghton, Glasgow, & Boyle, 2014). Despite this, there is a dearth of literature about transitions of children with additional support needs (see Hannah & Topping, 2013; Hughes et al., 2013; Jindal-Snape, Douglas, Topping, Smith & Kerr, 2006; Mays et al., 2016; Rosenkoetter et al., 2009), and what little exists largely focuses on post-school transitions (Richardson, Jindal-Snape, & Hannah, 2017). A systematic literature search in databases such as ERIC, PsycInfo and Fachportal Pädagogik clearly shows how the focus on transitions varies between different fields and different language areas. Take, for example, the transition from a special school for children with emotional and behavioural difficulties to mainstream education. Only a few empirical studies have been completed in this area in Germany (the country of this chapter's first author), despite the fact that the proportion of students educated outside the mainstream system remains steady and the originally defined role of such special schools was that of a preparatory or "transition" institution (Mays, 2014, 2017). As an example, North Rhine-Westphalia – the most populous state of Germany and commonly shortened to NRW – is, with a population of approximately 18 million, the fourth largest by area. Since 2009, around 15,000 students with additional support needs in the area of emotional and social development have been educated separately in special schools. However, it is not possible to ascertain any reduction in the number of students with Emotional and Behavioural Difficulties (EBD) schooled in special schools (MSW NRW, 2017). The re-integration of these children from the special school to the general school is a key challenge in the German school system even 10 years after the ratification of the UN Disability Rights Convention.

Notwithstanding the above, the issue of stress and anxiety for some children who are vulnerable as a result of the transition process is an important one to acknowledge as this may cause them to require additional support in school (Jindal-Snape, 2016). For example, this requirement for extra support when moving between schools can be more prevalent for students who are from refugee backgrounds due to their particularly unique set of circumstances both inside and outside of the school setting (Gunasekera et al., 2014). As the authors wrote this chapter in mid 2020, it is clear that the intake of refugees is an issue for many countries, most notably Germany. The reasons why many current refugees seek to leave their home country can be multifaceted, however it is clear that many will have experienced or witnessed violence as a result of oppression and/or war situations. Transitioning between schools is even more problematic for many of these students than would normally be expected and the issue of education with appropriate support provision through the lens of inclusive education is paramount to successful transitions and thus schooling.

Hattie (2013) put the main aspects which influenced student achievement in school in rank order. He found that "mobility" (which we can take to mean a transitional factor) was ranked last, with a negative effect of −0.34. His research was based on meta-analyses and individual studies which concluded that the most important fundamental factor for ensuring success in school is that of developing strong friendships within the first month of transitioning to a new school (Hattie, 2013). This importance of the social aspects of schooling can quite often be forgotten in the ever-prevalent rush to gain success in government initiated school metrics, which only focus on exam performance as opposed to the myriad of other factors relevant to student development (Boyle, 2014; Hardy & Boyle, 2011). This is despite repeated evidence that children and parents are more focussed on the social and interpersonal aspects of transitions rather than the academic aspects (Jindal-Snape, 2013).

The installation of professional and system-linking support might be a key factor in improving transition processes (e.g. for reliable information exchange about students). Professional support is required; however, this should transcend all levels from individual student support to that of interactional and contextual support.

This chapter will seek to set out the influence that transitions can have on children with additional support needs, indicate appropriate transition practice in this area, and finally to make recommendations for effective inclusive transition practice.

2 Impact of Transitions on Children with Additional Support Needs

One of the first major studies on school transitions was conducted by Nisbet and Entwistle (1969). Over 2,000 children from 33 schools in Scotland took part in the project. The researchers investigated the age at which the transition to secondary education appeared to be most appropriate, and whether moving schools affected a child's development. The study found that students who experienced difficulty in adapting at the transition phase performed worse at school than students who did not. It also concluded that less motivated students often came from working class families and had greater trouble adapting (Nisbet & Entwistle, 1969). It has also been indicated in various research studies (see Mays, 2014; Mays et al., 2018) that students who require additional support may be more at risk of being negatively affected during the transition periods. This section will discuss the different stages of educational transitions and consider research evidence related to the experience of students with additional support needs. The stages are:

1. Pre-school (nursery) to primary school
2. Primary school to secondary school
3. Post-school transitions.

2.1 *Pre-school (Nursery) to Primary School*

Although research is limited at this stage, studies have highlighted issues in relation to these transitions for children with additional support needs, especially due to variability in practice of professionals and views of staff. A US study suggested that children who were found to have more severe learning difficulties had more pronounced issues with making a successful transition into primary school than those with less severe learning difficulties (Carlson et al., 2009). They found that teachers in the regular primary school made use of five strategies in order to support the transition of students with additional support needs, whereas special educators were found to have used substantially more strategies. These particular strategies were found to have included supplying documented information to parents, encouraging advance school visits by both parents and students as well as teachers in the new school, conducting a 'reverse' visit to see the student in his/her current school, and providing students' school records in a timely manner. The study reported that the child's characteristics played a role in their successful transitions and school readiness, such as severity of disability, academic ability as well as social skills. In Scotland, Gorton (2012) reports a similar issue; parents of children with additional support needs were more willing to postpone the transition to primary school so that there would be more opportunity for the child to 'mature' and thus have more opportunity to attend the mainstream school rather than special school. This study suggests that the maturational approach to school readiness versus the interactionist approach may be more prevalent in many cases. In order for the transition to be inclusive it is necessary that the interactionist approach is accepted as this will incorporate the individual support needs necessary for each child. Readiness for school exists at various levels both inside and outside of school, community, and family. They are all essential in the transition process (Mayer, Amendum, & Vernon-Feagans, 2010). It is not surprising that the ecological and systemic perspective has received wide-ranging support for the analysis and transparent development of transition concepts. Advocates for this type of approach work on the assumption that the way in which a child or young person is prepared for and supported through changes by people from their immediate environment can have a significant influence on the success of the transition (Bronfenbrenner, 2009; Anderson, Boyle, & Deppeler, 2014).

2.2 *Transition to Secondary and High School*

A wide range of educational, developmental, emotional and cognitive transitions occurs at this stage; moving school, the onset of puberty, and the emergence of formal operational reasoning, all of which have to be managed by the students at the same time (Cole et al., 2001). Children are excited about the transition to secondary school due to the greater choice of subjects, social aspects, and sports. There are further opportunities to meet new people and, of course, leave some friends behind. Suddenly there are many teachers, instead of the same one throughout the year, and there are opportunities to gain more independence and to potentially have new or change to one's identity (Akos, 2010; Jindal-Snape & Foggie, 2008; Jindal-Snape, 2010). However, children can be anxious due to schools being generally larger, in a different location and with a different setup, as well as due to the loss of lifelong friendships, the requirement to make new friends, and suddenly having to understand the requirements of many teachers instead of a few (Jindal-Snape, 2016). This difficulty can be magnified many times for children who are on the autistic spectrum and have a detrimental effect on their wellbeing (Hannah & Topping, 2012).

Jindal-Snape, Douglas, Topping, Smith, and Kerr (2006) found that the five children with autistic spectrum disorder (ASD) in their small-scale study in Scotland had multiple routes when moving to secondary school, such as from mainstream primary to mainstream secondary school, mainstream primary school to a communication support unit attached to a mainstream secondary school, primary communication support unit to a secondary communication support unit, primary communication support unit to autism-specific day provision, and primary communication support unit to autism-specific residential provision. Parental choice played a role in the selection of the pathways. However, there were significant delays in placement, leading to stress for children and families, with two children experiencing a break in schooling, one for approximately ten months. Similarly, in the English context, parents highlighted that professionals and the local authority should view their child as the "whole person", with placement based on their wishes and needs, rather than the financial implications for the local authority (Poet, Wilkinson, & Sharp, 2011).

Furthermore, a new social environment can support development in transitional phases (see Mays, 2014). It is possible that a new start for children and young people with behavioural difficulties can be positive as the shifting peer affiliations provide youth who have previously experienced social difficulties an opportunity to establish new social relationships, roles, and identities which foster their adjustment and adaptation (Farmer et al., 2011). However, it has also been reported that those with behaviour problems are at an increased risk of being perpetrators and victims of bullying (Farmer, et al., 2012; Gumpel & Sutherland, 2010; Swearer, Grills, Haye, & Cary, 2004). Therefore, the new social context can be both a protective and a risk factor (Farmer et al., 2015). Similarly, Langenkamp (2010) suggests that students' social relationships at primary school (and their continuation) and ability to form new positive social relationships in secondary school protect them from not only emotional but also academic vulnerability.

2.3 *Post-School Transitions*

The post-school transition is one frought with many difficulties, especially for those young people who have some form of additional support need (Autorengruppe Bildungsberichterstattung, 2014). It seems that those with complex needs have limited options (or are only made aware of limited options) for moving on from school, with the most frequently mentioned destination being further education college, where they go on to take practically-oriented, skills-based courses, or vocational training as in the case of Germany (Autorengruppe Bildungsberichterstattung, 2014). It is not clear whether the young people who do move onto vocational training or further education end up in positive work environments and further research is required to follow this population more diligently.

At this stage, the collaboration between professionals from children's services and adult services becomes crucial. This can be problematic due to tensions surrounding inter-professional collaboration and a lack of clear responsibilities, the handing over of responsibilities and the lack of a feedback loop to see what has worked. For example, the post-school transition meetings in Scotland involve several professionals from different agencies, and young people and families can find such meetings to be overwhelming, with power dynamics making it difficult for young people and families to express their views. Also, there are several reports of young people *being invited* by the teacher but declining to participate (Aziz, 2014). There are only a small number of reports of young people being involved in a meaningful way, such as through the use of pre-prepared Power-Point presentations, taking a friend along with them, and/or the use of other visual and various creative ways of expression (Richardson et al., 2017).

This is also the time that the person is developing into a young adult with the accompanying need for independence and developing adult relationships. For those with complex needs, such as serious health problems, this might also involve the adaptation of their living space before such things can happen. Also, for some, having grown up in a relatively protected environment due to their complex needs, independent living might require gradual psychological adaptation, both for the young person and the significant others in their life (Jindal-Snape et al., 2015).

3 Effective Transition Practice

Mays (2014) argues that a good transition practice which is not firmly established at multiple systemic levels is highly likely to exacerbate the anxieties of the students. He highlights factors that can act as facilitators or barriers during transitions (see Table 10.1).

TABLE 10.1 Important transition factors (facilitators/barriers) at all systemic levels (from Mays, 2014)

Student level	Teacher level	Organisation level
Social skills	Specialist (integration) competence (psychological expertise; knowledge of the mainstream school system)	Human resources
Anxieties	Communication skills	How the transition concept is established at the school level
Work	Teacher's basic attitude to inclusion	How the transition concept is established at the education authority level
Intelligence	Subjective perception of workload	Regional structure (area with social problems, size of catchment area, types of school in the vicinity)
Self-concept	Scope for personal initiative	Time available
Developmental age		Incentive systems
Transition stress		Organisation of cooperation (special school/mainstream school)

Many students are at risk of exhibiting behaviour which impedes a successful transition as a result of ongoing feelings of anxiety. Students' anxieties about a transition can be a powerful variable in the transition process, and we need to listen very carefully to the voices of the children and young people to notice these fears (Wigfield et al., 1991; Yeboah, 2002). Repeated measures to strengthen students' self-concept in good time before the transition and to help young people to cope with the upcoming change processes could therefore be the first step in preparing children and young people at an early stage for more complex upheavals, and teaching them how to deal with transition stress (Mays, 2016a).

At the level of the teachers, educational and psychological expertise on the dynamics of transition processes, advisory and communication skills training, the optimisation of cooperation structures (e.g. clear personal contacts; set times for meetings) and greater authority to strengthen the position of the teachers involved in transition were found in the studies to have a positive overall effect (Cheney, 2012; Felner et al., 1993; Galton, 2010; Strnadová & Cumming, 2014; Tissue & Korz, 1998).

Strengthening the individual powers available to teaching staff – for example, by allowing a teacher to organise taster placements easily, individually and at short notice – could be another useful measure. A system should also be developed to offer incentives for teachers and head teachers to actively initiate transitions (Mays, 2015). Effective communication between teachers at the feeder school and transition school is a major aspect of professional transition management. As well as the time resources essential for holding transition meetings, the way in which those meetings are held can also be decisive for a child's educational progress. If certain aspects are communicated too late or not at all, or if advice on dealing with a given student is not accepted, taken as personal criticism or not even requested, there can be no talk of professional transition management.

The joint and targeted preparation of the teaching staff (for example, subject teachers, special school teachers and learning support staff) for transitions in terms of educational psychology, at universities and on placements or through subsequent professional development is essential if we are to achieve a sustainable improvement in permanence. Establishing close partnerships for developing joint transition practice is the most important tool for improving permanence at the contextual level. Such an approach must involve a clear definition of roles and responsibilities, agreement on the communication structures and the draft of a transparent "crisis management plan" for dealing with any difficulties that occur. For an effective collaboration to happen, research suggests that the following are important: the sharing of mental models, closing the communication loop and developing trust amongst the professionals (Salas, Rosen, Burke, & Goodwin, 2009), sharing knowledge and respectful relationships (Mays & Grotemeyer, 2014; Bamber, Gittell, Kochan, & von Nordenflycht, 2009), identifying and working towards shared goals as a team (Mays, 2016b; Hackman, 2002), as well as the provision of adequate resources, rewards, incentives (Baggs, Norton, Schmitt, & Sellers, 2004), and time and scheduling (Smith, Lavoei-Tremblay, Richer, & Lanctot, 2010).

The availability of sufficient human resources and a clear process for crediting any additional working time would also appear to be important. There should, moreover, be clear and logical requirements and incentive systems at the level of the school and education authority. Part of such an approach includes, for example, straightforward options for cooperation between schools and the students' gradual preparation for the new challenges facing them. Particular attention should be paid to the internal school procedures for class composition: for example, ten-year-old Lisa, who joins the same class as two friends from the same area and whose older sister is already at the transition school, will likely see the transition as more within her control and less unsettling than her fellow student Pascal, who travels alone from outside town every morning and was previously taught in a small group at a special school. Children and young people who have had traumatic experiences in early childhood or who display appreciable delays in their emotional and social development as a result of neglect or abuse must be actively protected from transition processes that are damaging to their development (Mays, 2014).

Parental participation and home-school partnership have been the focus of several transition studies with positive partnership and parental participation being seen to facilitate transitions (Hannah, Gorton, & Jindal-Snape, 2010). Parental participation can take the form of establishing buddy pairings between parents similar to student buddies, which are set up at the organisational level and could lead to effective transition support networks for children and families. We also need to be aware of the parents' own transitions, which occur due to the transition of their child. Parents should also be better supported through effective home-school partnerships.

Since transition is a dynamic process, it is vital that transition planning and preparation and the associated activities are carried out *across* the educational lifespan and beyond (see Akos, 2010; Galton, 2010; Jindal-Snape, 2016). Following a review of the good transition practices across the educational stages across the world, Jindal-Snape (2010, 2016), summarised some key aspects of effective transition practice. These include listening to the views of the child/young person more closely and actively involving them in their own transition, opportunities to create friendship networks prior to moving to a new context, and once there, a clear and transparent exchange of information between professionals and families, providing the child with opportunities for bonding with staff and peers (through a buddy system), the sharing of pedagogical approaches across all educational stages (this is even more important if it is not the case that all staff have been trained in inclusive education), meaningful parental participation, and information packs (where possible, with photographs and videos of the new environment and people). These transition practices have clear theoretical underpinnings. For example, opportunities to create social networks with other children starting at the same school or with staff can be linked to resilience theory, as they can provide opportunities to create strong, externally-protective factors through focusing on relationships and networking.

One aspect which is highlighted in the literature and legislation regarding effective transition is *person-centred planning*. This is an approach which places the person at the centre of the plan and assists them to plan their life and support, with a focus on their strengths and capacities. Person-centred planning involves listening and learning about what an individual wants, helping them to think about what they want now and in the future, and significant others such as family members, friends, professionals and services working together with the person to make sure their aspirations are met (O'Brien, 2004; Rasheed, Fore III, & Miller, 2006). Research suggests that person-centred planning for transitions has been considered to be effective by different stakeholders, for example, young people, families and professionals (Wertheimer, 2007), and is widely accepted as the most effective way of transition planning for those with disabilities (Kaehne, 2010).

Although studies cite its use for post-school transitions, person-centred planning could also be useful at all stages, especially if it is linked with Individual Education Plans and Transition Plans. It is seen to be beneficial due to choice, community involvement, contact with friends, contact with family, social networks and scheduled activities (Robertson, Emerson, Hatton, Elliot, McIntosh, Swift, et al., 2007; Sanderson, Thompson, & Kilbane, 2006). For example, Tobin et al. (2012) developed an ecological transition programme called STEP-ASD as a low-intensity intervention for reducing problem behaviours and distress in children with autism spectrum disorder as they transition to mainstream secondary school. This includes creating an individualised "transition management plan" (summary of the child's needs, the support strategies, and people responsible for delivering support) and "student profile" (one-page summary of the plan).

However, these studies also suggest that person-centred planning works differently for different people, and that the evidential basis for its effectiveness is limited, for example, in the context of employment. This might be due to it not being used effectively at present, despite great potential for its use (Aziz, 2014; Richardson, 2015). Furthermore, work is required to ensure that the person-centred planning approach is embedded from the very start.

4 Conclusion

Above all else, in the light of inclusive school development, there is an urgent need for new research projects to address the issue of transition in more detail. The methodological challenges (e.g. big-fish-little-pond effect, sample size, time required and costs) involved in this research must not prevent this important field from being investigated in the (special) education disciplines. The imbalance between the importance of transition processes in regards to emotional and social development on the one hand, and the almost complete absence of academic and scientific debate in (special) education disciplines on the other, is not acceptable: the issue is central to the debate about an inclusive society which seeks to focus on participation, opportunities and transparency. In the authors' view, the question could be approached with controlled case studies documenting longitudinal development in transition processes.

References

Akos, P. (2010). Moving through elementary, middle, and high schools: The primary to secondary shifts in the United States. In D. Jindal-Snape (Ed.), *Educational transitions: Moving stories from around the world* (pp. 125–142). Routledge.

Anderson, J., Boyle, C., & Deppeler, J. (2014). The ecology of inclusive education: Reconceptualising Bronfenbrenner. In Z. Zhang, P. W. K. Chan, & C. Boyle (Eds.), *Equality in education: Fairness and inclusion* (pp. 23–34). Sense Publishers.

Autorengruppe Bildungsberichterstattung. (2014). *Bildung in Deutschland 2014. Ein indikatorengestützter Bericht mit einer Analyse zur Bildung von Menschen mit Behinderungen.* Bielefeld. https://www.bildungsbericht.de/de/bildungsberichte-seit-2006/bildungsbericht-2014/pdf-bildungsbericht-2014/bb-2014.pdf

Aziz, A. (2014). *A longitudinal study exploring post-school transitions of young peolple with learning disabilities perspectives of young people, parents and professionals* (Doctoral dissertation). University of Dundee.

Baggs, J. G., Norton, S., Schmitt, M. D., & Sellers, C. (2004). The dying patient in the ICU: Role of the interdisciplinary team. *Critical Care Clinics of North America, 20*, 525–540.

Bamber, G., Gittell, J. D., Kochan, T. A., & Von Nordenflycht, A. (2009). Contrasting employment relations strategies in European Airlines. *Journal of Industrial Relations, 51*(5), 635–652.

Boyle, C. (2014). Labelling in special education: Where do the benefits lie? In A. Holliman (Ed.), *The Routledge international companion to educational psychology* (pp. 213–221). Routledge.

Bronfenbrenner, U. (2009). *The ecology of human development: experiments by nature and design.* Harvard University Press.

Carlson, E., Daley, T., Bitterman, A., Heinzen, D., Keller, B., Markowitz, J., & Riley, J. (2009). *Early school transitions and the social behavior of children with disabilities: Selected findings from the pre-elementary elementary education longitudinal study: Wave 3 overview report from the Pre-Elementary Education Longitudinal Study (PEELS).* Institute of Education Sciences. Retrieved from http://ies.ed.gov/ncser/pdf/20093016.pdf

Cheney, D. (2012). Transition tips for educators working with students with emotional and behavioral disabilities. *Intervention in School and Clinic, 48*, 22–29.

Cole, D. A., Maxwell, S. E., Martin, J. M., Peeke, L. G., Seroczynski, A. D., Tram, J. M., Hoffman, K. B., Ruiz, M. D., Jacquez, F., & Maschman, T. (2001). Age and gender effects in multiple domains of child and adolescent self-concept: A cohort sequential longitudinal design. *Child Development, 72*, 1723–1746.

Farmer, T. D., Hamm, J. V., Leung, M.-C., Lambert, K., & Gravelle, M. (2011). Early adolescent peer ecologies in rural communities: Bullying in schools that do and do not have a transition during the middle grades. *Journal of Youth and Adolescence, 40*, 1106–1117. doi:10.1007/s10964-011-9684-0

Farmer, T. D., Irvin, M. J., Motoca, L. M., Brooks, D. S., Leung, M.-C., & Hutchins, B. C. (2015). Externalizing and internalizing behavior problems, peer affiliations, and bullying involvement across the transition to middle school. *Journal of Emotional and Behavioral Disorders, 23*, 3–16.

Farmer, T. D., Petrin, R. A., Brooks, D. S., Hamm, J. V., Lambert, K., & Gravelle, M. (2012). Bullying involvement and the school adjustment of rural students with and without disabilities. *Journal of Emotional and Behavioral Disorders, 20*, 19–37. doi:10.1177/1063426610392039

Felner, R. D., Brand, S., Adan, A. M., Mulhall, P. F., Flowers, N., Sartain, B., & DuBois, D. L. (1993). Restructuring the ecology of the school as an approach to prevention during school transitions: Longitudinal follow-ups and extensions of the School Transitional Environment Project (STEP). *Prevention in Human Services, 10*, 103–136.

Galton, M. (2010). Moving to secondary school: What do students in england say about the experience? In D. Jindal-Snape (Ed.), *Educational transitions: Moving stories from around the world* (pp. 107–123). Routledge.

Galton, M., & Hargreaves, L. (2002). Transfer: An future agenda. In M. Galton & L. Hargreaves (Eds.), *Transfer from primary classroom: 20 years on* (pp. 185–208). RoutledgeFalmer.

Gorton, D. (2012). *"Are they ready? Will they cope?" An exploration of the journey from pre-school to school for children with additional support needs who had their school entry delayed* (Doctoral thesis). Dundee. http://discovery.dundee.ac.uk/portal/files/2112743/Gorton_dedpsych_2012.pdf

Griebel, D., & Niesel, R. (2004). *Transitionen. Fähigkeit von Kindern in Tageseinrichtungen fördern, Veränderungen erfolgreich zu bewältigen* (pp. 119–137). Beltz.

Gumpel, T. P., & Sutherland, K. S. (2010). The relation between emotional and behavioral disorders and school-based violence. *Aggression and Violent Behavior, 15*, 349–356. doi:10.1016/j.avb.2010.06.003

Gunasekera, S., Houghton, S., Glasgow, K., & Boyle, C. (2014). From stability to mobility: African secondary school aged adolescents' transition to mainstream schooling. *The Australian Educational and Developmental Psychologist, 31*(1), 1–17. doi:10.1017/edp.2014.4

Hackman, J. R. (2002). *Leading teams: Setting the stage for great performances*. Harvard Business School Press.

Hannah, E. F. S., Gorton, D., & Jindal-Snape, D. (2010). Small steps: Perspectives on understanding and supporting children starting school in Scotland. In D. Jindal-Snape (Ed.), *Educational transitions: Moving stories from around the world* (pp. 51–67). Routledge.

Hannah, E. F. S., & Topping, K. J. (2012). Anxiety levels in students with autism spectrum disorder making the transition from primary to secondary school. *Education and Training in Autism and Developmental Disabilities, 47*(2), 198–209.

Hannah, E. F. S., & Topping, K. J. (2013). The transition from primary to secondary school: Perspectives of students with autism spectrum disorder and their parents. *International Journal of Special Education, 28*(1), 145–160.

Hardy, I., & Boyle, C. (2011). My school? Critiquing the abstraction and quantification of education. *Asia-Pacific Journal of Teacher Education, 39*(3), 211–222. doi:10.1080/1359866X.2011.588312

Hattie, J. (2013). *Lernen sichtbar machen*. Überarb. dt.-sprachige Ausg. Schneider Verlag.

Hughes, L. A., Banks, P., & Terras, M. (2013). Secondary school transition for children with special educational needs: A literature review. *Support for Learning, 28*(1), 24–34.

Jindal-Snape, D. (Ed.). (2010). *Educational transitions: Moving stories from around the world*. Routledge.

Jindal-Snape, D. (2013). Primary-secondary transition. In S. Capel, M. Leask, & T. Turner (Eds.), *Learning to teach in the secondary school: A companion to school experience* (6th ed., pp. 200–213). Routledge.

Jindal-Snape, D. (2016). *A-Z of transitions*. Palgrave.

Jindal-Snape, D., Douglas, D., Topping, K. J., Kerr, C., & Smith, E. F. (2006). Autistic spectrum disorders and primary-secondary transition. *International Journal of Special Education, 21*(2), 18–31.

Jindal-Snape, D., & Foggie, J. (2008). A holistic approach to primary-secondary transitions. *Improving Schools, 11*, 5–18.

Jindal-Snape, D., Johnston, B., Pringle, J., Gold, L., Grant, J., Scott, R., Carragher, P., & Dempsey, R. (2015). *Multiple and multi-dimensional transitions: Understanding the life transitions of young adults cared for by CHAS and the impact on their parents, siblings and professionals*. University of Dundee.

Kaehne, A. (2010). Multiagency protocols in intellectual disabilities transition partnerships: A survey of local authorities in Wales. *Journal of Policy and Practice in Intellectual Disabilities, 7*(3), 182–188.

Kashima, E. S., & Sadewo, G. R. P. (2016). Need for cognitive closure and acculturation of international students: Recent findings and implications. In D. Jindal-Snape & B. Rienties (Eds.), *Multidimensional transitions of international students to higher education. EARLI new perspective on learning and instruction series* (pp. 37–52). Routledge.

Langenkamp, A. G. (2010). Academic vulnerability and resilience during the transition to high school: The role of social relationships and district context. *Sociology of Education, 83*(1), 1–19.

Lucey, D., & Reay, R. (2000). Identities in transition: Anxiety and excitement in the move to secondary school. *Oxford Review of Education, 26*, 191–205.

Mayer, K. L., Amendum, S. J., & Vernon-Feagans, L. (2010). The transition to formal schooling and children's early literacy development in the context of the USA. In D. Jindal-Snape (Ed.), *Educational transitions. Moving stories from around the world.* Routledge.

Mays, D. (2014). *In Steps! – Wirksame Faktoren schulischer Transition. Gestaltung erfolgreicher Übergänge bei Gefühls- und Verhaltensstörungen*. Julius Klinkhardt.

Mays, D. (2015). Transitionsprozesse gestalten – Faktoren eines inklusiven Übergangsmanagements. *Praxis Schule 5–10, 25*(2), 4–8.

Mays, D. (2016a). Transparenz als wirksamer Faktor schulischer Transition. In K. Moegling & S. Schude (Eds.), *Transparenz im Unterricht und in der Schule. Theorie und Praxis transparenten Unterrichts und transparenter Schulorganisation*. Prolog-Verlag.

Mays, D. (2016b). *Wir sind ein Team! Multiprofessionelle Kooperation in der inklusiven Schule. Ein Ratgeber für Lehrer, Förderpädagogen und Integrationshilfen*. Ernst Reinhardt Verlag.

Mays, D. (2017). Zur Notwendigkeit einer selbstkonzeptsensiblen und ökologisch-systemischen Reform der Übergangskonzepte zwischen der Förderschule für emotionale und soziale Entwicklung und der Allgemeinen Schule. In P. C. Link & R. Stein (Eds.), *Schulische Inklusion und Übergänge* (pp. 21–37). Frank & Timme.

Mays, D., Franke, S., Diezemann, E., & Kißgen, R. (Hrsg.). (2016). *Netzwerk Transition. Inklusion in Übergangsphasen bei Störungen des Sozialverhaltens.* Universi.

Mays, D., & Grotemeyer, M. (2014). Teamarbeit in der inklusiven Schule. Den Einzelnen entlasten – das Team stärken. *Praxis Schule 5–10, 24*(2), 4–8.

Mays, D., Schneider, L., Wichmann, M., Metzner, F., Pawils, S., Zielemanns, D., & Franke, S. (2018). Schulisches Selbstkonzept sowie Lern- und Leistungsmotivation bei Schülerinnen und Schülern mit einem prognostizierten ungünstigen Entwicklungsverlauf im Bereich der emotionalen und sozialen Entwicklung während der Transition in die Sekundarstufe I. *Zeitschrift für Heilpädagogik, 69*(3), 133–146.

Ministerium für Schule und Weiterbildung des Landes Nordrhein – Westfalen. (2017). *Das Schulwesen in NRW aus quantitativer Sicht. Schuljahr 2016/17. Statistische Übersicht Nr. 395–1.* Auflage (März 2017). Retrieved from https://www.schulministerium.nrw.de/docs/bp/Ministerium/Service/Schulstatistik/Amtliche-Schuldaten/Quantita_2016.pdf

Nisbet, J., & Entwistle, N. (1969). *The transition to secondary education.* University of London Press.

O'Brien, J. (2004). If person-centred lanning did not exist, valuing people would require its invention. *Journal of Applied Research in Intellectual Disabilities, 17*, 11–15.

Poet, D., Wilkinson, K., & Sharp, C. (2011). *Views of young people with SEN and their parents on residential education* (LG Group Research Report). NFER.

Rasheed, S. A., Fore III, C., & Miller, S. (2006). Person-centered planning: Practices, promises, and provisos. *The Journal for Vocational Special Needs Education, 28*(3), 47–59.

Richardson, T. D., Jindal-Snape, D., & Hannah, E. (2017). Impact of legislation on post-school transition practice for young people with additional support needs in Scotland. *British Journal of Special Education, 44*(3), 239–256. doi:10.1111/1467-8578.12178

Robertson, J., Emerson, E., Hatton, C., Elliott, J., McIntosh, B., Swift, P., Krinjen-Kemp, E., Towers, C., Romeo, R., Knapp, M., Sanderson, D., Routledge, M., Oakes, P., & Joyce, T. (2007). Person-centred planning: Factors associated with successful outcomes for people with intellectual disabilities. *Journal of Intellectual Disability Research, 51*(3), 232–243. doi:10.1111/j.1365-2788.2006.00864.x

Rosenkoetter, S., Schroeder, C., Rous, B., Hains, A., Shaw, J., & McCormick, K. (2009). *A review of research in early childhood transition: Child and family studies. Technical Report #5.* University of Kentucky, Human Development Institute, National Early Childhood Transition Center. Retrieved from http://www.niusileadscape.org/docs/FINAL_PRODUCTS/LearningCarousel/ResearchReviewTransition.pdf

Salas, E., Rosen, M. A., Burke, C. S., & Goodwin, G. F. (2009). The wisdom of collectives in organizations: An update of the teamwork competencies. In E. Salas, G. F. Goodwin, & C. S. Burke (Eds.), *Team effectiveness in complex organizations. CrossDisciplinary perspectives and approaches* (pp. 39–79). Psychology Press.

Sanderson, D., Thompson, J., & Kilbane, J. (2006). The emergence of person-centred planning as evidence-based practice. *Journal of Integrated Care, 14*(2), 18–25.

Smith, K., Lavoie-Tremblay, M., Richer, M.-C., & Lanctot, S. (2010). Exploring nurses' perceptions of organizational factors of collaborative relationships. *Health Care Manager, 29*, 271–278.

Strnadová, I., & Cumming, T. M. (2014). The importance of quality transition processes for students with disabilities across settings: Learning from the current situation in New South Wales'. *Australian Journal of Education, 58*(3), 318–336.

Swearer, S. M., Grills, A. E., Haye, K. M., & Cary, P. T. (2004). Internalizing problems in students involved in bullying and victimization: Implications for intervention. In D. L. Espelage & S. M. Swearer (Eds.), *Bullying in American schools: A social-ecological perspective on prevention and intervention* (pp. 63–83). Lawrence Erlbaum Associates.

Tissue, R., & Korz, A. (1998). Making a successful transition: Effects of a treatment – Based and school – Based program on emotionally troubled children and their adjustment to new placements. *Child Psychiatry Human Development, 28*, 199–210.

Tobin, D., Staunton, S., Mandy, D., Skuse, D., Hellriegel, J., Baykaner, O., Anderson, S., & Murin, M. (2012). A qualitative examination of parental experience of the transition to mainstream secondary school for children with an autism spectrum disorder. *Educational and Child Psychology, 29*(1), 75–85.

Wertheimer, A. (2007). *Person centred transition reviews – A national programme for developing person centred approaches to transition planning for young people with special educational needs.* Valuing People Support Team.

Wigfield, A., Eccles, J. S., Mac Iver, D., Reuman, D. A., & Midgley, C. (1991). Transitions during early adolescence: Changes in children's domain-specific self-perceptions and general self-esteem across the transition to junior high school. *Developmental Psychology, 27*, 552–565.

Yeboah, D. A. (2002). Enhancing transition from early childhood phase into primary education: Evidence from the research literature. *Early Years 2002, 22*, 51–68.

CHAPTER 11

Peers as Influential Agents of the Inclusion of Learners with Autism

Sofia Mavropoulou, Kirsten S. Railey and Jonathan M. Campbell

1 Introduction

As the identification of autism spectrum disorder (ASD) continues to increase and inclusive educational practice becomes more prevalent, students with ASD are interacting with peers within educational settings frequently (e.g., Sanford et al., 2008). Within inclusive educational settings, peers feature significantly in whether students with ASD experience a successful educational experience or not. Peers may view students with ASD as substantially different from social norms and view social communication and unusual behaviors as undesirable. For elementary school students, Bottema-Beutel and Li (2015) identify the role of peers as social 'gatekeepers' to social acceptance and social inclusion for students with ASD.

In this chapter, we provide a general overview of the evidence on the quantity and quality of peer relationships for students with ASD in inclusive settings. Next, we present a brief introduction to peers' knowledge of and attitudes towards students with ASD. The chapter concludes with a presentation of the empirical evidence on the effectiveness of peer-mediated interventions designed to enhance social inclusion for students with ASD.

2 Peer Interactions

Given legislative mandates and the work of advocates, students with autism are educated in settings with typical peers in steadily increasing numbers (Chamberlain & Locke, 2010). However, studies indicate that inclusive practices have failed to integrate students with disabilities into their typical peers' social networks (Chamberlain, Kasari, & Rotherham-Fuller, 2007). In addition, observational research in inclusive contexts has documented that children with autism were less engaged with peers in reciprocal activities in the playground or in the classroom (Locke, Shih, Kretzmann, & Kasari, 2016; Sparapani, Morgan, Reinhardt, Schatscheinder, & Wetherby, 2016).

 | DOI: 10.1163/9789004431171_011

2.1 *Social Experience of Students with Autism Spectrum Disorder*

Autism is a lifelong, neurodevelopmental disorder with social challenges at its core, which hinder an individual's ability to communicate with and relate to others and the world around them (American Psychiatric Association [APA], 2013). Although individuals with ASD demonstrate a wide range of social and communicative abilities, all individuals diagnosed with ASD display difficulties in developing, maintaining, and understanding relationships (APA, 2013). Due to difficulties navigating social interactions, students with ASD are often perceived as 'different', especially when educated alongside neurotypical peers in inclusive educational settings (Wainscot, Naylor, Sutcliffe, Tantum, & William, 2008). Despite the fact that many students with ASD are able to accurately define and describe social interactions, observational studies indicate that students with ASD are less socially engaged and display less positive interaction behaviors than neurotypical peers (Bauminger, Shulman, & Agam, 2003; Kasari, Locke, Gulsrud, & Rotherham-Fuller, 2011). Other studies indicate that students with ASD demonstrate less sharing, engage in more solitary play, participate in fewer social conversations, and were subject to more instances of verbal aggression than their neurotypical peers and students with dyslexia (Bauminger et al., 2008; Humphrey & Symes, 2011). In addition, gender seems to be associated with social acceptance. Dean and her colleagues (2014) found that boys were more overtly socially excluded than girls with autism, who seemed to be ignored rather than rejected.

2.2 *Nature of Peer Interactions and Friendships*

Research suggests that peer relationships are important to students' social and emotional development, overall school success, and quality of life (Rubin, Bukowski, & Laurensen, 2009). Additionally, successful peer interactions often require acknowledgement of shared interests, turn-taking, and social reciprocity, which may present complications for students with ASD. In addition, individuals with ASD may misperceive their own social involvement and inaccurately report on their friendships given their difficiulties in forming and maintaining friendships (Kasari, Locke, Gulsrud, & Rotherham-Fuller, 2011).

Despite the fact that children and adolescents with ASD seek friendships from peers without a disability (Sigman & Ruskin, 1999), these friendships tend to be characterized by less acceptance, companionship, and reciprocity than those between peers without a disability (Chamberlain et al., 2007; Daniel & Billingsley, 2010). Friendships between students with ASD and peers without a disability also tend to be less stable and less reciprocated than those of their peers (Bauminger-Zviely, 2013; Rotherham-Fuller et al., 2010). Although over half of children with ASD (n=100, 10–12 yrs) reported having friends in one study (Rowley et al., 2012), another national longitudinal study in the United States found that adolescents with ASD were less likely to see their friends, be called by their friends, or be invited to join in others' activities than students with other special educational needs (Shattuck et al., 2011).

In the United Kingdom, researchers utilized quantitative (e.g., Friendship Qualities Scale, Happe's Strange Stories and structured classroom observations), qualitative (e.g., semi-structured interviews with children with autism, their parents and teachers) and sociometric (e.g., a social cognitive mapping exercise) methods to compare friendship experiences of students with ASD with their peers without autism in primary mainstream schools (Calder, Hill, & Pellicano, 2013). Results suggested that some students with ASD were central to their social networks, others were deemed lower status members, and several students with ASD remained on the periphery of the classroom. With respect to students with ASD, input from teachers and parents indicated that motivation to interact with peers played a role in determining the degree of variation in the nature of their friendships. Although parents and teachers reported that friendships were less mature than those of their neurotypical peers, students with ASD reported being satisfied with their friends and described them in terms similar to a 'companion' (Calder et al., 2013). However, establishing friendships has been found to be the most difficult aspect about friendships for preadolescents and adolescents with autism and good verbal communication educated in general education classes (Daniel & Billingsley, 2010).

2.3 *Social Isolation, Loneliness, and Bullying*

For students with ASD, bullying and isolation are associated with decreased social skills and peer relationships, school refusal, academic difficulties, diminished self-esteem, and other mental health difficulties (Reid & Batten, 2006). Given their social difficulties, students with ASD are more often marginalized, rejected, and bullied than peers without any disabilities, particularly in inclusive settings where their peer interactions are more frequent (Symes & Humphrey, 2010). Research indicates that students with ASD are also more often socially isolated compared to both peers without any disabilities and students with other disabilities (Pisula & Lukowska, 2012; Wainscot et al., 2008). Kasari et al. (2011) found that elementary school students with ASD only engaged with peers about one-third of the time during playground activities. In other research, approximately one-third of students with autism were observed to be sitting alone during lunch time (Little, 2002). Research with younger children (4–7 yrs) has offered partial support for these findings (Zeedyk, Cohen, Eisenhower, & Blacher, 2016). Although a large majority of preschool children reported having kids to play with at school (78%) and having kids who liked them (72%), half of them reported that it was hard for them to make friends at school and a quarter reported feeling lonely and isolated at school.

High rates of social isolation among students with ASD may increase the likelihood that they are bullied by others, and social isolation on its own can be a type of bullying (i.e., ostracism). Further, research notes that students with ASD are more at risk for experiencing more bullying than peers without any disabilities (Cappadocia, Weiss, & Pepler, 2012; Carter, 2009; Humphrey & Hebron, 2015; Humphrey & Symes, 2010). Reported bullying prevalence rates, however, vary greatly depending on a number of factors such as informants, measurement tools, age of students with ASD, and definition of bullying that researchers choose to utilize in their studies (Schroeder, Cappadocia, Bebko, Pepler, & Weiss, 2014). One UK parental survey found that 40% of lower-functioning individuals with ASD and 59% of individuals diagnosed with Asperger syndrome (AS) experienced victimization (Reid & Batten, 2006). Comparatively, one study found that only 10.4% of middle school students without disabilities reported victizmiation in the 30 days prior to completing the survey (Rose, Espelage, Aragon, & Elliott, 2011). Another study in the United States found that 94% of students with AS were victimized by peers (Little, 2002) whereas a more recent study found that only 46.3% of children with ASD were classified as victims of bullying (Sterzing, Shattuck, Narendorf, Wagner, & Cooper, 2012). Additionally, Rowley et al. (2012) found that teachers reported greater frequency of bullying in inclusive educational settings as compared to special schools (mean scores: 0.71 vs 0.39) for students with autism.

Students with ASD who experience social isolation and poor peer relationships are also more likely to report loneliness. For example, high school students with ASD report more loneliness than peers without any disabilities (Locke, Ishijima, Kasari, & London, 2010), and 21% of adolescent boys with ASD reported "often" or "always" feeling lonely compared to 4% of typical peers (Lasgaard, Nielsen, Eriksen, & Gossens, 2010). As one way to understand social interactions of individuals with ASD, Humphrey and Symes (2011) proposed the Reciprocal Effects Peer Interaction Model (REPIM) to better understand the nature of peer interaction. The theoretical framework, incorporating endogeneous (within the child with autism, such as social cognition difficulties, poor social and communicative difficulties) and exogeneous (within the peer group, such as lack of awareness and understanding of autism and reduced acceptance of difference) factors, suggests that the social difficulties individuals with ASD experience coupled with peers' lack of awareness and acceptance of ASD lead to reduced quality and quantity of peer interactions between students with ASD and typical peers. After experiencing negative peer interactions, students with ASD may be less motivated to interact further with their typical peers, which may create a pattern of avoidance, isolation, and bullying. Neurotypical peers, too, will continue to have limited social contact with students with ASD, which will further limit opportunities to increase awareness and acceptance. This framework has important practical implications for the pivotal role of educators in inclusive settings. Teachers need to develop peers' autism awareness as well as facilitate positive social interactions with benefits for all children in their classrooms.

2.4 *Interventions to Facilitate Peer Interactions*

Currently, many early educational practices emphasize academic performance despite the fact social interactions are equally important in promoting learning and overall quality of life for students with ASD in inclusive settings (Bassok, Latham, & Rorem, 2014). Although facilitating peer interactions has many benefits, educators often find it difficult to promote social interactions and relationships within general education settings (Carter, Bottema-Beutel, & Brock, 2014). Given the complex nature of peer interactions and the negative social outcomes for students with ASD, multi-faceted, comprehensive interventions should be utilized to both promote social relationships and decrease isolation and bullying (Kasari et al., 2012). Four areas of action have been discussed in the literature as ways to promote peer interactions: (a) student-focused, (b) peer-focused, (c) school staff-focused, and (d) school climate-focused (Bellini, Peters, Benner, & Hopf, 2007).

To promote peer interactions, many student-focused interventions seek to improve social skills and social understanding of students with ASD. One program in Canada focused on teaching students with ASD social awareness, expression of feelings, importance of verbal and nonverbal communication, and ways to respond to bullying and teasing (Tse, Strulovich, Tagalakis, Meng, & Fombonne, 2007). In one study with children with ASD, Beaumont and Sofronoff (2008) found positive outcomes from using the Junior Detective Training Programme, which utilized a computer game and small-group therapy to teach emotion recognition and components of social interactions. Additionally, a meta-analysis identified social skill instruction and video-modeling as evidence-based practices for improving peer interactions (Wang & Spillane, 2009).

Peer-mediated interventions have also emerged as an effective method to improve both academic and social outcomes for students with ASD in inclusive settings (Hochman, Carter, Bottema-Beutel, Harvey, & Gustafson, 2015). Researchers have demonstrated that providing descriptive and explanatory information about ASD improves peer attitudes toward students with ASD;

however, results are mixed as to whether these interventions improve behavioral intentions (e.g., peers' willingness to engage in a behaviour with a student with ASD) towards those students with ASD (e.g., Staniland & Byrne, 2013). Kasari et al. (2012) found improvements in the social involvement of students with ASD using modeling, role-play, and rehearsal.

Apart from the larger peer group, school personnel also play a role in promoting peer interactions and preventing bullying (Frisén, Hasselblad, & Holmqvist, 2012). As an example of a way that teachers can prevent bullying, research has suggested that schools with more positive teacher-student relationships reported fewer bullying incidents (Richard, Schneider, & Mallet, 2012). Additionally, paraprofessionals who support students in inclusive settings play an important role in creating opportunities for social interaction and helping students with ASD navigate peer interactions (Feldman & Matos, 2012). Blood et al. (2013) further suggested that external support staff, such as Speech-Language Pathologists (SLPs), may also support the development of positive social experiences of students with ASD as a means for the reduction and elimination of bullying. They found that the majority of SLPs seemed to use the three intervention strategies of reporting, educating, and reassuring for handling all types of bullying incidents. In order to support students with ASD, teachers and other staff can encourage and support the student and their peers, reinforce inclusive messages, and provide opportunities for social learning and engagement.

Finally, the school climate and culture play a role in supporting peer interactions. Feldman and Matos (2012) found that staff often lack training to support social interactions, which is an important part of implementing successful social interventions. Highly inclusive settings that celebrate students' differences provide opportunities for positive social interactions between students with ASD and students without any disabilities which reflects a positive ethos and are an integral part of a whole school saturation model to inclusion (Morewood, Humphrey, & Symes, 2011). In particular, simple peer awareness-raising techniques in combination with formalized peer support interventions constitute essential elements of the inclusive model.

Given the complexity of the social-communication challenges of students with ASD, a combination of interventions may be necessary to facilitate successful peer interactions and decrease bullying. The development of social competencies and the importance of social outcomes, as opposed to a narrow focus on academic goals, have been identified as a high priority by parents of students on the autism spectrum educated in inclusive settings (Whitaker, 2007). Educators and school systems should be equipped to support the social development of all students by providing opportunities for and supporting meaningful social interactions and relationships. One example of an approach that schools can utilize is developing peer networks for students with ASD (Carter et al., 2013), which emphasize building a social network of peers that meet informally and formally. Research has found that implementing peer networks in a high school increased the percentage of time students with ASD were engaged in social interactions with peers at school (Hochman, Carter, Bottema-Beutel, Harvey, & Gustafson, 2015). Beyond facilitating peer interactions, educators should work to teach all students about friendships and strive to foster meaningful, lasting friendships between students with ASD and their peers without any disabilities.

In addition to involving teachers in taking measures to prevent bullying, caregivers can also play a role in school-based bullying prevention. Research suggests that caregiver involvement in anti-bullying programs has positive outcomes for schools such as (a) increasing the likelihood that caregivers tell the school about bullying incidents and (b) being able to punish bullying perpetration both in and outside of the school setting (Axford, Farrington, Clarkson, Bjornstad, Wrigley, & Hutchings, 2015). Other research has found that positive parenting behaviors (e.g., good communication between parent and child; sharing of affection; parental involvement, support, and supervision) are protective factors against peer victimization (Lereya, Samar, & Wolke, 2013). School systems may choose to involve parents in anti-bullying initiatives at school by providing information to them via newsletter, email, and other means by holding parent-teacher meetings to discuss any concerns (Farrington & Ttofi, 2009). For example, the Olweus Bullying Prevention Programme includes parent engagement that involves the following components: (a) psychoeducation regarding bullying, (b) parent-teacher meetings, (c) discussions between perpetrators and their caregivers, and (d) conversations between victims and their caregivers (Olweus & Limber, 2010).

3 Peer Awareness and Attitudes

Raising peer awareness about autism has been proposed as an important strategy for developing peers' behavioral control, which in turn can lead to more positive behavioral intentions for forming social interactions with students with autism (Freitag & Dunsmuir, 2015). Over the past 15 years, peers' basic awareness of autism has increased from 0% to 50–75% of elementary and middle school students being at least somewhat familiar with the term autism (see Campbell & Barger, 2011 for review). Even so, peers report critical inaccuracies about defining symptoms, etiology, and course of ASD, which may impact their understanding of autism and predict their willingness to interact with a student with ASD. For example, Campbell and Barger (2011) surveyed over 1,000 middle-school students and found that over 40% of students did not know that poor eye contact is associated with autism. More problematic, however, is the finding that roughly 5% of middle-school students reported that ASD was contagious.

Additional analysis of 450 middle schoolers' definitions of ASD revealed that most understood ASD as a disability (i.e., roughly 70%), however, few definitions reflected understanding of social, communicative, and restrictive interests that characterize ASD (Campbell et al., 2011). Understanding peers' lack of knowledge about ASD is important, as misunderstanding the core symptoms and etiology of ASD (e.g., brain-based social communicative impairment) may lead to isolation. For example, peers may interpret social difficulties as intentional actions which lead to negative appraisals and, ultimately, social isolation. Likewise, a peer that believes that he or she might 'catch' ASD may result in social exclusion.

Research identifying and describing peers' attitudes towards students with ASD typically measures three types of attitudes: affective, behavioral, and cognitive, the 'A-B-Cs' of attitudes (e.g., Campbell, 2006; Morton & Campbell, 2008). Affective attitudes refer to an individual's feelings towards an individual with ASD (e.g., "I feel happy when I think about a student with ASD"). Behavioral attitudes, or behavioral intentions, refer to an individual's willingness to engage in a behavior with an individual with ASD (e.g., "I would help a student with ASD finish his spelling homework"). Cognitive attitudes refer to an individual's appraisal about an individual with ASD (e.g., "Students with ASD are friendly"). Experimental research consistently documents that peers' initial attitudes towards students with ASD are negative when compared to peers without disabilities, and this is consistent across affective, behavioural, and cognitive domains (e.g., Campbell et al., 2004; Swaim & Morgan, 2001). International work in Greece (Mavropoulou & Sideridis, 2014), the United Kingdom (Freitag & Dunsmuir, 2015), and Australia (Ranson & Byrne, 2014; Staniland & Byrne, 2013) has documented benefits of educational programming in improving peers' knowledge of and attitudes towards students with ASD. There is some evidence, however, that peers' intentions to engage in shared behaviors are less responsive to educational intervention and, when changed, differ according to context. Campbell et al. (2004) found that a two-minute educational intervention consisting of information about autism improved students' willingness to engage in academic activities (e.g., study spelling words with a student with ASD) but not social or recreational activities (e.g., eat lunch with a student with ASD). Staniland and Byrne (2013) found that a 6-hr anti-stigma educational intervention improved knowledge and cognitive attitudes, but not intentions to engage in shared activities with individuals with autism.

Campbell and colleagues have approached peer attitudinal change from a general social persuasion framework to guide practical decision-making for how to educate peers about ASD. The framework considers factors such as message (i.e., what is said), source (i.e., who says it), audience (i.e., to whom) and channel (i.e., how is it delivered; Campbell, 2006). Within the framework, specific messages have been tested based on social psychological theories, such as cognitive consistency theory and attribution theory. Cognitive consistency theory (or balance theory) predicts that similarity occasions attraction and likability. As such, providing peers with information about that highlights similarities between themselves and students with ASD should increase attraction and attitudes. Attribution theory predicts that peers' perceptions of personal responsibility for undesirable behaviour occasions negative attitudes. For example, a peer may view repetitive behaviors associated with ASD as intentional, which results in annoyance and social distancing. In general, findings have highlighted the importance of establishing similarities between students with ASD and their peers as well as providing an explanation for the behavioural characteristics of ASD. An explanatory message has been shown to be useful for improving attitudes of students with no prior awareness of ASD (e.g., Campbell, 2006). Students also respond differently depending on who delivers the information, with some evidence that older students respond more favorably to messages delivered by a professional versus a student's mother, for exanple.

Outside of a general social persuasion framework, others have examined the role of attitudes within theories that link attitudes, behavioral intentions, and social behavior. For example, Freitag and Dunsmuir (2015) examined the utility of the Theory of Planned Behavior (TPB; Azjen, 1991) to understand linkages between peers' attitudes towards an unfamiliar child with ASD and their social behavior with classmates with ASD. The TPB predicts behavioral intention from a small set of variables: attitude, subjective norm, and perceived behavioral control. Behavioral intention, in turn, predicts behavior. Of particular interest are the roles of the subjective norm and perceived behavioral control in predicting one's intentions to perform the behavior of interest, e.g., interacting with a student with ASD. Subjective norm refers to an individual's perceptions of significant others' opinion about engaging in the behavior of interest. The subjective norm may incorporate beliefs about teachers', parents', and friends' attitudes towards interacting with students with ASD (e.g., "My teachers/parents/friends think I should be friends with students with ASD"). Prior work has documented significant correlations between parent attitudes towards children with disability and children's self-reported attitudes (Rosenbaum, Armstrong, & King, 1988). Perceived behavioral control refers to perceptions of control regarding the behavior of interest, such as, "Studying math with students with ASD is totally up to me".

Frietag and Dunsmuir (2015) found support for the TPB model with a sample of 8- to 11-year-olds in East London, with 74% of the variance explained for students' intentions to interact with a hypothetical student with ASD. Each component of the model contributed independently in accounting for student intentions. Behavioral intentions, in turn, predicted interactions between peers and classmates with ASD. Students' beliefs of how much control they had over interacting with peers with ASD strongly predicted behavioral intentions, such that greater controllability predicted greater intention. Students identified teachers as the most salient social norm to include students with ASD, followed by parents and peers. Findings from the TPB model yield practical recommendations. For example, the role of teacher expectations in including students with ASD in class activities is important in predicting students' intentions. As such, explicit teacher support for including students with ASD is likely to yield improved behavioral intentions, and actual behavior, towards students with ASD. Likewise, improving students' perceptions of control over efforts to include students with ASD may also produce benefits. Providing students with behavioral models of successful inclusion may improve perceptions of controllability of behavior towards students with ASD.

Recent important work has focused on understanding the reasons that elementary and middle school students may choose to include or exclude students with ASD, both within and outside of educational contexts (Bottema-Beutel & Li, 2015; Bottema-Beutel, Turiel, DeWitt, & Wolfberg, 2017). The domain theory of moral development and reasoning informs this line of inquiry (see Bottema-Beutel & Li, 2015 for a general overview of domain theory). Essentially, domain theory asserts that children's moral decision making is informed by various domains of social information: moral (i.e., welfare, justice, rights), societal (i.e., social norms), personal (i.e., personal choice), and prudential (i.e., personal well-being). From a practical standpoint, understanding students' reasoning for accepting or not accepting students with ASD may yield information to guide messaging and appeals.

Bottema-Beutel et al. (2017) shared vignettes with 44 elementary schoolers that depicted situations where a student with autism was not included: a classroom activity, a birthday party, a playground activity, and a playdate. The majority of elementary school students reported that not including the student with autism was equally unacceptable for each context. When asked to articulate their rationale, students invoked moral (e.g., students with autism should be treated equally), personal (e.g., it is up to the peer to decide to include the student with autism), societal (e.g., the decision to include hinges on social tradition, authority, or social influence), and prudential (e.g., the decision to include is based on health and safety considerations) explanations. In contrast, adolescents (ages 13–18) presented with similar vignettes reported the decision to not include the character with ASD as more frequently acceptable (Bottema-Beutel & Li, 2015). Their ratings of acceptability depended on the context, with failure to include the student in a general education classroom rated as least acceptable (3%) while failure to include the student in a recreational activity at home as most acceptable (45%). Adolescents provided justifications similar to elementary school students, but invoked an additional justification, categorized as "negation of welfare", meaning that exclusion is thought to be harmless to the individual. It is worth noting however, that an important distinction exists between the studies which may have impacted on the findings. Elementary school students were told that the student was diagnosed with autism; adolescents were told that the student had a disability that results in social difficulties. Furthermore, adolescents' attitudes towards hypothetical students with autism appear to be affected by social cues of acceptance, such as the student's social status and perceived similarity to their own peer group, rather than physical inclusion (Tonnsen & Hahn, 2016). Middle-school students' attitudes were less positive when the fictional peer with autism was socially excluded by his peers, regardless of whether those peers were also portrayed with disabilities.

Based on findings across studies, authors identify several implications for their evidence regarding peer attitudes. First, because elementary school students endorse exclusion of students with ASD as more unacceptable when compared to older students, and this was across all contexts, interventions delivered in elementary school may prove more beneficial when students are more receptive to inclusion across a greater number of contexts. Second, interventions may need to be tailored to the context due, in part, to the reasons articulated by students. For example, adolescents rated exclusion from the classroom or sports as less acceptable than that of the home environment. Bottema-Beutel and Li (2015) advocate for educating peers about ASD and supporting opportunities to interact with students with ASD in more private contexts. Given that adolescents invoked moral and personal preference reasoning when justifying decision-making, messaging might emphasize the well-being of students with ASD alongside personal decision-making. For example, Bottema-beutel and Li (2015) note the potential value of educating peers about the high rates of loneliness experienced by students with ASD due to limited contact with peers, which constitutes a moral appeal.

4 Peer-Mediated Interventions

Peer mediation has been widely implemented as a strategy for ameliorating the social difficulties experienced by students with autism in inclusive settings, with superior advantages compared to other classroom interventions. Peer-Mediated Interventions (PMI) have been recognized as an established intervention with mutual social benefits for children and adolescents with autism and their peers (National Center for Autism, 2015). More important, the development of peer interactions, as the core element of PMI, can facilitate the inclusion of students with ASD in school settings by removing the stigma of having a teacher assisting a student in a general education classroom (Chan et al., 2009; Hughes et al., 2011). Rooted in social learning theory and principles of behaviorism (Bandura, 1968), PMI encompasses a range of strategies where the peer can act as the teacher, the assistant, the buddy or tutor for a student with disabilities in specific tasks. It is recommended that the peer tutor can be the same age as the tutee or two or more years older (cross-age tutoring) than the student receiving the tutoring (Utley, Mortweet, & Greenwood, 1997). Peer-mediated interventions have important social goals for learners with ASD and their peers: a) to teach all students behaviours leading to frequent social interactions in their natural environments, b) to extend peers' skills for initiating and maintaining positive and natural social interactions social contact with their classmates with ASD in the classroom and beyond, and c) to lessen support from teachers and other adults for developing social interactions between students with ASD and their peers (Battaglia & Radley, 2014; Sperry, Neitzel, & Engelhardt-Wells, 2010).

4.1 *PMI in Autism: What Does the Evidence Say?*

The extant empirical evidence demonstrates the efficacy of PMI in developing social skills in boys and girls with autism in preschool, primary and high school settings (Hughes et al., 2013; Zhang & Wheeler, 2011). This section will report the major findings from meta-analytic and other literature reviews of PMI for students with autism.

Watkins and her colleagues (2015) reviewed 14 experimental (using multiple baseline single-subject designs) studies published from 2008 to 2014 with findings on the application of PMI only in inclusive settings, targeting social interaction skills of students with ASD, ranging from 4 to 21 years old. They concluded that peer initiation was the most commonly used intervention strategy, whereas peer proximity was the least commonly applied strategy. Peer initiation involves direct training of peers to initiate interactions with persons with autism. Peer proximity refers to strategies in which socially competent peers are placed in close proximity to classmates with autism to model appropriate social interactions, but they have not received explicit training in initiating social interactions with students with autism. Specifically, the evidence showed that preschool peers seemed to initiate simple joint play activities with young children with autism, primary school age peers-initiated interactions during games and activities in recess and high school students initiated conversations with peers with autism. Overall, one of the key findings of this review is that PMI strategies can lead to positive outcomes, as well as to generalization across peers and settings and maintenance of at least one taught social skill. It is worth noting that positive generalization and/or maintenance outcomes were documented in interventions where peers shared similar characteristics, such as having well-developed language and social skills, had expressed prior interest in interacting with the participants with ASD, were regularly attending school and showed high levels of compliance with directions. Besides, Watkins et al. (2015) concluded that there is not sufficient evidence about children with ASD at preschool ages and for those with higher learning needs. In addition, more rigorous research designs, such as randomized control trials and investigation of long-term outcomes will strengthen the existing empirical support for the effectiveness of PMI in inclusive contexts.

In a meta-analysis of 37 published studies reporting outcomes of school-based single-subject interventions targeting peer-related social competence of students with ASD (aged 3–12 yrs), Whalon and her colleagues (2015) found that PMI had positive outcomes [effect size indices: average NAP (percentage of nonoverlapping data) of .95 and Tau-U of .87] for all children, who maintained their gains and generalized their learning to new settings, untrained peers and other behaviours. Both NAP and Tau-U are considered a "complete" index of effect size, because they include all data points in single subject interventions (Rakap, 2015). NAP is a percentage of nonoverlapping data that compares each data point from phase a (e.g., baseline) to each in phase B (e.g., intervention) to obtain a percentage of nonoverlapping data that shows improvement; Tau-U is the percent of data that show improvement over time by comparing all data points in each phase (Rakap, 2015). However, Whalon et al. (2015) underlined the need for future intervention research to involve teachers or other school personnel (instead of researchers) and peers in authentic school settings during naturally occurring social opportunities. They also highlighted the need to implement future research with young children and in collaboration with other professionals (i.e. speech-language therapists) in preschool inclusive settings. Similar recommendations are included in another research review by Zagona and Mastergeorge (2018), which provided further support for the effectiveness of PMI for addressing the social-communication needs of children with autism.

In another meta-analysis by Chang and Locke (2016), PMI was further supported as a promising practice with established evidence base. Following the systematic review and evaluation of published research utilizing group designs in real-world community settings (schools and camps), PMI was found to lead to significant positive social gains for children and adolescents with autism with high levels of ability. Therefore, the effects of PMI on children with autism who have very limited language and social skills remain unexplored. Moreover, the researchers draw attention to critical methodological issues, such as the need for measuring implementation fidelity (especially when adults are not present), given that PMI are conducted in real-world settings, as well as the need to collect generalization and maintenance data to fully explore the sustainment of learned social skills.

Peer-mediated interventions encompass a range of focused strategies aimed to teach peers how to initiate and maintain positive social interactions with students with disabilities (Sperry, Neitzel, & Engelhardt-Wells, 2010). In Odom and Strain's (1984) first review of PMI, three different types of PMI were identified: proximity, prompting and peer initiation. Peer network interventions is a promising type of PMI which has been found to increase social interaction and foster friendships between children with autism and their peers. A peer network is a cohesive group of three to six peers who meet weekly within the classroom and across the school day with a student with a disability to share enjoyable activities based on common interests with initial guidance and ongoing support from an adult facilitator (Carter et al., 2013). Existing research (using single subject and randomized trial designs) has documented that young children and high school students on the autism spectrum, who seem to improve their communication skills, exhibit higher social engagement and participate in increased social interactions with their peers following peer network interventions (Gardner et al., 2014; Hockman et al., 2015; Kamps et al., 2015; Sreckovic, Hume, & Able, 2017). Platos and Wojaczek (2018) put forward an interesting research proposal to explore the wider scope of PMI through out-of-school activities aimed to build befriending relationships focused on friendship, social participation and well-being of adolescents and adults with autism.

The authors of the aforementioned literature reviews have identified several areas for future research to strengthen the empirical basis of PMI. First, a key priority is to conduct research with peers assisting young children with autism in inclusive kindergarten and preschool settings. Second, it remains unexplored whether PMI can be beneficial for children with more complex social communication needs, who need extensive supports for their academic and social engagement. Third, it is critical to include teachers as research participants who will implement PMI as part of their inclusive teaching strategies, thereby modelling acceptance and support for children with autism.

4.2 *Steps for Implementing Peer-Mediated Interventions*

For the successful implementation of PMI in schools and the reinforcement of rigorous intervention research, it is critical to follow a sequence of steps coupled with systematic instruction as outlined in the literature. Sperry et al. (2010) emphasize that careful selection of peers combined with systematic instruction of skills can lead to a successful intervention for promoting the social and academic progress of students with ASD. Battaglia and Radley (2014) describe in detail the four steps required for the application of PMI with children with ASD.

The first step involves the selection of peers, based on their high level of the targeted social skills and their willingness to follow adult instructions. It is recommended to use peers who have been classmates with the child with ASD and have a positive or even neutral history with the child with ASD. The second step focuses on the identification of socially significant target skills which present a challenge for the student with ASD. This stage is followed by direct observations of social skills in naturalistic settings to establish baseline levels of performance to be set as the aims of the intervention. For example, social skills rating scales, such as the Autism Social Skills Profile (Bellini, 2006) or self-developed observational schedules recording the frequency/duration of target behaviors or the prompts used for the expression of social skills, can be utilised. In the third stage, school personnel will have to consider which intervention strategy would be most appropriate to use for the participating children with ASD. Such a decision is based on the aims of the intervention, that is on whether it is to increase the performance of existing skills or to teach new skills in naturalistic contexts; in the first case, peers will be trained to initiate social interactions with the child with ASD, whereas in the latter case, peers will be trained to model the target skills and provide corrective feedback to the child with ASD. To this end, Battaglia and Radley (2014) underscore that the most commonly used types of PMI, such as peer modelling, peer initiation training and direct training for target student and peers, and need to be carefully selected to match specific target social skills. For example, peer modelling may be suitable for teaching how to ask for help, to share toys and follow directions, whereas peer initiation training would be more appropriate for taking turns in play activities and responding to questions. The last step involves the monitoring of progress through direct observations of target skills across different persons and settings, to allow the evaluation of the intervention and any troubleshooting if students with ASD do not make the desired progress towards objectives. Furthermore, Sperry et al. (2010) draw special attention to additional factors which can lead to the successful implementation of PMI in school and community-based settings. In particular, they underline the importance of setting up a consistent schedule and place for these activities in the classroom, carefully selecting the educational materials to promote social interaction, identifying staff with the responsibility to organize and supervise play, and providing prompts (i.e., explicit verbal instructions, physical guidance) and reinforcement for social initiations, as critical elements for a successful PMI in school and community contexts. With respect to the materials deemed conducive to increased peer social engagement, it is recommended to use unfamiliar materials, related with specific themes to encourage socio-dramatic play and requests for assistance for their operation.

5 Conclusion

Despite the increasing number of students with autism educated in inclusive educational settings, they seem to have persisting difficulties with their peers, which can lead to loneliness and social exclusion. As part of a whole-school approach to inclusion, teachers carry the weighty responsibility to gain knowledge of PMI and collaborate with other school staff to help all students establish positive relationships which can be the springboard for their learning in multiple domains. It is widely accepted that every academic lesson is a social skills lesson. PMI is a cost and time effective instructional strategy for fostering the social and academic competencies of all students at any educational level. The presence of peers in inclusive contexts provides to all students ample naturally occurring opportunities for academic support and social engagement. Through the systematic use of peer-mediated strategies, educators can play an instrumental role in facilitating peer interactions, increasing awareness of diversity and nurturing positive attitudes towards students with autism; these are all essential ingredients of respectful and inclusive school communities.

References

Ajzen, I. (1991). The theory of planned behavior. *Organizational Behavior and Human Decision Processes, 50*, 179–211. https://doi.org/10.1016/0749-5978(91)90020-T

American Psychiatric Association. (2013). *Diagnostic and statistical manual of mental disorders* (5th ed.). Author.

Axford, N., Farrington, D. P., Clarkson, S., Bjornstad, G. J., Wrigley, Z., & Hutchings, J. (2015). Involving parents in school-based programmes to prevent and reduce bullying: What effect does it have? *Journal of Children's Services, 10*, 242–251. http://dx.doi.org/10.1108/JCS-05-2015-0019

Bassok, D., Latham, S., & Rorem, A. (2016). Is kindergarten the new first grade? *AERA Open, 1*, 1–31. doi:10.1177/2332858415616358

Battaglia, A. A., & Radley, K. C. (2014). Peer-mediated social skills training for children with autism spectrum disorder. *Beyond Behavior, 23*, 4–13. https://doi.org/10.1177/107429561402300202

Bauminger, N., Shulman, C., & Agam, G. (2004). The link between perceptions of self and of social relationships in high-functioning children with autism. *Journal of Developmental and Physical Disabilities, 16*, 193–214. doi:10.1023/b:jodd.0000026616.24896.c8

Bauminger, N., Solomon, M., Aviezer, A., Heung, K., Gazit, L., Brown, J., & Rogers, S. J. (2008). Children with autism and their friends: A multidimensional study of friendship in high-functioning autism spectrum disorder. *Journal of Abnormal Child Psychology, 36*, 135–150. doi:10.1007/s10802-007-9156-x

Bauminger-Zviely, N. (2013). *Social and academic abilities in children with high-functioning autism spectrum disorders.* Guilford Press.

Beaumont, R., & Sofronoff, K. (2008). A multi-component social skills intervention for children with asperger syndrome: The junior detective training program. *Journal of Child Psychology and Psychiatry, 49*, 743–753. doi:10.1111/j.1469-7610.2008.01920.x

Bellini, S. (2006). *Building social relationships: A systematic approach to teaching social interaction skills to children and adolescents with autism spectrum disorders and other social difficulties.* Autism Asperger Publishing.

Bellini, S., Peters, J. K., Benner, L., & Hopf, A. (2007). A meta-analysis of school-based social skills interventions for children with autism spectrum disorders. *Remedial and Special Education, 28*, 153–162. https://doi.org/10.1177/07419325070280030401

Blood, G. D., Blood, I. M., Coniglio, A. D., Finke, E. D., & Boyle, M. P. (2013). Familiarity breeds support: Speech-language pathologists perceptions of bullying of students with autism spectrum disorders. *Journal of Communication Disorders, 46*, 169–180. doi:10.1016/j.comdis.2013.01.002

Bottema-Beutel, K., & Li, Z. (2015). Adolescent judgments and reasoning about the failure to include peers with social disabilities. *Journal of Autism and Developmental Disorders, 45*, 1873–1886. doi:10.1007/s10803-014-2348-7

Bottema-Beutel, K., Turiel, E., DeWitt, M. N., & Wolfberg, P. J. (2017). To include or not to include: Evaluations and reasoning about the failure to include peers with autism spectrum disorder in elementary students. *Autism, 21*, 51–60. doi:10.1177/1362361315622412

Calder, L., Hill, V., & Pellicano, E. (2013). 'Sometimes I want to play by myself': Understanding what friendship means to children with autism in mainstream primary schools. *Autism, 17*, 296–316. doi:10.1177/1362361312467866

Campbell, J. M. (2006). Changing children's attitudes toward autism: A process of persuasive communication. *Journal of Developmental and Physical Disabilities, 18*, 251–272. doi:10.1007/s10882-006-9015-7

Campbell, J. M., & Barger, B. D. (2011). Middle school students' knowledge of autism. *Journal of Autism and Developmental Disorders, 41*, 732–740. doi:10.1077/s10803-101-1092-x

Campbell, J. M., & Barger, B. D. (2014). Peers' knowledge about and attitudes towards students with autism spectrum disorders. In. V. B. Patel, V. R. Preedy, & C. R. Martin (Eds.), *Comprehensive guide to autism* (pp. 247–261). Springer. doi:10.1007/978-1-4614-4788-7_7

Campbell, J. M., Ferguson, J. E., Herzinger, C. V., Jackson, J. N., & Marino, C. A. (2004). Combined descriptive and explanatory information improves peers' perceptions of autism. *Research in Developmental Disabilities, 25*, 321–339. doi:10.1016/j.ridd.2004.01.005

Campbell, J. M., Morton, J. F., Roulston, K., & Barger, B. D. (2011). A descriptive analysis of middle school students' conceptions of autism. *Journal of Developmental and Physical Disabilities, 23*, 377–397. doi:10.1007/s10882-011-0234-4

Cappadocia, M. C., Weiss, J. A., & Pepler, D. (2012). Bullying experiences among children with autism spectrum disorders. *Journal of Autism and Developmental Disorders, 42*, 266–277. doi:10.1007/s10803-011-1241-x

Carter, E. D., Asmus, J., Moss, C. K., Cooney, M., Weir, K., Vincent, L., Born, T., Hochman, J. M., Bottema-Beutel, K., & Fesperman, E. (2013). Peer network strategies to foster social connections among adolescents with and without severe disabilities. *Teaching Exceptional Children, 46*, 51–59.

Carter, E. D., Bottema-Beutel, K., & Brock, M. E. (2014). Social interactions and friendships. In M. Agran, F. Brown, C. Hughes, C. Quirk, & D. Ryndak (Eds.), *Equity and full participation for individuals with severe disabilities: A vision for the future* (pp. 197–216). Brookes.

Carter, S. (2009). Bullying of students with asperger syndrome. *Issues in Comprehensive Pediatric Nursing, 32*, 145–154. doi:10.1080/01460860903062782

Chan, J. M., Lang, R., Rispoli, M., O'Reilly, M., Sigafoos, J., & Cole, D. (2009). Use of peer-mediated interventions in the treatment of autism spectrum disorders: A systematic review. *Research in Autism Spectrum Disorders, 3*, 876–889. doi:10.1016/j.rasd.2009.04.003

Chang, D., & Locke, J. (2016). A systematic review of peer-mediated interventions for children with autism spectrum disorder. *Research in Autism Spectrum Disorders, 27*, 1–10. https://doi.org/10.1016/j.rasd.2016.03.010

Chamberlain, B., Kasari, C., & Rotherham-Fuller, E. (2007). Involvement or isolation? The social networks of children with autism in regular classrooms. *Journal of Autism and Developmental Disorders, 37*, 230–242. doi:10.1007/s10803-006-0164-4

Daniel, L. S., & Billingsley, B. S. (2010). What boys with an autism spectrum disorder say about establishing and maintaining friendships. *Focus on Autism and Other Developmental Disabilities, 25*, 220–229. doi:10.1177/1088357610378290

Dean, M., Kasari, C., Shih, D., Frankel, F., Whitnet, R., Landa, R., Lord, C., Orlich, F., King, B., & Harwood, R. (2014). The peer relationships of girls with ASD at school: Comparison to boys and girls with and without ASD. *The Journal of Child Psychology and Psychiatry, 55*, 1218–1225. doi:10.1111/jccp.12242

Farrington, D. P., & Ttofi, M. M. (2009). School-based programs to reduce bullying and victimization: A systematic review. *Campbell Systematic Reviews, 2009*, 5. Retrieved from https://campbellcollaboration.org/library/school-based-programmes-to-reduce-bullying-victimisation.html

Feldman, E. K., & Matos, R. (2012). Training paraprofessionals to facilitate social interactions between children with autism and their typically developing peers. *Journal of Positive Behavior Interventions, 15*, 169–179. doi:10.1177/1098300712457421

Freitag, S., & Dunsmuir, S. (2015). The inclusion of children with ASD: Using the theory of planned behaviour as a theoretical framework to explore peer attitudes. *International Journal of Disability, Development and Education, 62*, 405–421. doi:10.1080/1034912X.2015.1046818

Frisén, A., Hasselblad, T., & Holmqvist, K. (2012). What actually makes bullying stop? Reports from former victims. *Journal of Adolescence, 35*, 981–990. doi:10.1016/j.adolescence.2012.02.001

Gardner, K. F., Carter, E. D., Gustafson, J. R., Hochman, J. M., Harvey, M. N., Mullins, T. S., & Fan, D. (2014). Effects of peer networks on the social interactions of high school students with autism spectrum disorders. *Research and Practice for Persons with Severe Disabilities, 39*, 100–118. doi:10.1177/1540796914544550rpsd.sagepub.com

Hochman, J. M., Carter, E. D., Bottema-Beutel, K., Harvey, M. N., & Gustafson, J. R. (2015). Efficacy of peer networks to increase social connections among high school students with and without autism spectrum disorder. *Exceptional Children, 82*, 96–116. doi:10.1177/0014402915585482

Hughes, C., Harvey, M., Cosgriff, J., Reilly, C., Heilingoetter, J., Brigham, N., Kaplan, L., & Bernstein, R. (2013). A peer-delivered social interaction intervention for high school students with autism. *Research and Practice for Persons with Severe Disabilities, 38*, 1–16. https://doi.org/10.2511/027494813807046999

Humphrey, N., & Hebron, J. (2015). Bullying of children and adolescents with autism spectrum conditions: A 'state of the field' review. *International Journal of Inclusive Education, 19*, 845–862. doi:10.1080/13603116.2014.981602

Humphrey, N., & Symes, D. (2010). Perceptions of social support and experience of bullying among pupils with Autistic Spectrum Disorders (ASD) in mainstream secondary schools. *European Journal of Special Education, 25*, 77–91. doi:10.1080/08856250903408 55

Humphrey, N., & Symes, D. (2011). Peer interaction patterns among adolescents with Autistic Spectrum Disorders (ASDs) in mainstream school settings. *Autism, 15*, 397–419. doi:10.1177/1362361310387804

Kamps, D., Thiemann-Bourque, K., Heitzman-Powell, L., Schwartz, I., Rosenberg, N., Mason, R., & Cox, S. (2015). A comprehensive peer network intervention to improve social communication of children with autism spectrum disorders: A randomized trial in kindergarten and first grade. *Journal of Autism and Developmental Disorders, 45*, 1809–1824. doi:10.1007/s10803-014-2340-2

Kasari, C., Locke, J., Gulsrud, A., & Rotherham-Fuller, E. (2011). Social networks and friendships at school: Comparing children with and without ASD. *Journal of Autism and Developmental Disorders, 41*, 533–544. doi:10.1007/s10803-010-1076-x

Kasari, C., Rotherham-Fuller, E., Locke, J., et al. (2012). Making the connection: Randomized controlled trial of social skills at school for children with autism. *Journal of Child Psychology and Psychiatry, 53*, 431–439. doi:10.1111/j.1469-7610.2011.02493.x

Lasgaard, M., Nielsen, A., Eriksen, & Goossens, L. (2010). Loneliness and social support in adolescent boys with autism spectrum disorders. *Journal of Autism and Developmental Disorders, 40*, 218–226. doi:10.1007/s10803-009-0851-z

Lereya, S., Samara, M., & Wolke, D. (2013). Parenting behavior and the risk of becoming a bully/victim: A meta-analysis study. *Child Abuse & Neglect, 37*, 1091–1108. doi:10.1016/j.chiabu.2013.03.001

Little, L. (2002). Middle-class mothers' perceptions of peer and sibling victimization among children with asperger's syndrome and nonverbal learning disorders. *Issues in Comprehensive Pediatric Nursing, 25*, 43–57. doi:10.1080/01460860275350 4847

Locke, J., Ishijima, E., Kasari, C., & London, N. (2010). Loneliness, friendship quality and the social networks of adolescents with high-functioning autism in an inclusive school setting. *Journal of Research in Special Educational Needs, 10*, 74–81. doi:10.111/j.1471-3802.2010.01148.x

Locke, J., Shih, D., Kretzmann, M., & Kasari, C. (2016). Examining playground engagement between elementary school children with and without autism spectrum disorder. *Autism, 20*, 653–662. doi:10.1177/1362361315599468

Mavropoulou, S. M., & Sideridis, G. D. (2014). Knowledge of autism and attitudes of children towards their partially integrated peers with autism spectrum disorders. *Journal of Autism and Developmental Disorders, 44*, 1867–1885. doi:10.1007/s10803-014-2059-0

McLeskey, J., Landers, E., Williamson, P., & Hoppey, D. (2012). Are we moving toward educating students with disabilities in less restrictive settings? *The Journal of Special Education, 46*, 131–140. doi:10.11177/0022466910376670

Morewood, G. D., Humphrey, N., & Symes, D. (2011). Mainstreaming autism: Making it work. *Good Autism Practice, 12*, 62–68. doi:10.1177/1362361310387804

Morton, J. F., & Campbell, J. M. (2008). Information source affects peers' initial attitudes toward autism. *Research in Developmental Disabilities, 29*, 189–201. doi:10.1016/j.ridd.2007.02.006

National Autism Center. (2015). Report.

Odom, S. L., & Strain, P. S. (1984). Peer-mediated approaches to promoting children's social interaction: A review. *American Journal of Orthopsychiatry, 54*, 544–557. doi:10.1111/j.1939-0025.1984.tb01525.x

Olweus, D., & Limber, S. P. (2010). Bullying in school: Evaluation and dissemination of the Olweus Bullying Prevention Program. *American Journal of Orthopsychiatry, 80*, 124–134. doi:10.1111/j.1939-0025.2010.01015.x

Pisula, E., & Lukowska, E. (2012). Perception of social relationships with classmates and social support in adolescents with asperger syndrome mainstream schools in Poland. *School Psychology International, 33*, 185–206. doi:10.1177/0143034311415784

Platos, M., & Wojaczek, K. (2018). Broadening the scope of peer-mediated interventions for individuals with autism spectrum disorders. *Journal of Autism and Developmental Disorders, 48*, 747–750. https://doi.org/10.1007/s10803-017-3429-1

Rakap, S. (2015). Effect sizes as result interpretation aids in single-subject experimental research: Description and application of four nonoverap methods. *British Journal of Special Education, 42*, 11–33. doi:10.1111/1467-8578.12091

Ranson, N. J., & Byrne, M. K. (2014). Promoting peer acceptance of females with higher-functioning autism in a mainstream education setting: A replication and extension of the effects of an autism anti-stigma program. *Journal of Autism and Developmental Disorders, 44*, 2778–2796. doi:10.1007/s10803-014-014-2139-1

Reid, B., & Batten, A. (2006). *B is for bullied.* National Autistic Society.

Richard, J. F., Schneider, B. D., & Mallet, P. (2012). Revisiting the whole-school approach to bullying: Really looking at the whole school. *School Psychology International, 33*, 263–284. doi:10.1177/0143034311415906

Rose, C. A., Espelage, D. L., Aragon, S. R., & Elliott, J. (2011). Bullying and victimization among students in special education and general education curricula. *Exceptionality Education International, 21*, 2–14.

Rosenbaum, P. L., Armstrong, R. D., & King, S. M. (1988). Determinants of children's attitudes toward disability: A review of the evidence. *Children's Health Care, 17*, 32–39.

Rotherham-Fuller, E., Kasari, C., Chamberlain, B., & Locke, J. (2010). Social involvement of children with autism spectrum disorders in elementary school classrooms. *Journal of Child Psychology and Psychiatry, 51*, 1227–1234. doi:10.1111/j.1469-7610.2010.02289.x

Rowley, E., Chandler, S., Baird, G., Simonoff, E., Pickles, A., Loucas, T., & Charman, T. (2012). The experience of friendship, victimization, and bullying in children with an autism spectrum disorder: Associations with child characteristics and school placement. *Research in Autism Spectrum Disorders, 6*, 1126–1134. doi:10.1016/j.rasd.2012.03.004

Rubin, K. D., Bukowski, D. M., & Laurensen, B. (Eds.). (2009). *Handbook of peer interactions, relationships, and groups.* Guilford Press.

Sanford, C., Levine, P., & Blackorby, J. (2008). *A national profile of students with autism: A special topic report from the special education elementary longitudinal study.* SRI International.

Schroeder, J. D., Cappadocia, M. C., Bebko, J. M., Pepler, D. J., & Weiss, J. A. (2014). Shedding light on a pervasive problem: A review of research on bullying experiences among children with autism spectrum disorders. *Journal of Autism and Developmental Disorders, 44,* 1520–1534. doi:10.1007/s10803-013-2011-8

Shattuck, P. T., Orsmond, G. I., Wagner, M., & Cooper, B. P. (2011). Participation in social activities among adolescents with an autism spectrum disorder. *PLoS ONE, 6,* e27176. doi:10.1371/journal.pone.0027176

Sigman, M., & Ruskin, E. (1999). Continuity and change in the social competence of children with autism, down syndrome, and developmental delays. *Monographs of the Society for Research in Child Development, 64,* 256–264. doi:10.1111/1540-5834.00001

Sparapani, N., Morgan, L., Reinhardt, V. P., Schatscheinder, C., & Wetherby, A. M. (2016). Evaluation of classroom active engagement in elementary students with autism spectrum disorder. *Journal of Autism and Developmental Disorders, 46,* 782–296. doi:10.1007/s10803-015-2615-2

Sperry, L., Neitzel, J., & Engelhardt-Wells, K. (2010). Peer-mediated instruction and intervention strategies for students with autism spectrum disorders. *Preventing School Failure, 54,* 256–264. doi:10.1080/10459881003800529

Sreckovic, M. A., Hume, K., & Able, D. (2017). Examining the efficacy of peer network interventions on the social interactions of high school students with autism spectrum disorder. *Journal of Autism and Developmental Disorders, 47,* 2556–2574. doi:10.1007/s10803-017-3171-8

Staniland, J. J., & Byrne, M. K. (2013). The effects of a multi-component higher-functioning autism anti-stigma program on adolescent boys. *Journal of Autism and Developmental Disorders, 43,* 2816–2829. doi:10.1007/s10803-01301829-4

Sterzing, P. R., Shattuck, P. T., Narendorf, S. C., Wagner, M., & Cooper, B. P. (2012). Bullying involvement and autism spectrum disorders: Prevalence and correlates of bullying involvement among adolescents with an autism spectrum disorder. *Archives of Pediatrics & Adolescent Medicine, 166,* 1058–1064. doi:10.1001/archpediatrics.2012.790

Symes, D., & Humphrey, N. (2010). Peer-group indicators of social inclusion among pupils with Autistic Spectrum Disorders (ASD) in mainstream secondary schools: A comparative study. *School Psychology International, 31,* 478–494. doi:10.1177/0143034310382496

Swaim, K. F., & Morgan, S. B. (2001). Children's attitudes and behavioral intentions toward a peer with autistic behaviors: Does a brief educational intervention have an effect? *Journal of Autism and Developmental Disorders, 31*, 195–205. doi:10.1023/A:1010703316365

Tonnsen, B. L, & Hahn, E. R. (2016). Middle school students' attitudes toward a peer with autism spectrum disorder: Effects of social acceptance and physical inclusion. *Focus on Autism and Other Developmental Disabilities, 31*, 262–274. doi:10.1177/1088357614559213focus.sagepub.com

Tse, J., Strulovitch, J., Tagalakis, V., Meng, L., & Fombonne, E. (2007). Social skills training for adolescents with asperger syndrome and high-functioning autism. *Journal of Autism and Developmental Disorders, 37*, 1960–1968. doi:10.1007/s10803-006-0343-3

Utley, C. A., & Mortweet, S. L. (1997). Peer-mediated instruction and intervention. *Focus on Exceptional Children, 29*, 1–23.

Wainscot, J. J., Naylor, P., Sutcliffe, P., Tantam, D., & Williams, J. V. (2008). Relationships with peers and use of the school environment of mainstream secondary school pupils with asperger syndrome (High-functioning autism): A case-control study. *International Journal of Psychology and Psychological Therapy, 8*, 25–38.

Wang, P., & Spillane, A. (2009). Evidence-based social skills interventions for children with Autism: A meta-analysis. *Education and Training in Developmental Disabilities, 44*, 318–342.

Watkins, L., O'Reilly, M., Kuhn, M., Gevarter, C., Lancioni, G. E., Sigafoos, J., & Lang, R. (2015). A review of peer-mediated social interaction interventions for students with autism in inclusive settings. *Journal of Autism and Developmental Disorders, 45*, 1070–1083. doi:10.1007/s10803-014-2264-x

Whalon, K., Conroy, M. A., Martinez, J. R., & Werch, B. L. (2015). School-based peer-related social competence interventions for children with autism spectrum disorders: A meta-analysis and descriptive review of single case research design studies. *Journal of Autism and Developmental Disorders, 45*, 1513–1531. doi:10.1007/s10803-015-2373-1

Whitaker, P. (2007). Provision for youngsters with autism spectrum disorders in mainstream schools: What parents say – and what parents want. *British Journal of Special Education, 34*, 170–178.

Zeedyk, S. M., Cohen, S., R., Eisenhower, A., & Blacher, J. (2016). Perceived social competence and loneliness among young children with ASD: Child, parent and teacher reports. *Journal of Autism and Developmental Disorders, 46*, 436–449. doi:10.1007/s10803-015-2575-6

Zagona, A. L., & Mastergeorge, A. M. (2018). An empirical review of peer-mediated interventions: Implications for young children with autism spectrum disorders. *Focus on Autism and Other Developmental Disabilities, 33*, 131–141, doi:10.1177/1088357616671295

Zhang, J., & Wheeler, J. J. (2011). A meta-analysis of peer-mediated interventions for young children with autism spectrum disorders. *Education and Training in Autism and Developmental Disabilities, 46*, 62–77.

CHAPTER 12

Using Social Skills Training to Enhance Inclusion for Students with ASD in Mainstream Schools

Kelly-Ann Allen, Christopher Boyle, Fraser Lauchlan and Heather Craig

1 Introduction

It could be regarded as a necessary survival skill that individuals are able to display appropriate social skills within the rules of their culture. Conforming to the often-unspoken rules of sociability enables the formation and maintenance of relationships that will help individuals to be independent and successful. Social skills have been defined as a set of learned, identifiable behaviours that contribute to an individual's functioning in society (Johns, Crowley & Guetzloe, 2005). Those who display inappropriate social behaviours may be less appealing to their peers and have problems throughout life, such as loneliness or a poor sense of belonging (Sha'ked & Rokach, 2015; Allen & Boyle, 2018). For example, without adequate social skills an individual may experience difficulties with employment, daily and independent living, and connectedness to society.

Improving social skills is often an area of emphasis for those who work with students who have Autism Spectrum Disorders (ASD). Impaired social functioning in individuals with ASD is well documented as being a commonly recognised indicator of difficulties especially when children transition through the years of school including through adolescence and then ultimately, adulthood (Matthews et al., 2015). Research has demonstrated that employers often believe that social competency is more important than the actual experience in the workplace (Deloitte, 2017). Moreover, deficits in social skills have been linked to school dropout, juvenile deviancy, suicide, and police intervention (Merrell & Gimpel, 1998). Therefore, when considering a systemic approach to social competencies, the development of necessary social skills should be an essential part of the educational curriculum to support the functioning of all students within the school, family, and wider socio-ecological systems (AACTE, 2010). This chapter argues that current approaches to social skills training through schools is not sufficient for children with ASD and calls for a multi-systemic approach to address social skills intervention in order to drive authentic inclusive practices for all children and young people.

 | DOI: 10.1163/9789004431171_012

2 The Problem

In an attempt to teach social competencies to all students in mainstream educational settings, many schools have implemented programmes to compensate for curriculum shortcomings in this area (e.g., Stop, Think, Do; Petersen & Adderley, 2002; Friends for Life, Kösters et al., 2012; Calmer Classrooms, Brodzeller, Ottley, Jung, & Coogle, 2018), or when an identified need has emerged. The majority of these programmes have focused on teaching a broad range of social skills including greetings and farewells, initiating and maintaining appropriate conversations, giving and receiving compliments, and sharing. Research on friendship and social skill-based programmes have shown that they help reduce anxiety (Moharreri & Yazdi, 2017), improve problem-solving skills (da Silva et al., 2016), promote the use of self-regulation strategies (Blair & Raver, 2015), and increase social competence (Spence, 2003). Despite the success of these programmes in the general school population, the efficacy of interventions for children with ASD attending mainstream school is limited (Barry et al., 2003; Zainal & Magiati, 2016).

In general, interventions that aim to increase the overall social competencies in the general classroom are not designed to specifically target children with ASD (Barry et al., 2003; Boyle, 2007). Further, in studies where improvements in social skills have been made, children with ASD still tend to have difficulty when adapting the skills to new or different environments and situations (Ooi et al., 2016). While social skills programmes aim to address the deficits typically exhibited by children with ASD, these programmes are usually implemented over short periods of time (Paul, 2008). Due to the brief nature of the interventions, children with ASD may not master the skill being taught before a new topic is introduced. Therefore, a more longitudinal approach may be more beneficial. Programmes should be properly evaluated using scientific principles so as to ensure their effectiveness in inclusive settings.

The difficulties that some children and young people with ASD have with social interactions result in atypical social development that may have a devastating effect on their ability to establish positive relationships at home, at school, and in other community settings. Deficits in cognitive functioning, negative perceptions by peers, and the engagement in obsessive interests and negative (or aberrant) behaviours may further contribute to social isolation (Barnhill, 2001). School safety issues are also of concern (The National Association of School Psychologists [NASP], 2007). Social skills that relate to school safety, such as anger management, conflict management, and peer negotiation, may affect both personal safety and the safety of the general school population. Given the many sociability issues faced by individuals with ASD, especially when attending mainstream school settings, greater efforts are needed to improve the social skills of these children to create an inclusive environment where they can effectively interact with other children.

Hidden social rules and norms are manifested in every aspect of mainstream schools and daily life (e.g., classroom, playground, and bathroom) and create great difficulties for the child with ASD. Individuals with ASD may behave in ways that are reactive and do not conform to social or group norms within mainstream educational settings. Rules surrounding acceptable and non-acceptable behaviours often need to be taught, as do social cues that inform us when others may be disapproving of our behaviour (Adreon & Durocher, 2007; Holt, Lea, & Bowlby, 2012). For example, children with ASD not only need to be taught the appropriate distance at which to stand when talking to someone, but also the subtle cues that an interlocutor might display when that distance is breached. Once these protocols have been taught, further efforts must be made to generalise them. Behaviour that is acceptable in one setting may not be necessarily acceptable in another. While explicitly stated norms (e.g., school starting time) are usually easier for the child with ASD to understand – partially due to their predictability and routine nature – non-explicit norms can be particularly challenging. Informal silent norms dominate all social settings and can be overlooked by children and adults with ASD. Howlin et al. (1999) state that, when these norms are transgressed, individuals can become socially excluded. It is not surprising, therefore, that many children with ASD experience social isolation, a low sense of belonging, and bullying in the classroom and schoolyard (Erin, 2015).

2.1 *ASD in Mainstream Settings*

According to Baio et al. (2018), in 2014, the overall occurrence of ASD among the 11 Autism and Developmental Disabilities Monitoring (ADDM) locations was 16.8 per 1,000 (one in 59) children. Total ASD frequency estimates varied among locations, from 13.1–29.3 per 1,000 children. ASD prevalence estimates also varied by sex and race/ethnicity. Males were four times more likely than females to be identified with ASD and Hertz-Picciotto and Delwiche (2009) contend that the arguably inflated estimations of incidence in recent years can be attributed to the inclusion of milder cases. Current evidence also indicates that females are under identified in the population due to the misunderstanding of the manifestation of ASD in females (Fulton, Paynter, & Trembath, 2017). The incidence and increase of ASD, however, appears to be equally represented in populations throughout the world. The Autism Society of America (2007) reports a 10 to 17% increase in the number of children with ASD every year. In Australia, the situation is similar where there are increasing numbers of children with ASD being included in mainstream-classrooms across the country. In the UK, 70% of children with ASD attend mainstream education (DfE, 2016). For all children with ASD, regardless of which country they are living, adequate social skills are vital to successful inclusion (Laushey & Heflin, 2000).

2.2 *Perceptions in Educational Settings*

Perceptions differ when discussing the social skill deficits of children with ASD. Some educators perceive the teaching of social skills to be the role for parents and the community (Anderson, 2000). Many think social competency is readily acquired.

The notion of inclusion as applied to children with ASD in a mainstream setting has been marked by controversy. Many parents in the UK have reported that school leaders in mainstream schools claim that limited resources render them unable to accommodate the additional needs of a child with ASD (Macbeath et al., 2006). Alternatively, Barnard, Broach, Potter, and Prior (2002) found strong support for the policy of inclusion in the UK, with 65% of the mainstream schools surveyed reporting that the inclusion of children with ASD into their student populations had been successful. Interestingly the one third (32%) of schools that reported negative feelings about inclusion also admitted to having insufficient training in ASD. This specific finding has been identified as being a general issue in mainstream schools with some teaching staff in the UK not even being sure if they had received any training on inclusion (Boyle, Topping, & Jindal-Snape, 2013; Boyle, Topping, Jindal-Snape, & Norwich, 2012), which is a damning indictment of the support that teachers received to facilitate inclusion in mainstream schools. Without adequate training and knowledge of ASD, the formation of incorrect stereotypes is more likely. Mainstream schools that have never catered for a child with ASD may have preconceived ideas as to how these children think, behave, and impact on the school curriculum (Roberts & Simpson, 2016; Symes & Humphrey, 2011). It can also be argued that there is an over-reach of measuring whether schools are inclusive or not (Boyle & Anderson, in press). However, the real issue is about systems (Anderson, Boyle, & Deppeler, 2014; Anderson & Boyle, 2019) and resources (Kraska & Boyle, 2014). Schools are not operating in an environment with unlimited resources and the focus on schools is almost pointless as it is on the local authority, and by extension the government, where the real success of inclusion can be measured.

2.3 *Curriculum Priorities*

Most of the skills required for successful navigation through school systems are academically related. Therefore, teachers, educators, and educational departments regard academic competence as a high priority. Teaching social and interpersonal skills, on the other hand, tends not to be the focus for most teachers, including those with special education backgrounds. Further, social skills are often not included in individualised education or integration plans or in the basic school curriculum (UNESCO, 2001). Anderson (2000) reported that only 37% of students who required social skills training had it written into their education plans. Alberta Teachers' Association (2015), however, revealed that teachers consider the teaching of social skills such as following directions, completing tasks, and dealing with emergencies and ethics to be very important. Nevertheless, these skills continue not to be addressed by the school curriculum in a way that is meaningful and achievable for a child with ASD. Kebapci and Erkal (2009) suggest that all systems are resistant to change and, when a need arises, tend to resort back to the status quo. In addition, teachers may not recognise that they too can contribute to students' problems. This can lead to a failure to grasp their role in helping students achieve greater social competencies. Social skills are necessary for students to become successful and independent in the world outside the school system and need to be incorporated into the curriculum for all children (Alberta Teachers' Association, 2015).

2.4 *Resource Issues*

For funding and educational reasons, modern schools tend to focus on interventions that result in tangible outcomes (Corey, 2005). Thus, schools usually favour short-term programs relating to cognitive skills rather than the development of affective skills. Educational systems also place a greater value on diagnosis and formal psychological testing than on the operation of long-term interventions, professional development for staff, and ongoing teacher training (Boyle, 2007; Boyle & Lauchlan, 2009). The National Autistic Society (2007) reports that 80% of parents of children with ASD in mainstream schools believe that their child's teachers have undergone some training in ASD. Despite this, only 35% are satisfied with the understanding of issues related to ASD within the school system. Without an understanding of ASD, teachers are unable to adjust the curriculum and school environment for students with ASD in order to help them cope more successfully and improve their wellbeing. In schools where teachers have had training in ASD awareness, the impact on the child, their family and the school system has been positive. The lack of adequate training seems to be an ongoing issue in inclusive education (Boyle, Topping, & Jindal-Snape, 2013).

3 Possible Resolutions

The notion that individuals with ASD lack an interest in social interactions is often inaccurate. Many individuals with ASD do indeed desire social involvement, however these individuals typically lack the necessary skills to interact effectively (White, Keonig, & Scahill, 2007; Watkins, Leadbetter-Cho, O'Reilly, Bernard-Brak, & Garcia-Grau, 2019). Further research is also suggesting that there exist significant differences between gender in people diagnosed with ASD, with females demonstrating greater competencies in social skills than males, which may also have implications for intervention (Head, McGillivray, & Stokes, 2014). Some progress in teaching social skills to children with ASD has been made through behaviour modification techniques such as those influenced by the early work of B. F. Skinner and more recently, Applied Behavioural Analysis (ABA) and the related Functional Behaviour Analysis (FBA). While behaviourist interventions have been found to be empirically validated and valuable in school systems, they are often criticised for creating short-term solutions that emphasise extrinsic controls (Plas, 1986) and can be at the mercy of pervasive negative attitudes (Allen & Bowles, 2013).

Plas (1986) argues for a systemic approach to mainstream education whereby a *focus group*, such as a group of students experiencing social skill deficits, is recognized in terms of its position in a larger system. For example, a group of students may be part of a classroom that in turn is geographically and culturally contained within an even larger system such as the school. A student also belongs to a family system; the family system and school system both belong to larger units of state, country, and culture (Fish & Jain, 1988; Whitchurch & Constantine, 2009). For interventions to be effective, systems theory guide practitioners and educators to understand that schools are organisations, where influential members of the system (e.g., principals, teachers, and parents) are jointly responsible for issues faced by students (Hong, Al-Khatib, Magagna, McLoughlin, & Coe, 1997). A systemic approach to addressing social skills training in students with ASD may use a focus group based around developing necessary social skills. Results may then be applied to the classroom and related participants of the wider system, that is, peers, parents, teachers, and principals.

4 Belonging

The psychological concept of belonging, and in particular, the concept of 'school belonging' is particularly relevant to the current discussion. The concept of school belonging can be viewed as having strong links with inclusion, since it regards the notion that students, and one might argue especially those with additional support needs (ASN), should feel accepted and valued by others in the school, not only by their fellow students and their teachers, but by everyone connected to the school: parents, ancillary staff and anyone else who might be considered part of the wider school community. Promoting a sense of belonging places much responsibility on the teaching staff to foster a supportive environment of trust, fairness, and security within the school (Hattie, 2018; Grove & Laletas, 2019). Creating such a climate in a school is challenging, and an important aspect of belonging is not only to have positive relations between teachers and students, but also amongst the students themselves. Developing these positive relationships requires carefully planned intervention work and the importance of social skills training is clear.

Laursen and Yazdgerdi (2012) outline the intervention approach they use in trying to foster a sense of belonging to students with ASD. Their work centres on helping students to develop their social skills in relationships with adults and peers. Some of the interpersonal interactions they describe might be considered simple but, as they outline in their article, it is essential that the students remain in their 'comfort zone'. Some examples they provide are the following: a consistent greeting and a few friendly words each day, offering to help another student, sharing a success and offering praise to another. The key thing is for staff to acknowledge any attempts that a young person may make to connect with another person. Attempts to connect by a young person with ASD require courage; courage to trust others and courage in the face of potential rejection. Laursen and Yazdgerdi (2012) emphasise the importance of relationships in promoting personal growth and development as well as serving as "catalysts for change and success" (p. 46).

The importance of fostering strong relationships for children with support needs in school is also underlined by a recent study by Pollock (2019), albeit that the research investigated the school experiences of learners identified as having literacy difficulties rather than ASD. The research used an exploratory case study methodology using several case studies. An original aspect of this research was the use of the participatory method of photovoice, whereby the students were asked to take photographs that were illustrative of their school experience. The findings showed that there were very few photos taken by the participants that were explicitly about literacy and learning 'tools'. Instead the students' photographs highlighted the importance they placed on relationships with peers and key staff. This indicated an important connection between their social and learning experiences. In other words, it is the importance placed on an atmosphere of belonging and the development of social relationships that was significant for these learners, rather than the provision of specific 'learning tools'. The same argument can be made for children with ASD regarding the value of promoting strong relationships and fostering a sense of belonging within the school environment. Thus, the significance of developing and teaching social skills to children with ASD in mainstream settings cannot be over-emphasised.

5 A Multi-Systemic Approach to Teaching Social Skills

A multi-systematic approach to teaching social skills provides a way for children with ASD to learn appropriate social skills in a small group that facilitates cohesive and comfortable interactions with their peers, but also recruits the resources within the broader systems that surround the child in order to teach, consolidate, and master new skills (Simpson, Smith-Mykes, Sasso, & Kamps, 1991). In order for this to be successful in mainstream schools appropriate resources, including staffing, need to be provided.

Anderson et al. (2018) carried out a literature review of the connection between social-ecological features and transition in youth with ASD. They systematised variables used in studies through five influence levels: interpersonal, community, family, policy and institutional level factors. Their results showed that both the breadth and depth of social-ecological factors that are used in autism research is inadequate because of the overreliance on an inadequate amount of national data sets, the slender addition of variables across social-ecological levels, and the general absence of variation in research design.

Bellini (2004) suggests that social skills are acquired through observation, modelling, coaching, and social problem solving as well as rehearsal, feedback, and reinforcement-based strategies. Moreover, social skills groups that are most successful tend to focus on one social skill at a time and involve a systemically orientated approach as opposed to a *stand-alone* or pull-out intervention (McMahon, Vismara, & Solomon, 2014).

6 Conclusion

Social ineffectiveness translates into an inability to relate to others and interact appropriately within the various systems and groups that constitute society. Applying systems perspectives to students with ASD gives students and educators in whole school systems and sub-systems (e.g., classrooms and groups) responsibility for teaching and learning appropriate behaviours relating to social expectations and acceptable social behaviour. A systems approach increases the understanding of relationships between systems by creating a shared, ongoing responsibility towards the problem. Children, adolescents, and adults must be able to deal with a wide range of societal situations to be successful in life and in order to do this, knowledge of social skills and competencies is essential. Social competency is correlated with academic success, positive peer relationships, and greater satisfaction in adulthood. For typical students, these skills are learnt through natural experience and interaction;

however students with ASD tend to have less opportunity for such interactions. To address this growing problem in schools, systemic interventions must be considered to provide increased teaching opportunities for the development of necessary social skills. All students benefit from social skill interventions as a way of creating more successful interactions in the schools, families, and wider cultural systems of which society is comprised. The difficult question as to whether pupils with ASD are able to receive the required resourcing in a mainstream environment is a moot point and is unlikely to be concluded soon.

References

AACTE. (2010). *21st century knowledge and skills in educator preparation.* Retrieved from https://files.eric.ed.gov/fulltext/ED519336.pdf

Adreon, D., & Durocher, J. S. (2007). Evaluating the college transition needs of individuals with high-functioning autism spectrum disorders. *Intervention in School and Clinic, 42*(5), 271–279.

Alberta Teachers' Association. (2015). *Teachers and educational assistants: Roles and responsibilities.* The Alberta Teachers' Association (ATA).

Allen, K., & Bowles, T. (2013). Belonging as a guiding principle in the education of adolescents. *Australian Journal of Educational and Developmental Psychology, 12*, 108–119.

Allen, K., Bowles, T., & Weber, L. (2013). Mothers' and fathers' stress associated with parenting a child with autism spectrum disorder. *Journal of Autism Insights, 5*, 1–11.

Allen, K., & Boyle, C. (2018). The varied pathways to belonging. In K. Allen & C. Boyle (Eds.), *Pathways to school belonging* (pp. 1–6.). Brill | Sense.

American Psychiatric Association. (2013). *Diagnostic and Statistical Manual of mental disorders (DSM-5®).* American Psychiatric Publishers.

Anderson, K. A., Roux, A. M., Kuo, A., & Shattuck T. (2018). Social-ecological correlates in adult autism outcome studies: A scoping review. *The American Academy of Pediatrics, 141*(4). S306–S317.

Anderson, J., & Boyle, C. (2015). Inclusive education in Australia: Rhetoric, reality, and the road ahead. *British Journal of Support for Learning, 30*(1), 4–22. doi:10.1111/1467-9604.12074

Anderson, J., & Boyle, C. (2019). Looking in the mirror: Reflecting on 25 years of inclusive education in Australia. *The International Journal of Inclusive Education, 23*(7–8), 796–810. doi:10.1080/13603116.2019.1622802

Anderson, J., Boyle, C., & Deppeler, J. (2014). The ecology of inclusive education: Reconceptualising Bronfenbrenner. In Z. Zhang, P. D. K. Chan, & C. Boyle (Eds.), *Equality in education: Fairness and inclusion* (pp. 23–34). Sense Publishers.

Anderson, P. L. (2000). Using literature to teach social skills to adolescents with learning disabilities. *Intervention in School and Clinic, 35*(5), 271–279.

Baio, J., Wiggins, L., Christensen, D. L., Maenner, M. J., Daniels, J., Warren, Z., ... Durkin, M. S. (2018). Prevalence of autism spectrum disorder among children aged 8 years – Autism and developmental disabilities monitoring network, 11 sites, United States, 2014. *MMWR Surveillance Summaries, 67*(6), 1.

Barnard, J., Broach, S., Potter, D., & Prior, A. (2002). *Autism in schools, crisis or challenge.* The National Autistic Society.

Barnhill, G. (2001). Social attribution and depression in adolescents with Asperger Syndrome. *Focus on Autism and Other Developmental Disabilities, 16*, 46–53.

Barry, T. D., Klinger, L. G., Lee, J. M., Palardy, N., Gilmore, T., & Bodin, S. D. (2003). Examining the effectiveness of an outpatient clinic-based social skills group for high-functioning children with autism. *Journal of Autism and Developmental Disorders, 33*, 685–701.

Bellini, S. (2004). Social skill deficits and anxiety in high functioning adolescents with autism spectrum disorders. *Focus on Autism and Other Developmental Disabilities, 19*, 78–86.

Blair, C., & Raver, C. C. (2015). School readiness and self-regulation: A developmental psychobiological approach. *Annual Rev Psychol, 66*, 711–731. doi:10.1146/annurev-psych-010814-015221

Blankenship, K., & Minshawi, N. F. (2010). Behavioral therapy with an individual with asperger's disorder. *Psychiatry (Edgmont), 7*(8), 38–41.

Boyle, C. M. (2007). An analysis of the efficacy of a motor skills training programme for young people with moderate learning difficulties. *International Journal of Special Education, 22*(1), 11–24.

Boyle, C., & Anderson, J. (in press). Inclusive education and the progressive inclusionists. In U. Sharma & S. Salend (Eds.), *The Oxford research encyclopedia of education.* Oxford University Press.

Boyle C., Topping, K., & Jindal-Snape, D. (2013). Teachers' attitudes towards inclusion in high schools. *Teachers and Teaching: Theory and Practice, 19*(5), 527–542. doi:10.1080/13540602.2013.827361

Boyle, C., Topping, K., Jindal-Snape, D., & Norwich, B. (2012). The importance of peer-support for teaching staff when including children with special educational needs. *School Psychology International, 33*(2), 167–184. doi:10.1177/0143034311415783

Brodzeller, K. L., Ottley, J. R., Jung, J., & Coogle, C. J. (2018). Interventions and adaptations for children with autism spectrum disorder in inclusive early childhood settings. *Early Childhood Education Journal, 46*(3), 277–286. doi:10.1007/s10643-017-0859-5

Brumariu, L. E., & Kerns, K. A. (2008). Mother-child attachment and social anxiety symptoms in middle childhood. *Journal of Applied Developmental Psychology, 29*(5), 393–402. doi:10.1016/j.appdev.2008.06.002.

Corey, G. (2005). *Theory and practice of counseling and psychotherapy* (7th ed.). Brooks/Cole-Thomson Learning.

da Silva, J. L., de Oliveira, D. A., Braga, I. F., Farias, M. S., da Silva Lizzi, E. A., Gonçalves, M. F. C., … Silva, M. A. I. (2016). The effects of a skill-based intervention for victims of bullying in Brazil. *International Journal of Environmental Research and Public Health, 13*(11), 1042. doi:10.3390/ijerph13111042

Deloitte. (2017). *What key competencies are needed in the digital age? The impact of automation on employees, companies and education.* Retrieved from https://www2.deloitte.com/content/dam/Deloitte/ch/Documents/innovation/ch-en-innovation-automation-competencies.pdf

Department for Education. (2016). Absence and exclusions additional analysis for pupils with Special Educational Needs (SEN). Retrieved from www.gov.uk/government/publications/sen-absences-and-exclusions-additional-analysis

Dukpa, D. (2015). A critical perspective on inclusion of children with autism spectrum disorder in a mainstream classroom: Lessons for Bhutan. *Rabsel: The CERD Educational Journal, XVI*(I).

Erin, O. (2015). *Perceptions about bullying of students with autism spectrum disorder: A survey of school-based speech-language pathologists* (Master's thesis). Graduate Faculty of Auburn University.

Fish, M., & Jain, S. (1988). Using systems theory in school assessment and intervention: A structural model for school psychologists. *Professional School Psychology, 3*(4), 291–300. doi:10.1037/h0090569

Fulton, A. M., Paynter, J. M., & Trembath, D. (2017). Gender comparisons in children with ASD entering early intervention. *Research in Developmental Disabilities, 68*(1), 27–34. doi:10.1016/j.ridd.2017.07.009

Grové, C., & Laletas, S. (2019). Promoting student wellbeing and mental health through social and emotional learning. In L. Graham (Ed.), *Inclusive education in the 21st century*. Allen & Unwin.

Gus, L. (2000). Autism: Promoting peer understanding. *Educational Psychology in Practice, 16*(4), 461–468.

Hattie, J. (2018). Foreword. In K. A. Allen & C. Boyle (Eds.), *Pathways to belonging: Contemporary research in school belonging.* Brill | Sense.

Head, A. M, McGillivray, J. A., & Stokes, M. A. (2014). Gender differences in emotionality and sociability in children with autism spectrum disorders. *Molecular Autism, 5*(1), 19. doi:10.1186/2040-2392-5-19

Hertz-Picciotto, I., & Delwiche, L. (2009). The rise in autism and the role of age at diagnosis. *Epidemiology, 20*(1), 84–90. doi:10.1097/EDE.0b013e3181902d15

Holt, L., Lea, J., & Bowlby, S. (2012). Special units for young people on the autistic spectrum in mainstream schools: Sites of normalisation, abnormalisation, inclusion, and exclusion. *Environment and Planning A, 44*(9), 2191–2206.

Hong, N., Al-Khatib, D., Magagna, B. C, McLoughlin, A., & Coe, B. (1997). *Summary of systems theory*. Pennsylvania State University.

Howlin, P., Baron-Cohen, S., & Hadwin, J. (1999). *Teaching children with autism to mind-read*. Wiley.

Johns, B. D., Crowley, E. P., & Guetzloe, E. (2005). The central role of teaching social skills. *Focus on Exceptional Children, 37*(8).

Kaiser, A. P., & Hancock, T. B. (2003). Teaching parents new skills to support their young children's development. *Infants & Young Children, 16*(1), 9–21.

Kebapci, S., & Erkal, D. (2009). *Resistance to change a constructive approach for managing resistant behaviors* (Master thesis). Baltic Business School, Baltic Business School, University of Kalmar, Kalmar, Sweden.

Koegel, L., Matos-Fredeen, R., Lang, R., & Koegel, R. (2011). Interventions for children with autism spectrum disorders in inclusive school settings. *Cognitive and Behavioral Practice, 19*(3), 401–412.

Kösters, M. P., Chinapaw, M. J., Zwaanswijk, M., van der Wal, M. F., Utens, E. M., & Koot, D. M. (2012). Study design of 'Friends for Life': Process and effect evaluation of an indicated school-based prevention programme for childhood anxiety and depression. *BMC Public Health, 12*(1), 86. doi:10.1186/1471-2458-12-86

Kraska, J., & Boyle, C. (2014). Attitudes of pre-school and primary school pre-service teachers towards inclusive education. *Asia-Pacific Journal of Teacher Education, 42*(3), 228–246. doi:10.1080/1359866X.2014.926307

Laursen, E. K., & Yazdgerdi, S. (2012). Autism and belonging. *Reclaiming Children and Youth, 21*(2), 44–47.

Laushey, K. M., & Heflin, L. J. (2000). Enhancing social skills of kindergarten children with autism through the training of multiple peers as tutors. *Journal of Autism and Developmental Disorders, 30*, 183–193.

Leaf, R., & McEachin, J. (1999). *A work in progress: Behavior management strategies and a curriculum for intensive behavioral treatment of autism*. DRL Books.

Macbeath, J., Galton, M., Steward, S., Macbeath, A., & Page, C. (2006). *The costs of inclusion report prepared for the National Union of teachers*. Retrieved from https://www.educ.cam.ac.uk/people/staff/galton/Costs_of_Inclusion_Final.pdf

Matthews, N. L., Smith, C. J., Pollard, E., Ober-Reynolds, S., Kirwan, J., & Malligo, A. (2015). Adaptive functioning in autism spectrum disorder during the transition to adulthood. *Journal of Autism and Developmental Disorders, 45*(8), 2349–2360. doi:10.1007/s10803-015-2400-2

McMahon, C. M., Vismara, L. A., & Solomon, M. (2014). Measuring changes in social behavior during a social skills intervention for higher-functioning children and adolescents with autism spectrum disorder. *Journal of Autism and Developmental Disorders, 43*(8), 1843–1856. doi:10.1007/s10803-012-1733-3

Merrell, K., & Gimpel, G. (1998). *Social skills of children and adolescents.* Psychology Press.

Moharreri, F., & Yazdi, A. S. D. (2017). Evaluation of the effectiveness of the friends for life program on children's anxiety and depression. *Iranian Journal of Psychiatry, 12*(4), 272–280.

Ooi, K. L., Ong, D. S., Jacob S.A., & Khan, T. M. (2016). A meta-synthesis on parenting a child with autism. *Neuropsychiatric Disease and Treatment, 12*, 745–762. doi:10.2147/NDT.S100634

Paul, R. (2008). Interventions to improve communication. *Child and Adolescent Psychiatric Clinics of North America, 17*(4), 835–843. doi:10.1016/j.chc.2008.06.011

Petersen, L., & Adderley, A. (2002). *Stop think do social skills training: Primary years of schooling ages 8–12.* Nelson.

Pisula, E., Kawa, R., Danielewicz, D., & Pisula, D. (2015). The relationship between temperament and autistic traits in a non-clinical students sample. *PLoS ONE, 10*(4), e0124364. https://doi.org/10.1371/journal.pone.0124364

Plas, J. M. (1986). *Systems psychology in the schools.* Pergamon.

Pollock, S. (2019, in press). Literacy difficulties: What are learners' experiences? *Educational and Child Psychology, 36*(1).

Rimland, B., & Edelson, S. M. (1999). *Autism Treatment Evaluation Checklist (ATEC).* Retrieved from https://www.autism.org/autism-treatment-evaluation-checklist/

Roberts, J., & Simpson, K. (2016). A review of research into stakeholder perspectives on inclusion of students with autism in mainstream schools. *International Journal of Inclusive Education, 20*(10), 1084–1096.

Sayorwan, D., Phianchana, N., Permpoonputtana, K., & Siripornpanich, V. (2018). A study of the correlation between VEP and clinical severity in children with autism spectrum disorder. *Autism Research and Treatment.* https://doi.org/10.1155/2018/5093016

Sha'ked, A., & Rokach, A. (2015). *Addressing loneliness: Coping, prevention and clinical interventions* (3rd ed.). Routledge.

Simpson, R. L., Smith Myles, B., Sasso, G. M., & Kamps, D. M. (1991). *Social skills for students with autism.* The Council for Exceptional Children.

Soorya, L. V., Arnstein, L. M., Gillis, J., & Romanczyk, R. G. (2003). An overview of imitation skills in autism: Implications for practice. *The Behavior Analyst Today, 4*(2), 114–123. http://dx.doi.org/10.1037/h0100108

Spence, S. D. (2003). Social skills training with children and young people: Theory, evidence and practice. *Child and Adolescent Mental Health, 8*(2), 84–96.

Symes, D., & Humphrey, N. (2011). School factors that facilitate or hinder the ability of teaching assistants to effectively support pupils with Autism Spectrum Disorders (ASDs) in mainstream secondary schools. *Journal of Research in Special Educational Needs, 11*(3), 153–161.

The Autism Society of America. (2007). *Improving the lives of all affected by autism*. Retrieved from https://ectacenter.org/~pdfs/meetings/national2009/120809OSEP.pdf

The National Association of School Psychologists (NASP). (2007). *Social skills: Promoting positive behavior, academic success, and school safety*. Retrieved from https://www.naspcenter.org/factsheets/socialskills_fs.html

The National Autistic Society. (2007). *The right training for every teacher*. Author.

Tomanik, S., Harris, G. E., & Hawkins, J. (2004). The relationship between behaviours exhibited by children with autism and maternal stress. *Journal of Intellectual & Developmental Disability, 29*, 16–26.

UNESCO. (2001). *Understanding and responding to children's needs in inclusive classrooms: A guide for teachers*. Inclusive Education, Division of Basic Education; United Nations Educational, Scientific and Cultural Organization.

Watkins, L., Ledbetter-Cho, K., O'Reilly, M., Barnard-Brak, L., & Garcia-Grau, P. (2019). Interventions for students with autism in inclusive settings: A best-evidence synthesis and meta-analysis. *Psychological Bulletin, 145*(5), 490–507. doi:10.1037/bul0000190

Whitchurch, G. G., & Constantine, L. L. (2009). Systems theory. In P. Boss, W. J. Doherty, R. La Rossa, D. R. Schumm, & S. K. Steinmetz (Eds.), *Sourcebook of family theories and methods* (pp. 325–355). Springer.

White, S. D., Keonig, K., & Scahill, L. (2007). Social skills development in children with autism spectrum disorders: A review of the intervention research. *Journal of Autism and Developmental Disorders, 37*(10), 1858–1868. doi:10.1007/s10803-006-0320-x

Xiao, Z., Qiu, T., Ke, X., Xiao, X., Xiao, T., Liang, F., … Zhang, J. (2014). Autism spectrum disorder as early neurodevelopmental disorder: Evidence from the brain imaging abnormalities in 2–3 years old toddlers. *Journal of Autism and Developmental Disorders, 44*(7), 1633–1640. doi:10.1007/s10803-014-2033-x

Zainal, D., & Magiati, I. (2016). A comparison between caregiver-reported anxiety and other emotional and behavioral difficulties in children and adolescents with autism spectrum disorders attending specialist or mainstream schools. *Journal of Autism and Developmental Disorders, 49*(7), 2653–2663. doi:10.1007/s10803-016-2792-7

CHAPTER 13

An Inclusive Model of Targeted Literacy Teaching for 7–8-Year-Old Children Who Are Struggling to Learn to Read: The Integrated Group Reading (IGR) Approach

Brahm Norwich and George Koutsouris

1 Introduction

This chapter draws on the background thinking and research which has informed a current research project that has been evaluating an additional literacy teaching programme designed for 7–8-year-old children who are struggling to learn to read. The rationale for the chapter is to illustrate challenges and practices in inclusive teaching in a very important area of teaching and learning. The framework of thinking that informs the design of the Integrated Group Reading (IGR) approach is the wave model (Griffiths & Stuart, 2013; Rose, 2006). In its UK form the wave model distinguishes between wave 1 (or universal or *Quality First* teaching), wave 2 or targeted teaching and wave 3 specialist teaching. In its typical presentation and use, the model is unclear about important questions in relation to what characterises each wave and what their relationship is to each other. One of the key issues is to what extent wave 1 teaching is meant to be adapted or differentiated for the diversity of children in a class. Is wave 1 teaching meant to provide for children who struggle to learn to read, for example for more than a year, and whose reading is well below some notional average? It is widely assumed that wave 1 teaching differentiates to some degree for different rates and styles of learning, but if some children cross a cut-off (say, well below average attainment for a year) and move to wave 2 (targeted teaching) how is this to be organised? In targeted teaching, designed to be supplementary to wave 1 teaching, are the identified children also participating in wave 1 teaching? Or does wave 2 teaching become their main form of literacy teaching? Also, how does the kind of teaching of reading in wave 2 (in terms of assumptions about reading and how to learn to read) relate to the kind of teaching done in wave 1? And, who teaches the wave 2 identified children and where does this teaching take place?

 | DOI: 10.1163/9789004431171_013

In this chapter, we will focus more on the relationship between waves 1 and 2 than wave 3. We will consider these questions with respect to a particular form of inclusive targeted literacy teaching, the IGR approach, and in doing so examine issues about the wave model and the relationship between assumptions about inclusivity and where teaching takes place, who is involved and how. We will also consider curriculum questions about what is involved in learning to read and the deployment of teaching assistants (TA). The chapter is organised into three parts. The first part will summarise a review of recent international literature about current models of additional support in the context of reading teaching (or instruction, to use the US term). In the second part, we outline the IGR programme as an alternate model of inclusive provision, explaining the significance of the term 'integrated'. In the third and final part, we discuss the implications of the IGR approach for teaching the diversity of children who are struggling to learn to read in terms of what inclusive teaching means.

2 Current Models of Additional Support in the Context of Early Reading Teaching

2.1 *Literature Search Methods and Main Findings*

This section builds on the findings of a literature review that was conducted by the authors to explore the nature of additional support for children struggling to learn to read. The particular focus of the search was the delivery arrangements of early literacy interventions that have been evaluated systematically and reflect the current models of provision for pupils who struggle in their learning to read.

ERIC and BEI (and Google Scholar as a supplementary resource) were searched for reading-related literacy interventions published between 2006 and 2016. Studies were included only if they used an experimental (randomised control trials and quasi-experimental studies) or a pre- and post-test design and the sample was primary age struggling or delayed readers. Studies focusing on particular SEN categories were not included. We focused on school-based interventions and studies published in English.

Using these criteria, 29 studies were found, which were then categorised according to the levels of the wave model in the UK (Griffiths & Stuart, 2013; Rose, 2006) or the tier model in the US (Fuchs & Fuchs, 2006), also sometimes called the response to intervention (RTI) model. As mentioned above, the basic model describes most often three waves of support: *wave 1* whole class teaching (or *Quality First* to highlight that each child is entitled to quality teaching); *wave 2* additional (most often group) support for some pupils; and *wave 3* highly intensive and personalised intervention for a few pupils. In terms of the RTI model approach, the nature of teaching is expected to change at each wave to become more intensive, and this is achieved by: '(a) using more teacher-centred, systematic, and explicit instruction; (b) conducting it more frequently; (c) adding to its duration; (d) creating smaller and more homogenous student groupings; (e) relying on instructors with greater expertise' (Fuchs & Fuchs, 2006, p. 94).

From these 29 studies, seven were categorised as targeting wave 1, 11 studies wave 2 and nine wave 3 (the remaining two combined more than one wave). More specifically:

2.1.1 Wave 1

Seven studies evaluated reading interventions offered in whole class teaching with the aim to improve reading outcomes for all pupils. These interventions were delivered during whole class sessions by the class teacher (e.g. Boardman et al., 2016) or involved computer-based delivery (as for instance Shannon et al., 2015).

2.1.2 Wave 2

All 11 wave 2 interventions were delivered outside of the regular classroom sessions. The majority (seven out of 11 studies) were delivered by specially hired and trained instructors (most often non-regular school staff) (e.g. Vaughn et al., 2016; Wanzek & Roberts, 2012), or by special educational needs (SEN) teachers (Lovett et al., 2008) while the rest were computer-based. These interventions were delivered in addition to the wave 1 literacy teaching, outside of the regular class, and at a time that would not conflict with this teaching (Cirino et al., 2009; Ritchey et al., 2012). Torgesen et al. (2010), for example, wrote that 'none of the students were pulled out of the classroom when students were receiving reading instruction from their classroom teachers as a whole class' (p. 44). The examined wave 2 interventions were delivered by people other than the class teacher, thus it was seen as important to ensure that the pupils would be able to attend their wave 1 teacher-delivered whole classroom sessions.

2.1.3 Wave 3

Wave 3 interventions were delivered one-to-one, and mostly in a way similar to the wave 2 interventions (in addition to core teaching, and out of the regular literacy sessions). Ardoin et al. (2016) notes in relation to this that 'to ensure that intervention was supplementary (i.e., additional to typical instruction), sessions took place during teacher-selected intervals in which students were not receiving reading/language arts instruction. Specifically, sessions generally occurred in the morning prior to the official start of the school day or during morning announcements' (p. 20). Wave 3 interventions were delivered by a combination of specially trained tutors, SEN teachers and TAs (there was also a computer-based intervention). As the majority of the UK-based studies (four out of five studies) were targeting wave 3, a pattern emerged: with reference to the people responsible for delivering the intervention, most UK-based studies (three out of four studies) used TAs (regular school staff), whereas specially hired and trained tutors (most likely non-regular school staff) were only used in US-based studies. From the remaining wave 3 interventions, one from Netherlands used TAs and another from Sweden, SEN teachers. This, and especially the US/UK difference, seems to reflect cultural differences in delivery arrangements for school-based interventions across contexts.

2.2 *The Current Model of Providing Additional Support*

Waves 2 and 3 interventions not involving computer-based delivery were all administered in addition to the wave 1 teaching in withdrawal sessions run by people other than the class teacher (TAs, trained tutors or SEN teachers). The people responsible for teaching wave 2 and 3 interventions were either regular school staff (most likely in the UK) or specially recruited (most likely in the US). By using regular school staff such as TAs to deliver an intervention (the model mostly used in the UK) (as in See et al., 2015; Clarke et al., 2010; Duff et al., 2008; Hatcher et al., 2006), schools were making a long-term investment. This is because most TA-delivered intervention programmes included training, meaning that the schools would be able to continue using the intervention in the long term if they wished to. By contrast, all US studies that did not involve computer-based delivery used some form of specially hired tutors to deliver interventions targeting wave 2 or 3 (for example Vaughn et al., 2016; Fien et al., 2015). It is likely in a research context that this approach would be considered preferable, as it allowed US researchers to have better control over fidelity of intervention implementation. Cirino et al. (2009), for example, highlighted in relation to the trained tutors who delivered a wave 3 intervention: 'ratings of tutors were found to have adequate validity, and tutors were found to exhibit a high degree of adherence to positive instructional practices (e.g., materials were ready, high instructor enthusiasm, consistent redirection of off-task behavior)' (p. 762). This level of control might not be achievable in the UK-based studies where interventions were delivered by regular school staff (teachers or TAs) as part of a demanding school timetable. Yet, with the US model, schools might find it difficult to continue to use an intervention after a trial has finished, since regular class teachers would not have knowledge and experience of its delivery.

2.3 *The Over-Reliance on TAs*

So, using regular school staff to deliver an intervention can offer certain advantages. However, the use of pull-out sessions and a reliance on people other than the classroom teacher (such as TAs) to provide extra support can invite 'a separation effect' (EEF, 2015, p. 15), with certain pupils spending considerably less time with the teacher and having fewer opportunities for peer interaction. The Making a Statement (MaSt) study (Webster & Blatchford, 2013), designed to explore the teaching, support and interactions experienced by pupils with statements of Special Educational Needs (SEN), found that the educational experiences of pupils holding a statement was characterised by a high degree of separation and TA support:

> Compared to average attaining pupils, statemented pupils experienced less time in whole class contexts and a much higher degree of one-to-one interaction with TAs – often at the expense of interactions with teachers and peers. (Webster & Blatchford, 2013, p. 2)

The result of this practice is that TAs can have more responsibility than class teachers for pupils with SEN statements. Therefore these pupils are likely to receive a less appropriate and lower quality pedagogic experience – for example, the Deployment and Impact of Support Staff (DISS) found that that the more support pupils received from support staff (including TAs), the less progress they made (Blatchford & Webster, 2014). Though there is a risk of over-generalising this study to situations where appropriate support is provided by TAs, such a finding is not surprising if additional support involves inadequately trained and supported TAs and a lack of on-going class teacher involvement (as the literature discussed earlier indicates). Though the above review of school-based interventions might involve the adequate training of TAs or tutors, the current model of evaluated support is still based on pull-out sessions which do not involve class teachers in teaching those children who are struggling in their literacy.

2.4 *Teaching Differentiation in Quality First*

This review and discussion also raises the question of whether *Quality First* wave 1 programmes are sufficiently differentiated for those struggling to learn, and why it is that programmes at wave 2 or 3 are offered as supplementary programmes. When *Quality First* provision does not necessarily offer sufficient differentiation, lesson attendance could be seen as learning time lost for those who are struggling. Though there has not been much research on this topic, a US study by Al Otaiba et al. (2014) found that children who had immediate access to wave 2 and 3, rather than a wait of eight weeks within typical RTI procedures before receiving support, had improved reading outcomes at the end of first grade (Year 1 in UK). But, even in the model of this study, as in the other reviewed studies, wave 2/3 support is delivered as supplementary teaching, often done outside the regular class and/or by someone other than the class teacher. Is it possible for children in need of more targeted wave 2 teaching to receive this in a regular class setting during wave 1 teaching and be taught by the class teacher? What organisational arrangements would make this possible and how would TAs be deployed to support such an arrangement?

3 The IGR Programme as an Alternate Model of Inclusive Provision

The IGR programme was designed and developed in response to these ongoing issues. It is an early intervention for delayed Year 2 and 3 readers (Stebbing, 2016) which attempts to provide wave 2 targeted teaching in a regular class setting during wave 1 teaching, taught by the class teacher and supported by a TA. By using a whole class group reading organisation model, the programme enables the teacher to support those children struggling to learn to read in the regular class and attempts to address an overreliance on pull-out sessions and TA support.

The programme provides teachers with a core set of story-based materials (a set of 52 short books with accompanying story-specific games and supplementary phonics games), and a language-based methodology and lesson structure which teachers deliver on a twice-weekly basis in the classroom. In between the teacher-led IGR lessons there are in addition two highly structured TA-led one-to-one consolidation sessions for the children.

The IGR programme is 'integrated' in two key senses of the term: integrated in IGR refers not only to the inclusive aspect of the classroom-based organisation but also to the integration of several discrete research-informed teaching approaches that underpin and justify its methodology, as we will discuss below.

3.1 *IGR Organisation and Relevance to Schools*

Not only does the teacher have the main role in teaching the wave 2 IGR programme (rather than the TA, as is frequently found), but IGR with its teacher and TA sessions takes the place of typical wave 1 provision for those most struggling with reading in the class. IGR adopts a group reading model of classroom organisation (influenced by Guided Reading discussed in the next section) where a class is organised into several groups (four-five), one of which is the IGR group. The intensity of this wave 2 teaching is achieved through four

30-minute sessions each week (two with the teacher and two with the TA) as part of the usual group reading organisation for all pupils. After initial screening using a teacher scoring scale, three to four pupils who would benefit from literacy support are selected to form an IGR reading group. The teacher teaches the IGR group twice a week using the programme materials and a structured teaching routine. The TA works with the group in-between the teacher sessions for consolidation, also using the programme materials and a TA-specific routine. Teacher and TAs have very discrete roles, with the teacher preserving the main role. Teachers and TAs communicate regarding the fine detail of IGR pupils' reading progress or difficulties on a daily basis, using a Teacher-TA Daily Record book. In this way, IGR is designed to be part of the usual group reading schedule but it also allows teachers to organise their group reading rota in a more structured and efficient way for all the pupils in the class. It also enables them to teach each group at least once a week while working twice a week with the IGR group. During teacher-led IGR, the rest of the classroom works with the support of a TA on well-planned and structured group reading-related activities (such as independent reading, comprehension tasks, dictionary work, and computer literacy programmes).

As discussed, this organisation model stands in contrast to many of the evaluated wave 2 intervention programmes where a TA or a specially hired tutor has the main teaching role. With IGR organisation, the role of the TA is an integral aspect of the programme but follows on in a clearly specified way from the work of the teacher.

3.2 *Beyond Guided Reading*

Guided Reading can be a useful context for the teaching of early reading (Iaquinta, 2006), yet other research suggests that teachers are often confused about its purposes (Ford & Opitz, 2008). It might also be argued that the purposes and strategies of Guided Reading might be less relevant to pupils who are still in the early stages of learning to read.

The focus and aim of Guided Reading has been interpreted to be the development and cultivation of self-monitoring and independence in reading (NLS, 1998; Pinnell & Fountas, 2010), often meaning that books or parts of books are introduced to the children with the aim of ensuring maximum levels of text comprehension (and the teacher assuming the role of guide/inquisitor). Such an approach can mean that there is little time for reading itself, which in this context is not the main aim of the lesson. By contrast, the IGR programme is a self-contained learning-to-read programme with its own materials and story- and play-based methodology, with the teacher as participant/leader. IGR helps teachers proceed in a systematic and very gradual way with pre-literate children needing to make progress in a step-by-step way. In other words, IGR is for pupils who have not yet mastered reading, whereas Guided Reading focuses on the development of comprehension strategies and complex text exploration with pupils who have reached the stage of being relatively independent as readers.

3.3 *Systematic Integration of Current Approaches to Reading*

As indicated above, the second key sense of 'integrated' in IGR is the systematic integration of current research evidence on the teaching of reading that informs and underpins its programme design.

3.3.1 Phonics teaching

Substantial recent research shows that phonics teaching is not only the most examined teaching approach, but the one with the greatest efficacy for reading and spelling gains (for example Galuschka et al., 2014; Torgerson et al., 2006). However, the efficacy of different phonics approaches is still debated (Henbest & Apel, 2017). A number of studies consistently report no difference between synthetic and analytic phonics (Di Stasio et al., 2012; Ehri et al., 2001; Kyle et al., 2013), yet there are few studies supporting a difference (synthetic over analytic phonics: Christensen & Bowey, 2005; Johnston & Watson, 2004; and analytic over synthetic: Walton et al., 2001). The IGR programme adopts a mainly analytic phonics component based on onset and rhyme, but it is currently being developed to also include story-specific synthetic phonics activities.

In addition, IGR incorporates the support of phonic skill development within a comprehensive, story-based approach. It exists in a context of UK national 'one way only' synthetic phonics teaching but seeks to offer children who have proved unresponsive to this teaching a whole-to-parts route to reading where synthetic phonics becomes meaning-based and 'a posteriori' as well as an 'a priori' route to word learning. It is also open to whatever lessons are learned in its application and is designed to respond and adapt to new research findings (such as the importance of the explicit teaching of phonics). For example, *Reading Recovery* has been criticised by some commentators (such as Reynolds & Wheldall, 2007) who have an issue with programmes that have been trademarked and become more difficult to subsequently change.

3.3.2 Oral Language Skills

In addition, early progress in reading has been shown to depend on children's oral language skills (Bowyer-Crane et al., 2008; Clarke et al., 2010; Nation & Snowling, 2004). For example, Clarke et al. (2010) found that in a comparison between three treatment groups, an oral language training treatment group made better gains in reading comprehension from the end of the intervention to an eleven-month follow-up. They concluded that difficulties in reading comprehension partly reflect underlying oral language weaknesses calling for suitable teaching. Bowyer-Crane et al. (2008) also found that oral language training programmes can improve vocabulary and grammatical skills.

IGR also has a strong story-telling aspect aiming to enable the development of children's oral skills. Story-telling has particularly been explored as a way to promote language and literacy development, especially in the early years, with various study designs (Dickinson & Smith, 1994; Isbell et al., 2004; Peck, 1989; Sulzby, 1985; Valencia & Sulzby, 1991).

3.3.3 Word Games

Research shows that word games can support the reading skills and engagement of children who struggle to learn to read (Raffaele Mendez et al., 2016; Jasmine & Schiesl, 2009; Charlton et al., 2005). For instance, Raffaele Mendez et al. (2016) report significant pre- and post-test gains for a reading intervention named *Reading by Design* that involves board games to practice sight words and word attack skills, and foster engagement. In addition, Charlton et al. (2005) found that games can accelerate learning when they are combined with teacher instruction. IGR includes four reading games, each with a distinct pedagogic role (overlearning consolidation at the level of word and sentence, phonics practice, and advance organisation at the level of unfamiliar vocabulary).

3.3.4 Elements Associated with Reading Recovery

The importance of detailed responses to reading in small group as well as one-to-one contexts, and the monitoring of reading over time are elements that are associated with *Reading Recovery* (Clay, 1994; Doyle, 2013; What Works Clearinghouse, 2013). Clay (2001) argued that teachers can foster and support active constructive problem-solving through the regular monitoring of reading; self-monitoring, and self-correction from the first lesson, are also emphasised, to help learners understand that they must take over the expansion of their own competencies. Like *Reading Recovery*, IGR operates by engaging children at the cognitive level through word and phrase game-playing dynamics and group reading, encouraging collaborative problem solving, and enabling teachers to monitor progress closely.

3.3.5 Elements Associated with Paired Reading (PR)

A key element of the IGR approach to small group reading is its collaborative approach to reading and problem solving with the teacher as leader/participant. Experience from *Paired Reading* (*PR*) suggests that this is a valuable approach (Miller et al., 2010; Topping et al., 2011; Topping, 2014;

Topping & Lindsay, 1992). Topping (2014) describes the *PR* method as 'a form of supported oral reading which enables students to access and comprehend texts somewhat above their independent readability level [...] This structured support used with high motivation texts offers dysfluent readers a flow experience, which is likely to impact on their reading style and socio-emotional aspects of the reading process' (p. 59). Topping et al. (2011) report significant gains from a randomised control trial exploring *PR* in reading and self-esteem measures. Miller et al. (2010) also found significant gains in self-esteem using a pre-and post-test design.

The delivery of structured, teacher-led supported oral reading in IGR groups of four children (group not too big for personalised support, but not too small to allow for whole class teacher-led delivery) contrasts with intervention programmes of similar intensity that have mainly a one-to-one focus (Brooks, 2016). This aspect of the design of the IGR programme can be seen in the context of the Elbaum et al. (2000) meta-analysis finding that comparing one-to-one with small-group supplemental instruction showed no advantage for the one-to-one programmes.

In sum, the IGR programme responds to some of the key contemporary challenges in teaching early literacy to a diversity of pupils in primary classrooms and addresses/includes evidence-based strategies as integral in its design. Using the guided or group organisational model it enables children who are significantly delayed in learning to read (selected by their teacher or standardised assessment as reading below their classmates) to engage in an intensive programme geared to their needs in a wave 1 teaching setting (*wave 2 programme integrated into a wave 1 setting*). It does not expose these children to a wave 1 programme that might not suit their learning needs and give them additional teaching at wave 2 as a supplementary programme, often taught by a TA. IGR is taught by the teacher and the TA complements rather than substitutes for the class teacher. As an intensive group-based programme it is based on research informed principles and practices (*research-informed principles integrated into teaching practice*).

4 Implications of IGR for Inclusive Teaching

In the final section we consider to what extent and in what ways the IGR approach is an inclusive teaching approach. To answer this question, we will start by considering what is meant by inclusive education and teaching. For the purposes of this chapter we will analyse two positions that illustrate the perspective we adopt. The first comes from the Salamanca Statement (UNESCO, 1994) which said of inclusive education that it is: 'All children learning together, *wherever possible*, regardless of any difficulties or difference they have' (Salamanca Statement. UNESCO, 1994). The second is a more recent statement about inclusive pedagogy which is defined as: 'An approach to teaching and learning that supports teachers to respond to individual differences between learners, *but avoids* marginalisation' (Black-Hawkins & Florian, 2012).

Based on these statements, inclusive teaching is about togetherness in learning and responding to individual differences. Yet, both statements in their own way involve qualifications. In the Salamanca Statement it is 'wherever possible', implying that there might be some limits to togetherness. In the second statement, responding to individual differences has to be in a way that 'avoids marginalisation'. We suggest that possible limits to togetherness might be the value of responding to individual differences, on one hand, and that recognising differences, or what is commonly called differentiation, has the potential to be enabling and stigmatising (marginalising). We interpret the above statements as pointing to a dilemma or a balance of risks about how to respond to difference/differentiation. This is the *dilemma of difference* perspective on inclusive teaching (Norwich, 2014) which recognises that teaching involves trying to achieve several values, such as responding to individual differences (or needs) and being positive and respectful of learners (not marginalising or devaluing). When these values clash there are dilemmas that require a balancing of risks; so, though the aim is to have it 'all ways' there may be limits which are to do with the tension between values (responding to differences/needs and avoiding marginalisation). This balancing of risks involves finding creative ways to resolve the tension, something which will depend on both context and resources.

One way to examine whether the IGR programme achieves inclusive teaching and how it deals with dilemmas of difference is to examine IGR in terms of a contemporary perspective of inclusive pedagogy – *Inclusive pedagogical approach in action* (Florian & Black-Hawkins, 2011). This approach to inclusive pedagogy makes two key assumptions: that difference is part of the human condition and all children can make progress in their learning; and that there is a commitment to support all learners while rejecting that the presence of some holds back others. Regarding teachers' beliefs, it is also assumed that teachers are capable of teaching all learners and this involves replacing a 'fixed view' of 'ability' with an open-ended learning potential perspective. When translated into an approach in action, these authors identify several key practical principles:

– Making learning opportunities for *all* to participate in classroom life

- Extending what is ordinarily available for all; rather than learning activities for *most* alongside additional/different activities for *some* who experience difficulties
- Differentiation by pupil choice for everyone and rejection of ability grouping
- A flexible approach is required driven by needs of learner rather than by curriculum coverage
- Seeing difficulties in learning as professional challenges rather than learner deficits

It is possible to criticise these principles as overly fixed and prescriptive and also as tending to identify false oppositions. For example; here are some questions about these inclusive teaching principles: (i) 'differentiation by pupil choice' – is there a place for pupil choice and teacher determination? (ii) 'reject ability grouping' – are there no benefits to temporary subject ability grouping? (iii) 'seeing difficulties ... as professional challenges' – can some difficulties related to persistent child factors still be considered professional challenges? Nevertheless, these inclusive pedagogic principles are a useful basis for examining the inclusivity of the IGR approach, since they represent important values (such as respect for all, placing the learner first, believing that all learners can progress) that can however be translated into different pedagogical approaches/decisions.

In relation to these principles, IGR is designed to make opportunities to learn to read open to children struggling to read in a class and to do so through participating in a group or guided reading classroom organisation model. It can also be seen to extend the teaching of reading to those who are struggling to read in Years 2 and 3 into a wave 1 setting. The teaching approach used in IGR has been designed using research-informed principles and strategies based on a combination of approaches to reading (as discussed earlier) including phonics, as opposed to phonics-only approaches, i.e. the approach to reading used most often with children in years 2 and 3 in England (Rose, 2006).

The IGR approach and materials can be used with other groups to the extent that they are relevant to them (e.g. phonics games), not just with those most struggling with reading. Using IGR materials more broadly can address the issue that there is a continuum of progress in learning to read and some children might benefit from using elements of an IGR approach even if they do not need the full programme. This flexibility of IGR shows that the supposed dichotomy between 'extend what is ordinarily available for all' and 'learning activities for *most*' alongside 'different activities for some' is a false distinction.

Furthermore, IGR is clearly based on current reading ability grouping in the group organisation model, but in practice there can be flexibility in how children are grouped depending on how they respond to teaching. Nor is there an assumption in IGR that children cannot learn to read and nor is there a 'fixed' view about ability. In grouping children and using a particular set of materials that are visibly different from those used with other children, there is a risk that these children will be marked out as different and possibly seen as marginal and so devalued by others. However, given that the teacher in the IGR approach rotates around all class reading groups, this not only gives struggling readers the privilege of being taught by their teacher, but could also serve to 'normalise' wave 2 intensive teaching programmes. Whether there is any devaluation in the IGR approach is an empirical matter and will depend on how IGR is implemented; it is not something to be decided in advance by overly prescriptive 'inclusive pedagogy' principles.

Finally, as IGR involves teachers who take the lead in teaching those who struggle most in learning to read, such a teaching approach also supports teachers themselves in their continuing professional development. This in turn can result in wider gains for other children in their classes. Professional challenge is not the opposite of recognising the presence of learner difficulties. The IGR programme is also a flexible approach in being driven by monitoring the responses of children in groups of four, while also being driven by a particular curriculum model of learning to read and a corresponding tightly sequenced range of learning activities (reading stories, collaborative problem-solving, word games, drawing, etc.) which are research-informed. As stated, 'driven by needs of learner rather than by curriculum coverage' is a false opposition, in the sense that curriculum can be flexible (as in the case of IGR) to adjust to learner needs.

5 Conclusion

This chapter has been about the principles, theory and research underlying the IGR approach. To what extent IGR can be an inclusive approach to wave 2 early reading teaching is partly an empirical matter, the results of which will be reported in other papers at the end of the evaluation project. Questions such as these and many others – whether IGR teachers accept responsibility for teaching all pupils; in what way can a class management model involve the work of TAs; whether the IGR group having teaching in usual lesson time affect the way children and parents feel about visibility in a 'struggling readers' group – will be answered through the evaluation of the IGR programme (main project report: Norwich et al., 2018). Whatever the answers, it will still be evident that the issues raised by an IGR type approach will continue to challenge future theory and practice about general and additional teaching that will have a bearing on the future of inclusive teaching.

References

Al Otaiba, S., Connor, C. M., Folsom, J. S., Wanzek, J., Greulich, L., Schatschneider, C., & Wagner, R. K. (2014). To wait in tier 1 or intervene immediately: A randomized experiment examining first-grade response to intervention in reading. *Exceptional Children, 81*(1), 11–27.

Ardoin, S. P., Binder, K. S., Foster, T. E., & Zawoyski, A. M. (2016). Repeated versus wide reading: A randomized control design study examining the impact of fluency interventions on underlying reading behavior. *Journal of School Psychology, 59*, 13–38.

Blatchford, P., & Webster, R. (2014). *Support staff: The role and effective deployment of teaching assistants in schools in England and Wales* (IOE Research Briefing No. 88). IOE.

Boardman, A. G., Vaughn, S., Buckley, P., Reutebuch, C., Roberts, G., & Klingner, J. (2016). Collaborative strategic reading for students with learning disabilities in upper elementary classrooms. *Exceptional Children, 82*(4), 409–427.

Bowyer-Crane, C., Snowling, M. J., Duff, F. J., Fieldsend, E., Carroll, J. M., Miles, J., Götz, K., & Hulme, C. (2008). Improving early language and literacy skills: Differential effects of an oral language versus a phonology with reading intervention. *Journal of Child Psychology and Psychiatry, 49*(4), 422–432.

Brooks, G. (2016). *What works for pupils with literacy difficulties: The effectiveness of intervention schemes* (5th ed.). The Dyslexia-SpLD Trust.

Charlton, B., Williams, R. L., & McLaughlin, T. F. (2005). Educational games: A technique to accelerate the acquisition of reading skills of children with learning disabilities. *International Journal of Special Education, 20*(2), 66–72.

Christensen, C. A., & Bowey, J. A. (2005). The efficacy of orthographic rime, grapheme–phoneme correspondence, and implicit phonics approaches to teaching decoding skills. *Scientific Studies of Reading, 9*(4), 327–349.

Cirino, P. T., Vaughn, S., Linan-Thompson, S., Cardenas-Hagan, E., Fletcher, J. M., & Francis, D. J. (2009). One-year follow-up outcomes of spanish and english interventions for English language learners at risk for reading problems. *American Educational Research Journal, 46*(3), 744–781.

Clarke, P. J., Snowling, M. J., Truelove, E., & Hulme, C. (2010). Ameliorating children's reading-comprehension difficulties: A randomized controlled trial. *Psychological Science, 21*(8), 1106–1116.

Clay, M. M. (1994). Reading recovery: The wider implications of an educational innovation. *Literacy, Teaching and Learning, 1*(1), 121–141.

Dickinson, D. K., & Smith, M. D. (1994). Long-term effects of preschool teachers' book readings on low-income children's vocabulary and story comprehension. *Reading Research Quarterly, 29*(2), 105–122.

Di Stasio, M. R., Savage, R., & Abrami, P. C. (2010). A follow-up study of the ABRACADABRA web-based literacy intervention in grade 1: ABRACADABRA: A follow-up study. *Journal of Research in Reading, 35*(1), 69–86.

Doyle, M. A. (2013). Marie M. Clay's theoretical perspective: A literacy processing theory. In D. E. Alvermann, N. J. Unrau, & R. B. Ruddell (Eds.), *Theoretical models and processes of reading*. International Reading Association.

Duff, F. J., Fieldsend, E., Bowyer-Crane, C., Hulme, C., Smith, G., Gibbs, S., & Snowling, M. J. (2008). Reading with vocabulary intervention: Evaluation of an instruction for children with poor response to reading intervention. *Journal of Research in Reading, 31*(3), 319–336.

EEF. (2015). *Making best use of teaching assistants: Guidance report*. EEF.

Ehri, L. C., Nunes, S. R., Stahl, S. A., & Willows, D. M. (2001). Systematic phonics instruction helps students learn to read: Evidence from the national reading panel's meta-analysis. *Review of Educational Research, 71*(3), 393–447.

Elbaum, B., Vaughn, S., Tejero Hughes, M., & Watson Moody, S. (2000). How effective are one-to-one tutoring programs in reading for elementary students at risk for reading failure? A meta-analysis of the intervention research. *Journal of Educational Psychology, 92*(4), 605–619.

Fien, D., Smith, J. L. M., Smolkowski, K., Baker, S. K., Nelson, N. J., & Chaparro, E. (2015). An examination of the efficacy of a multitiered intervention on early reading outcomes for first grade students at risk for reading difficulties. *Journal of Learning Disabilities, 48*(6), 602–621.

Florian, L., & Black-Hawkins, K. (2011). Exploring inclusive pedagogy. *British Educational Research Journal, 37*(5), 813–828.

Ford, M. P., & Opitz, M. F. (2008). A national survey of guided reading practices: What we can learn from primary teachers. *Literacy Research and Instruction, 47*(4), 309–331.

Fuchs, D., & Fuchs, L. S. (2006). Introduction to response to intervention: What, why, and how valid is it? *Reading Research Quarterly, 41*(1), 93–99.

Galuschka, K., Ise, E., Krick, K., & Schulte-Körne, G. (2014). Effectiveness of treatment approaches for children and adolescents with reading disabilities: A meta-analysis of randomized controlled trials. *PLoS ONE, 9*(2), e89900.

Griffiths, D., & Stuart, M. (2013). Reviewing evidence-based practice for pupils with dyslexia and literacy difficulties. *Journal of Research in Reading, 36*(1), 96–116.

Hatcher, P. J., Hulme, C., Miles, J. N. V., Carroll, J. M., Hatcher, J., Gibbs, S., Smith, G., Bowyer-Crane, C., & Snowling, M. J. (2006). Efficacy of small group reading intervention for beginning readers with reading-delay: A randomised controlled trial: Efficacy of small group reading intervention. *Journal of Child Psychology and Psychiatry, 47*(8), 820–827.

Henbest, V. S., & Apel, K. (2017). Effective word reading instruction: What does the evidence tell us? *Communication Disorders Quarterly, 18*, 1–9.

Iaquinta, A. (2006). Guided reading: A research-based response to the challenges of early reading instruction. *Early Childhood Education Journal, 33*(6), 413–418.

Isbell, R., Sobol, J., Lindauer, L., & Lowrance, A. (2004). The effects of storytelling and story reading on the oral language complexity and story comprehension of young children. *Early Childhood Education Journal, 32*(3), 157–163.

Jaeger, E. L. (2016). Intensity of focus, richness of content: Crafting tier 2 response to intervention in an era of the common core. *The Reading Teacher, 70*(2), 179–188.

Jasmine, J., & Schiesl, P. (2009). The effects of word walls and word wall activities on the reading fluency of first grade students. *Reading Horizons; Kalamazoo, 49*(4), 301–314.

Johnston, R. S., & Watson, J. E. (2004). Accelerating the development of reading, spelling and phonemic awareness skills in initial readers. *Reading and Writing, 17*(4), 327–357.

Kyle, F., Kujala, J., Richardson, U., Lyytinen, D., & Goswami, U. (2013). Assessing the effectiveness of two theoretically motivated computer-assisted reading interventions in the United Kingdom: GG rime and GG phoneme. *Reading Research Quarterly, 48*(1), 61–76.

Lovett, M. D., De Palma, M., Frijters, J., Steinbach, K., Temple, M., Benson, N., & Lacerenza, L. (2008). Interventions for reading difficulties: A comparison of response to intervention by ELL and EFL struggling readers. *Journal of Learning Disabilities, 41*(4), 333–352.

Miller, D., Topping, K., & Thurston, A. (2010). Peer tutoring in reading: The effects of role and organization on two dimensions of self-esteem. *British Journal of Educational Psychology, 80*(3), 417–433.

Nation, K., & Snowling, M. J. (2004). Beyond phonological skills: Broader language skills contribute to the development of reading. *Journal of Research in Reading, 27*(4), 342–356.

NLS. (1998). *National literacy strategies: Framework for teaching*. DfEE.

Norwich, B. (2014). *Addressing tensions and dilemmas in inclusive education: Living with uncertainty*. Routledge.

Norwich, B., Koutsouris, G., & Bessudnov, A. (2018). *An innovative classroom reading intervention for year 2 and 3 pupils who are struggling to learn to read: Evaluating the Integrated Group Reading (IGR) programme – Project report*. Retrieved from http://www.integratedgroupreading.co.uk

Peck, J. (1989). Using storytelling to promote language and literacy development. *The Reading Teacher, 43*(2), 138–141.

Pinnell, G. S., & Fountas, I. C. (2010). *Research base for guided reading as an instructional approach*. Scholastic.com.

Raffaele Mendez, L. M., Pelzmann, C. A., & Frank, M. J. (2016). Engaging struggling early readers to promote reading success: A pilot study of reading by design. *Reading & Writing Quarterly, 32*(3), 273–297.

Reynolds, M., & Wheldall, K. (2007). Reading Recovery 20 years down the track: Looking forward, looking back. International Journal of Disability, Development and Education, *54*(2), 199–223.

Ritchey, K. D., Silverman, R. D., Montanaro, E. A., Speece, D. L., & Schatschneider, C. (2012). Effects of a tier 2 supplemental reading intervention for at-risk fourth-grade students. *Exceptional Children, 78*(3), 318–334.

Rose, J. (2006). *Independent review of the teaching of early reading: Interim report.* DFES.

See, B. D., Gorard, S., & Siddiqui, N. (2015). Best practice in conducting RCTs: Lessons learnt from an independent evaluation of the response-to-intervention programme. *Studies in Educational Evaluation, 47*, 83–92.

Shannon, L. C., Styers, M. K., Wilkerson, S. B., & Peery, E. (2015). Computer-assisted learning in elementary reading: A randomized control trial. *Computers in the Schools, 32*(1), 20–34.

Stebbing, J. (2016). *Integrated group reading project website.* Retrieved January 20, 2017, from http://www.integratedgroupreading.co.uk

Sulzby, E. (1985). Children's emergent reading of favorite storybooks: A developmental study. *Reading Research Quarterly, 20*(4), 458–481.

Torgerson, C., Brooks, G., & Hall, J. (2006). *A systematic review of the research literature on the use of phonics in the teaching of reading and spelling.* DfES Publications.

Torgesen, J. K., Wagner, R. K., Rashotte, C. A., Herron, J., & Lindamood, P. (2010). Computer-assisted instruction to prevent early reading difficulties in students at risk for dyslexia: Outcomes from two instructional approaches. *Annals of Dyslexia, 60*(1), 40–56.

Vaughn, S., Solís, M., Miciak, J., Taylor, D. P., & Fletcher, J. M. (2016). Effects from a randomized control trial comparing researcher and school-implemented treatments with fourth graders with significant reading difficulties. *Journal of Research on Educational Effectiveness, 9*(Suppl. 1), 23–44.

Topping, K. J. (2014). Paired reading and related methods for improving fluency. *International Electronic Journal of Elementary Education; Kutahya, 7*(1), 57–69.

Topping, K. J., & Lindsay, G. A. (1992). Paired reading: A review of the literature. *Research Papers in Education, 7*(3), 199–246.

Topping, K. J., Miller, D., Thurston, A., McGavock, K., & Conlin, N. (2011). Peer tutoring in reading in Scotland: Thinking big: Peer tutoring in reading. *Literacy, 45*(1), 3–9.

UNESCO. (1994, June 7–10). *The Salamanca statement and framework for action on special needs education: Adopted by the world conference on special needs education; Access and quality.* UNESCO, Salamanca, Spain.

Valencia, S. D., & Sulzby, E. (1991). Assessment: Assessment of emergent literacy: Storybook reading. *The Reading Teacher, 44*(7), 498–500.

Walton, P. D., Walton, L. M., & Felton, K. (2001). Teaching rime analogy or letter recoding reading strategies to prereaders: Effects on prereading skills and word reading. *Journal of Educational Psychology, 93*(1), 160–180.

Wanzek, J., & Roberts, G. (2012). Reading interventions with varying instructional emphases for fourth graders with reading difficulties. *Learning Disability Quarterly, 35*(2), 90–101.

Webster, R., & Blatchford, P. (2014). *The making a statement project: Final report.* IOE.

What Works Clearinghouse. (2013). *Updated intervention report: Reading recovery.* U.S. Department of Education, Institute of Education Sciences.

CHAPTER 14

Understanding Issues in Inclusive Education in the Basque Country

Zuriñe Gaintza, Leire Darretxe and Christopher Boyle

1 Introduction

Promoting school diversity is a goal shared by many countries, but actually achieving this goal in the day-to-day lesson is often difficult to do and each country attempts to achieve this goal by different means. Having reviewed features of the Basque Country and its educational system, this chapter describes how this region of Europe is able to respond to the diversity of students in an inclusive way. Firstly, the evolution of the laws which make inclusion possible is considered; and secondly, the wide range of measures that can be applied in order to cater for the needs of students in the environment of mainstream education is analysed. Although there may be some aspects which can be improved, the data referred to in this chapter demonstrates the success of the Basque Educational system which is able to give an inclusive response to student diversity.

2 Euskal Herria

In order to understand education and moreover inclusive education in the Basque Country, it is important to have an overview of this semi-autonomous region of Spain. According to Collins (1990) and Watson (2003), the Basque Country or in the Basque language, Euskal Herria, is a region in the western Pyrenees that spans the Spanish-French border. The northern part, under French administrative control, is made up of the territories of Labourd, Lower Navarre and Soule, which forms part of the Department of Pyrénées Atlantiques. The southern part of the Basque Country (within the Spanish border) is made up of the provinces of Vizcaya, Guipúzcoa, Álava and Navarra. It is only Vizcaya, Guipúzcoa, and Álava which constitute the autonomous region of Euskadi (Mansvelt, 2005). In this chapter, the term Basque Country refers to these three provinces.

In 1979, as a result of the Statute known colloquially as the Statute of Gernika, the Basque Country gained a level of self-government, becoming an autonomous community within Spain, and today it has, amongst other things,

 | DOI: 10.1163/9789004431171_014

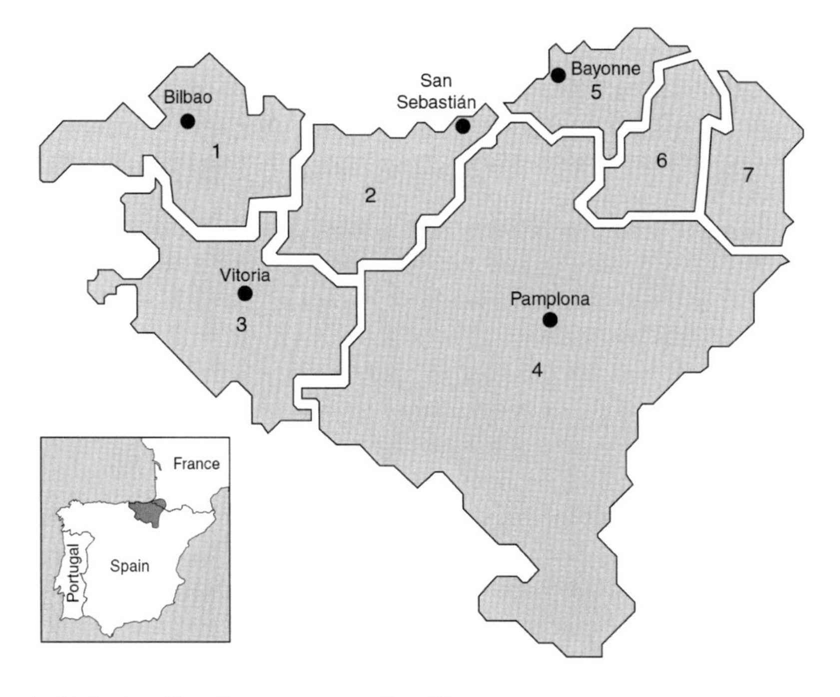

1 + 2 + 3 + 4	Hegoalde	*Hegoalde*
1 + 2 + 3	Euskadi	
5 + 6 + 7	French Basque Country	*Iparralde*
1	Vizcaya	*Bizkaia*
2	Guipúzcoa	*Gipuzkoa*
3	Álava	*Araba*
4	Navarra	*Nafarroa*
5	Labourd	*Lapurdi*
6	Lower Navarre	*Nafarroa Beheroa*
7	Soule	*Zuberoa*

FIGURE 14.1 Euskal Herria: regions and important towns (from Mansvelt, 2005, p. 3)

its own tax, health, police and education systems. However, in all these areas, Spanish laws must be implemented and can then be 'amended' by the parliament of the Basque Country. This issue not only subordinates and limits the evolution of the legal framework, but also creates an educational reality different from other Spanish regions.

3 Features of the Basque Educational System

The education system is organised in levels so that students progress from one to another each year. The main stages are Pre-school (age 0–6 years) and Basic education: Primary education (age 6–12), and Secondary education (age 12–16)

(Basque Government, 2007). Education is compulsory and free. Classroom groups are made according to age. Students do not have to complete a test to progress through the educational system. After finishing secondary education, students can advance to upper secondary (necessary to enter university) or to vocational training.

In the Basque Country there are two official languages, Basque and Spanish. As a result of this situation, an act of parliament (Decree 138/1983) was undertaken to address the issue and to regulate their use, and three language models were established as follows:

- Model A: all subjects – except Basque itself – are taught in Spanish.
- Model B: some subjects are taught in Spanish and others in Basque.
- Model D: all subjects – except the Spanish language – are taught in Basque (note that the letter 'C' does not exist in the Basque alphabet).

Parents are free to enrol their children in the model that best suits them. According to the Basque Statistical Institute (Eustat, 2016), in the school year 2015–2016, 221,904 students were enrolled in pre-school and primary education. The majority of students (73.2%) followed model D and 21% model B. This means that by the end of statutory schooling, nearly all students had become at least bilingual. It is important to state that the work of the education system in the training of Basque speakers has been fundamental. In fact, the last Sociolinguistic Survey points out that there are currently 223,000 more Basque speakers than in 1991. This increase starts from the youngest stages of the population, with more than 7 out of 10 young people between 16 and 24 years old having Basque as their first language (Basque Government, Government of Navarra & Euskararen Erakunde Publikoa, 2016).

As the Basque country is an autonomous bilingual region with its own legal system, it has a special educational reality which differs from other regions of Spain. According to the Spanish government's report entitled *Data and Numbers* (2015), in 2014 the dropout rate from compulsory Basque secondary school education was only 9.4%, being the only region that reached the European 2020 target (the average of Spain stands at 21.9% and EU-28 countries at 11.1%). Additionally, it is the region with the highest percentage of the population with higher education qualifications (Spanish School Committee, 2017), and according to the Education First English Proficiency Index, the citizens of the Basque Country have the highest level of English in Spain. Finally, after analyzing inclusive measures which have been developed in the Spanish Compulsory Secondary School System, Martínez (2011) concludes that the Basque Country is one of the most inclusive regions in Spain and a *Save the Children Report* finds that Basque Country presents the highest level of educational equity among Spanish autonomous regions (Assiego & Ubrich, 2015).

Taking this into account, it is important to describe the legal framework that facilitates the Basque Country school system's response to student diversity.

4 The Legal Framework of Inclusive Education in the Basque Country

According to Orcasitas (2005), the commitment to inclusive, quality education in the Basque Country dates back to the 1980s. In 1982, The Special Education Plan was published by the Basque Government, a policy that went beyond clinical and specialisation approaches to propose a radical (at the time) change: mainstream schools which would be designed to include all children. Although the separation and categorisation arguments have still continued to pervade education systems around the world (Boyle, 2014), the plan stipulated that there would be no parallel education systems, such as one for mainstream students and another for students with disabilities. This plan was subsequently reviewed, and the results and recommendations were set forth in the report by the Special Education Commission (Basque Government, 1988) entitled *An Understanding of the Integrated School.* This report stated that, '... the goals of education for children and young people with special educational needs are the same as for all the others' (p. 99).

Later on, the Spanish legislative act entitled Ley de Ordenación General del Sistema Educativo (LOGSE, 1990), enabled students with Special Educational Needs (SEN) to be educated in their local mainstream school. In line with international general practice this would now be regarded as an integration approach. The need to adapt the Spanish legislation to the autonomous region led the Basque Government to develop the Basque Public School Act (Law 1/1993), which tried to go further and indeed recognised the need to take measures to help redress inequalities and integrate diversity. Furthermore, Decree 118/1998 (incorporating the LOGSE in the Basque Country) ensured that students with SEN would be integrated into mainstream schools.

In 2006, a new Spanish legislative act entitled, Ley Orgánica de Educación (LOE), facilitated a strengthening of the inclusive approach. The concept of SEN was replaced by a new one: students with Specific Educational Support Needs (SESN). This term expands the SEN term by including other groups of students who, without being classified as disabled, also require specific educational support (Table 14.1).

The aforementioned LOE (2006) was implemented in the Basque Country through Decrees 175/2007 and 97/2010. Later on, the Basque Government

TABLE 14.1 Classification of students with specific educational support needs

	Students with
Students with Specific Educational Support Needs (SESN)	– Special Educational Needs (SEN). – Disabilities and serious behaviour disorders – Specific learning difficulties – Gifted – Have entered the education system late – Have special personal circumstances or school history – In circumstances of social inequality throughout the educational stages

(2012a) edited the 'Strategic Plan for Attention to Diversity within the framework of the inclusive school'. This Plan sets out a series of measures, resources and guidelines for creating the correct conditions to ensure appropriate schooling for all students and removing barriers to learning and participation. The plan conceptualises and manages resources to cater for the needs of these students within the ordinary school setting. Due to the plan, students with SESN are present within the framework of the Basque school system. In the school year 2014–2015, there were 16,076 students with specific educational support needs. Table 14.2 shows the number of students with SEN arising from a disability or serious behaviour disorders and, Table 14.3

TABLE 14.2 Trend in students with special educational needs across all stages (pre-school, primary, secondary and upper secondary 2–18 years old) by type of disability

Disability type	2014–2015
Hearing disability	398
Motor disability	791
Intellectual disability	2,070
Visual disability	215
Pervasive developmental disorders	1,904
Serious behavioural disorders	1,337
Multiple disabilities	245
Total students with *SESN*	*6,960*

TABLE 14.3 Distribution of students with specific educational support needs by educational stages

	2014–2015
Language and communication disorders	1,442
Specific learning difficulties	1,292
Slow maturing	1,243
ADD-D.	928
Borderline intellectual capacity	3,165
Gifted	379
Uncategorised	667
Total students	*9,116*

shows students in the rest of SESN categories (Basque School Committee, 2016).

A final change of law happened in 2013 with the Ley Orgánica para la Mejora de la Calidad Educativa (LOMCE, 2013) which is federal legislation for the improvement of educational quality. There is still no clear evidence of the impact that this law could have vis-à-vis an inclusive approach, although some authors say that it could be a setback in the strive for an inclusive path (Hayas & Rojas, 2017) and coeducation (Fernández & González, 2015). In order to implement the new law in the Basque Country, and minimising the possible negative consequences, in 2014 the Basque Government developed the Heziberri 2020 plan, and this will now be explored in some detail.

5 Measures for Responding to Diversity

The Basque State School Act (1993, art.10) states that 'wherever possible, all students will be schooled in mainstream units close to their home'. In order to enable the inclusion of all students in ordinary schools, and preferably, in ordinary classrooms, different measures, which will be explained in this section, were designed.

These measures (general and exceptional) aim to respond to all students' educational needs and help them to achieve the objectives of the curriculum (Mendia, 1999), and will be implemented gradually in a realistic manner, taking into account the nuances of the school and moving towards an individualised response to each pupil.

5.1 *General Measures*

The curriculum (meaning the sum of objectives, competences, contents, methodologies and evaluation system) that has to be applied in schools of the Basque Country is quite open and flexible. That means that each autonomous region and, specifically, each school community have the chance to set the general framework established by the administration according to its own features. In fact, there are three documents that each school has to develop in order to specify the final curriculum that will be implemented, always maintaining the final objectives that students have to reach at the end of each stage. These three documents are:

- *The school-based education project,* which the major guidelines that will follow the school in order to work in the community where it is placed. This document is designed by the school direction team, teachers, parents, and other agents of the community. Among other things, it defines the measures of attention to diversity.
- *The school-based curriculum project* (PCC), which all the educational stages teach at least, the objectives, contents, methods, resources, and evaluation systems that will be implemented in each subject.
- *The school plan* (*and the final annual report*) that sets out the school year design for each year.

The general measures to respond to diversity are based on the setting of the general curriculum defined by administration with regard to the social, economic and cultural context of the school community. When this occurs the educational needs of the majority of students are attended to. In accordance with the aforementioned documents, school departments draw up their teaching programmes where teachers specify their daily work, taking into account that the ordinary classroom is the place that makes inclusion possible.

5.2 *Ordinary Specific Measures*

When the ordinary setting of the curriculum is not enough, the school considers running ordinary specific measures that are based on the idea of reinforcement or support. There are different forms of collective reinforcement such as: to divide the natural group of students into two different groups in order to teach some subjects; to offer a new optional subject so as to work contents that can be more complex for some students; to increase the rate of teachers per group in order to help students that struggle with achieving a level's objectives, (Decree 175/2007).

From the school year 2012–2013 onwards, when a student needs to receive individual support, a 'personal educational reinforcement plan' known as PIRE

(Basque Government, 2012b) is designed and implemented. Coordinated by the class teacher, the PIRE is drawn up by the teaching team, and it includes the most appropriate actions and strategies to cater for students' educational needs: the reinforcement measures planned, specifying rooms, times and teaching staff available. In addition, it ensures that parents are involved in the reinforcement plan, an essential aspect in student success (Ziomek, 2010).

This plan is appropriate for students who are in any of the following categories: (1) Students who have repeated the school year; (2) Students who have not passed some school subjects at the previous level; or (3) Students who have difficulties in learning essential subjects. The aim of PIRE is for students to achieve basic skills and, thus, the objectives of the standard curriculum, as well as students progressing without implementing more segregated measures such as those discussed in the next section.

5.3 *Exceptional Specific Measures*

When specific measures are not enough to achieve the objectives of the curriculum, the following exceptional measures are implemented.

5.3.1 Repeat a Year

In primary education, at the end of each year, teaching staff make the relevant decisions regarding progression, taking into account students' assessment results. Students will progress to the next level only when they have attained the maturity for that level and also when the basic skills required in each level have been achieved. Whenever the above conditions, having enough maturity or achieving basic skills are not met, the students are not promoted and have to repeat their current level. Before implementing this measure, parents are informed by their child's teacher. This measure can be taken only once throughout a student's primary education. To be a productive and appropriate measure, the specific reinforcement and the support that the student will receive is carefully planned by drawing up the PIRE, so that the student can achieve the subjects in which she or he has previously failed.

Certainly, this can be seen as quite controversial and an unpopular measure. Research shows that repeating a level can increase the risk of school failure as well as the dropout rate (Cordero, Manchón, & Simancas, 2014; Rumberger, 2011). For this reason, it is only considered under exceptional circumstances and it is only applied when previous measures prove ineffective or if there are extenuating reasons, e.g. long-term hospitalisation. In fact, the Basque Country has one of the lowest repetition rates (Arregi, Martínez, Sainz, & Ugarriza,

2009) and the suitability rate of students (which refers to the percentage of students who are enrolled in the course that corresponds to the age) in primary education is higher than the Spanish average. This may be as a result of the fact that before the repeating of a year, schools develop measures to help students at risk of failing academically (Arregi et al., 2009). Future research will be required so as to understand the effectiveness of repeating with PIRE reinforcement.

5.3.2 Skip a Year

When a student is classified as gifted, one measure that can be taken is to reduce primary education by one year, enrolling the student in a higher level. Another option is to keep the gifted student within the classroom group, applying another two measures in any area that is required: (1) the curriculum of one subject/area can be adapted; (2) the student's level can be changed for the affected area. Whatever measure is taken, it must be the most appropriate for the personal and social development of the student. Despite the law, a study which focuses on identifying the best practices related to the organisation of attention to diversity in the Basque Country suggests that, there is no systematic use of any diagnostic or intervention method for gifted students (Intxausti, Etxeberria, & Barbau, 2017), and international research shows that there are many barriers such as: the lack of classroom management skills, teachers' attitudes and beliefs about learning, or the lack of administrative support, to carry out a real adaptation of the curriculum (e.g. VanTassel-Baska & Stambaugh, 2005). It follows that some improvements are required in order to more effectively respond to gifted students.

5.3.3 Curricular Diversification Program

This program can be implemented when students are at the end of their secondary education and are able to achieve the general objectives for the award of the certificate of education. There are some criteria that guide the implementation of this program, e.g. limiting the number of students to create a small group that can receive more personal attention, and the use of proactive methods such as Project Based Learning or grouping different subjects in order to create major areas so as to facilitate the acquisition of knowledge. Aramendi, Vega, and Bujan (2012) point out that these programs could be an accurate way to reduce the drop out rate of students, and results reveal that the level of satisfaction amongst students that participate in this program is higher than would be the case if taught in the more traditional manner.

5.3.4 Individualised Curricular Adaptations

When the classroom programme is not sufficient to meet the needs of students with SEN, an adaptation of the curriculum is conducted. According to the 118/1998 Decree, there are two kinds of adaptations to respond to the specific needs of a student enrolled in a mainstream classroom:

- *Individualised curricular adaptation to* access. This type of adaptation is especially designed for students with motor, visual and hearing impairments who can achieve the general objectives of each level. When this adaption is launched specific materials (Braille books), tools (tablets, computers, etc.) and personal resources (specialist teaching staff, speech therapists or physiotherapists, occupational therapists, specialists in visual impairment) can be used in order to make the student's work in the ordinary curriculum possible. In any case, only non-prescriptive elements like teaching methodology, activities, resources, timetables or spaces can be adapted.
- *Significant individualised curricular adaptation* (*ACI*). This is the most exceptional measure for students that are enrolled in regular classrooms. The ACI determines the accessible curriculum for students with cognitive disabilities, modifying not only methods, resources, times, but general aims, contents and assessment criteria as well. If students have significant cognitive disabilities, a global ACI will be implemented in order to support basic life skills. If the students have moderate cognitive disabilities the ACI will be based on the curriculum of the previous levels, and if the students achieve the objectives that the law establishes, they can get the certificate of education.

Different studies show the efficacy of this adaptation, for example, in students with autism (Brodzeller, Ottley, Jung, & Coogle, 2017; Domingo & Palomares, 2013). But as this last study showed, to be effective, it must be combined with other measures such as better teacher training, specific and sufficient material resources, and accurate coordination among teachers. According to Browder, Spooner, Wakeman, Trela, and Baker (2006) collaboration with general educators is essential to creating access to the general curriculum and collaboration is possible through good planning (Intxausti et al., 2017).

The high rate of inclusion in the Basque Country mentioned in the first part of this chapter leads us to suggest that applying this exceptional measure only when it is needed could help SEN students to access and participate in the general education curriculum. However, further research should be conducted in order to evaluate the applicability of the ACI in the ordinary classroom, specifically the designed education programme planned to address the needs of a particular student. These studies could complement others, which consider the strength of various individualised education programs (Blackwell & Rossetti, 2014; Zeitlin & Curcic, 2014).

6 Alternative forms of Schooling for SEN Students

The Basque State School Act (1993, art.10) also states that, only where necessary, students should be schooled in special education units within mainstream schools. This option is chosen when all other measures have not met the needs of the student and the school does not have enough resources to cater for SEN students with complex needs in ordinary classrooms. These special education units are known in Basque as 'gela egonkorra'.

The special education unit is a separate class within the mainstream school, for no more than five students with severe disabilities. It has specific, permanent resources, a physical space and is made up of a stable group of students, with a special education tutor and specialists in educational support (ancillary staff). On the basis of the group programme, an Individual Education Plan is developed for each pupil. This allows individualised attention tailored to any student's particular support needs, and at the same time facilitates socialisation and inclusion as the special classes are part of the mainstream school. These special classes cater for students up to 16 years, however they can stay until 18 years of age (Sainz, 2000). After completing this schooling, there are two possibilities for these students. (1) If their needs derived from limitations on autonomy, they can continue in mainstream school in a Task Learning Classroom where they perform a basic apprenticeship (16–18 years) and on the job training with placement in companies (18–21 years) (Ruiz, 2008). These classrooms aim to promote work preparation and the transition to adult life (Ugarriza & Mendia, 1997). (2) If the students have a severe disability, Social Services make up the priority regulatory reference framework for them. The role of Social Services is to promote personal autonomy and support the family in ensuring that professional support is provided as is necessary.

In the whole of the Basque Country, during the 2014–2015 year, 737 students were in special rooms and 475 in Task Learning Classrooms (Basque School Committee, 2016). These numbers are in line with the six European Union countries (Italy, Greece, Portugal, Norway, Cyprus, and Iceland) with greater rates of educational inclusion (López, 2009) where the percentage of the number of students in specific centres is low (0.53%). However, in recent years the number of students in these centres has increased and López (2009) states two reasons (that this departure from full inclusion practices could affect the

Basque Country if the correct decisions are not made): the clear irreversibility of these special measures which almost never refer students back to the mainstream school and the issue with some mainstream schools not wanting to receive some students who have severe behavioural difficulties.

Currently, to avoid these risks, legislation in the Basque Country facilitates the enrolment of SEN students in mainstream schools chosen by their parents (in ordinary classrooms whatever this is possible). However, research in this area has demonstrated that students with Down Syndrome have more chance of being placed in a mainstream school and to continue their schooling there (Fernández & Benitez, 2016; Gaztelumendi, 2002) than students with some medical conditions or difficulties (Aróstegui & Gaintza, 2014). Intxausti et al. (2017, p. 12) state that 'there may be a certain kind of hidden selection agenda in some schools'. In the near future, that risk of a shift towards special placement as an alternative to mainstream schooling should be faced in order to maintain the high level of inclusion in the Basque Country. With this aim the Department of Education, Language policy and Culture of the Basque Government will evaluate the success of the 'Strategic Plan for Attention to Diversity within the framework of the inclusive school, 2012–2018', and will update the priorities for successful inclusion in the 'Strategic Plan for an inclusive education II – 2018–2022'.

7 Conclusion

In conclusion, the response to diversity in the Basque Country has been, and continues to be, a gradual and continuous process. The aim is to both improve and promote inclusive schooling where the participation in the educational process of all children from the community is supported. The different approaches and measures used to ensure diversity have been detailed in this chapter.

Despite inclusive education being a fundamental component of the Basque government's general education policy, there still remain some gaps. One of them is the need to establish new legislation for children with special needs in education. Although there have been significant improvements in recent years concerning children with special needs in schools, the legal changes have not been completed and the Decree 118/1998 is still in force. New legislation could significantly and relevantly effect the schooling of SEN students and attempt to increase and improve the diversity in a wide range of settings without the need to resort to the perfunctory labelling of children. Nevertheless, in the Basque Country educational inclusion is stronger now than it has been in the past.

References

Aramendi, P., Vega, A., & Buján, K. (2012). Los programas de diversificación curricular doi los programas de cualificación profesional inicial ¿una alternativa al fracaso escolar? *Revista española de pedagogía, 70*(252), 237–255.

Aróstegui, I., & Gaintza, Z. (2014). La voz de un grupo de familiares de personas con enfermedades minoritarias de Bizkaia: Análisis de su experiencia en el proceso de escolarización, de la evolución doi necesidad de mejora. *Revista de Educación Inclusiva, 7*(3), 50–67.

Arregi, A., Martínez, P. A., Sainz, A., & Ugarriza, J. R. (2009). *Efecto de las repeticiones de curso en el proceso de enseñanza-aprendizaje del alumnado*. ISEI_IVE. Retrieved from http://www.isei-ivei.net/cast/pub/Repeticiones_cas.pdf

Assiego, V., & Ubrich, T. (2015). *Iluminando el futuro: invertir en educación es luchar contra la pobreza infantil: País Vasco*. Save the Children report.

Basque Government. (1982). *The special education plan for the basque country*. Department of Education, Language Policy and Culture.

Basque Government. (1988). *Una escuela comprensiva e integradora*. Department of Education, Language Policy and Culture.

Basque Government. (2007). *Structural organization and features of the Basque educational system*. Department of Education, Language Policy and Culture.

Basque Government. (2012a). *Plan estratégico de atención a la diversidad en el marco de una escuela inclusiva*. Department of Education, Language Policy and Culture.

Basque Government. (2012b). *Orientaciones para la elaboración del plan individual de refuerzo educativo (PIRE) en la educación básica*. Department of Education, Language Policy and Culture.

Basque Government. (2014). *Heziberri 2020. Marco del modelo educativo doi pedagógico*. Department of Education, Language Policy and Culture.

Basque Government, Government of Navarra and Euskararen Erakunde Publikoa. (2016). *VI sociolinguistic survey of the whole territory of the Basque language*. Retrieved from http://www.soziolinguistika.eus/files/euskararen_bilakaera_soziolinguistikoa_eng_2.pdf

Basque Government Organic Law. (1979). *The statute of autonomy for the Basque country. Statute of Gernika*. Retrieved from https://www.basquecountry.eus/contenidos/informacion/estatuto_guernica/en_455/adjuntos/estatu_i.pdf

Basque Public School Act. (Law 1/1993). *BOPV 25-11-1993*. https://www.legegunea.euskadi.eus/x59-preview/es/contenidos/ley/bopv199300650/es_def/index.shtml

Basque School Committee. (2016). *La Educación en Euskadi. Informe 2013–2015*. Department of Education, Language Policy and Culture.

Blackwell, D. D., & Rossetti, Z. S. (2014). The development of individualized education programs: Where have we been and where should we go now? *Sage Open, 4*(2), 1–15.

Boyle, C. (2014). *Labelling in special education: Where do the benefits lie?* In A. Holliman (Ed.), *The Routledge international companion to educational psychology* (pp. 213–221). Routledge.

Brodzeller, K. L., Ottley, J. R., Jung, J., & Coogle, C. G. (2017). Interventions and adaptations for children with autism spectrum disorder in inclusive early childhood settings. *Early Childhood Education Journal, 45*(3), 403–410.

Browder, D. M., Spooner, F., Wakeman, S., Trela, K., & Baker, J. N. (2006). Aligning instruction with academic content standards: Finding the link. *Research and Practice for Persons with Severe Disabilities, 31*, 309–321.

Collins, R. (1990). *The Basques* (2nd ed.). Basil Blackwell.

Cordero, J. M., Manchón, C., & Simancas, R. (2014). La repetición de curso doi sus factores condicionantes en España. *Revista de Educación, 365*, 12–37.

Decree 118/1998. (1998, June 23). *The organization of the educational response to SEN students within the framework of an understanding, integrating school* (BOPV, 13-07-1998).

Decree 138/1983. (1983, July 11). *Regulating the use of official languages in non-university education in the Basque Country* (BOPV 19-07-1983).

Decree 175/2007. (2007, October 16). *Establishing the basic education curriculum and implementing it in the Basque Country* (BOPV 13-11-2007).

Decree 236/2015. (2015, December 21). *Establishing the basic education curriculum and implementing it in the Basque Country* (BOPV 15-01-2016).

Decree 97/2010. (2010, March 30). *Modifying the Decree establishing the basic education curriculum and implementing it in the Basque Country* (BOPV 20-04-2010).

Domingo, B., & Palomares, A. (2013). La necesidad de nuevas estrategias metodológicas en la educación inclusiva del alumnado autista. *Revista de la Facultad de Educación de Albacete, 28*, 15–23.

Education First. English Proficiency Index. (2015). *Toronto: Education First; 2013*. https://www.ef.com/wwen/epi/regions/europe/spain/

Eustat. (2016). *Alumnado matriculado en enseñanzas de régimen general no universitarias en la C.A. de Euskadi por ámbitos territoriales, según nivel de enseñanza doi modelo lingüístico*. 2014-15. https://www.eustat.eus/indice.html

Fernández, J. M., & Benitez, A. M. (2016). Respuesta educativa de los centros escolares ante alumnado con síndrome de Down: precepciones familiares doi docentes. *Profesorado, 20*(2), 296–311.

Fernández, N., & González N. (2015). La LOMCE a la luz de la CEDAW: Un análisis de la coeducación en la última reforma educativa. *Journal of Supranational Policies of Education, 3*, 242–263.

Gaztelumendi, A. (2002) ¿Qué opinan las familias sobre la Integración Escolar de sus hijos/as? *Revista Síndrome de Down del País Vasco, 11*, 34–42.

Hayas, I., & Rojas, S. (2017). Una mirada inclusiva hacia la normativa educativa: limitaciones, posibilidades doi controversias. *Revista de Educación Inclusiva, 9*(2), 155–170.

Intxausti, N., Etxeberria, F., & Bartau, I. (2017). Effective and inclusive schools? Attention to diversity in highly effective schools in the autonomous region of the Basque Country. *International Journal of Inclusive Education, 21*(1), 14–30.

López, M. (2009). La inclusión educativa de los alumnos con discapacidades graves doi permanentes en la Unión Europea. *Revista Electrónica de Investigación doi Evaluación Educativa, 15*(1), 1–20.

Mansvelt, J. (2005). *Territory and terror: Conflicting nationalisms in the Basque Country*. Routledge.

Martínez, B. (2011). Luces doi sombras de las medidas de atención a la diversidad en el camino de la inclusión educativa. *Revista Interuniversitaria de Formación del profesorado, 25*(1), 165–183.

Mendia, G. R. (1999). Gradación de las medidas de tratamiento de la diversidad. *Organización doi Gestión Educativa, 2*, 13–16. Retrieved from http://rafaelmendia.com/mendia/Hemeroteca-2_files/OG199921316.pdf

Orcasitas, J. R. (2005). *20 años de integración escolar en el País Vasco: Haciendo historia, construyendo un sistema educativo de calidad para todos*. Department of Education, Language Policy and Culture.

Order of 24th July 1998. *Regulating authorisation for adapting the curriculum to make it accessible and significant individual curricular adaptations for SEN students* (BOPV, 31-08-1998).

Organic Act on the General Organization of the Education (LOGSE). (1990). Retrieved from https://www.boe.es/eli/es/lo/1990/10/03/1

Organic Law of Education (LOE). (2006). BOE, 04-04-2006. Retrieved from https://www.boe.es/eli/es/lo/2006/05/03/2/con

Organic Law on the Improvement of the Quality of Education (LOMCE). (2013). Retrieved from https://www.boe.es/boe/dias/2013/12/10/pdfs/BOE-A-2013-12886.pdf

Ruiz, C. (2008). Retos de la inclusión educativa en los próximos años en la Comunidad Autónoma del País Vasco. *Revista Iberoamericana sobre Calidad, Eficacia doi Cambio en Educación, 6*(2), 45–57.

Rumberger, R. D. (2011). *Dropping out. Why students drop out of high school and what can be done about it.* Harvard University Press.

Sainz, A. (2000). *Las aulas estables para el alumnado con necesidad de apoyos generalizados en centros de ESO.* Department of Education, Language Policy and Culture.

Spanish Government. (2015). *Report: Datos doi cifras*. Secretaría General Técnica. http://www.educacionyfp.gob.es/ministerio.html

Spanish School Committee. (2017). *Informe 2016 sobre el estado del sistema educativo. Curso 2014–2015*. Ministerio de Educación, Cultura doi Deporte.

Ugarriza, J. R., & Mendia, R. (1997). *La transición a la vida activa de jóvenes con necesidades educativas especiales*. Instituto para el Desarrollo Curricular doi la Formación del Profesorado.

VanTassel-Baska, J., & Stambaugh, T. (2005). Challenges and possibilities for serving gifted learners in the regular classroom. *Theory into Practice, 44*(3), 211–217.

Watson, C. (2003). *Modern Basque history: Eighteenth century to the present*. Center for Basque Studies.

Zeitlin V. M., & Curcic, S. (2014) Parental voices on individualized education programs: 'Oh, IEP meeting tomorrow? Rum tonight!' *Disability & Society, 29*(3), 373–387.

Ziomek, J. (2010). Schools, families, and communities affecting the dropout rate: Implications and strategies for family counselors. *The Family Journal, 18*(4), 377–385.

PART 4

Conclusion

CHAPTER 15

The Perpetual Dilemma of Inclusive Education

Christopher Boyle, Joanna Anderson, Angela Page and Sofia Mavropoulou

'Inclusive education' is almost universally regarded as positive educational practice (Boyle, Scriven, Durning, & Downes, 2011), and for this reason, past decades have seen scholars and advocates arguing the merits of the construct. The Salamanca Statement (UNESCO, 1994) brought the idea of inclusive education to the fore in the mid 1990's, and since this time it has been the prevailing philosophy for the education of students globally (Anderson & Boyle, 2019). However, rather than providing a guidebook of step by step instructions, it offered a loose framework for governments to create successful, inclusive systems. Different countries took different paths, and 25 years on, despite some positive changes (such as students who were once considered uneducable now accessing schools in some countries (Boroson, 2017)), it can be argued that we are not much further along the path towards inclusive education than we were two decades ago (Boyle & Anderson, in press). Why? This volume has attempted to provide some insights and answers to this complex question.

Inclusive education has proven difficult to define and thus difficult to effectively research and evaluate (Boyle & Anderson, in press). Despite inclusive education appearing in education policies around the globe (Slee, 2018), many very real challenges and barriers have been identified and described within the pages of this book that make enacting these policies within the confines of the local school fence, problematic. Most authors in this volume are positive about inclusive education, but temper this with the reality that exists in implementing a construct for which there is no globally agreed upon definition in a period of educational reform that is working within the current neoliberal socio-political climate. The destination of inclusive education, which once seemed achievable, has become like Scott Fitzgerald's *green light at the end of the pier*; something which can be imagined, but will always and forever remain out of reach.

To better understand the controversies and issues that surround inclusive education, this book invited contributions across three broad areas: the philosophical underpinnings of the construct, what barriers are preventing more inclusive practices, and finally, what existing and aspirational practices have

 | DOI: 10.1163/9789004431171_015

been implemented and what can be learnt from these. Distinct ideas have emerged from within the pages of this book, some from a number of different authors, others from within a single chapter. The breadth of these hint at the complexity of inclusive education, whether the discussion is framed around a philosophical or theoretical idea, or the application of inclusive strategies in the classroom. To unpack each of these again here is unnecessary as they have been explained in detail within the preceding pages, however what is worth exploring are the ideas that transcend across chapters, and therefore provide an insight into some of the big controversies and issues that proponents of inclusive education are facing, two decades into this new century.

It is clear from what has been presented in this book, that any debate about inclusive education must have at its core a discussion about what it actually is that children and young people are being included into, and whether or not it is of value and worth to them – it must be about what constitutes a 'good' education. Educational discourse has shifted over the past decades, from once containing language with a focus on the 'what' of providing a 'good' education, to now being about the 'how well', or the effectiveness of education. This change in rhetoric has moved the focus in education from what is being studied within schools, to how well students are achieving, regardless of whether or not what they are learning is 'good'. This shift in rhetoric is in part explained by the influence of the neoliberal paradigm under which current education reform has been developed and enacted. Neoliberal principles, which have driven recent educational change, such as marketisation, competition and choice, seem to sit in direct contradiction to the principles of inclusive education, those of social justice, equity and fairness. It becomes evident very quickly that inclusive education, within the socio-political climate of today, faces some big challenges, even before its implementation is considered.

Another interesting notion to come out of the discussion presented within this book is the nexus between special education and inclusive education. It is evident that much of the debate around inclusive education is still setting the construct up as being in direct competition with special education, and therefore as being about the education of students with a disability (or other diagnosable learning needs), rather than about all children and young people. While there are arguments against this perspective of inclusive education (Jackson, Fitzpatrick, Alazemi, & Rude, 2018), the reliance on both labels, and of systems on enrolments in special education settings to allow successful inclusive practices in their mainstream schools, it is not difficult to see why proponents of special education view the ideal of 'full inclusion' as being something that is unattainable, and even undesirable.

Next, we move into the schools themselves, and those working to develop and enact inclusive practices – the school leaders and teachers. Numerous authors identify the key role school leaders (in particular principals), have in the development of policies, processes and structures that promote an inclusive school culture. Leaders must reflect upon their values, attitudes and practices, perhaps challenging the status quo, to ensure all students are participating and succeeding in every facet of school life. Teachers also have an important part to play, with the attitudes they hold being a direct determinant of the success (or not) of inclusive practices in their classrooms. School leaders, teachers, and the values they hold, matter.

Finally, the importance of all student outcomes, not just academic success, is examined across a number of chapters. While this is not surprising given that inclusive education is bound by principles of social justice, it is an area that is not always considered in the climate of reliance on measured, standardised test results. Yet positive social, behavioural and emotional outcomes directly impact the success of students at school, whether they are considered to have additional needs or not, and positive outcomes in these areas will have a positive influence on the future of these students, as they transition from primary to secondary school, and then onto post school life.

This book has considered various aspects of inclusive education. Some of these consider whether we are doing enough to achieve an effective inclusive education environment at both a system and school level, while others question whether the construct is even something worth striving for. Whilst this book does not and cannot provide solutions to the controversies and issues raised within its pages, it has brought to the fore a group of leading academics who are forthright in their ideas, considerations and opinions. Exploring inclusive education through the different lenses of each individual part of the book, has allowed some of the more challenging, and perhaps less considered, aspects to be raised. Amongst the continuing debates, we should not forget the important role that the inclusive education agenda has played in increasing the reach of education globally. Nelson Mandela stated that *education is the most powerful weapon you can use to change the world.* It cannot be disputed that inclusive education has improved access to schooling, within many education systems in various countries across the globe. Let us end this book where it began, with advice proffered by Professor Adrian Ashman. Further research, rigorous research, exploring the impacts of inclusive approaches on the schooling success of all students, is needed. Then, and only then, can we have a more informed debate as to the merits, or not, of inclusive education.

References

Anderson, J., & Boyle, C. (2019). Looking in the mirror: Reflecting on 25 years of inclusive education in Australia. *The International Journal of Inclusive Education, 23*(7–8), 796–810. doi:10.1080/13603116.2019.1622802

Boroson, B. (2017). Inclusive education: How has education evolved from exclusion to inclusion, from judgment to acceptance, and from disability to difference? *Educational Leadership, 74*(7), 18–23.

Boyle, C., & Anderson, J. (in press). Inclusive education and the progressive inclusionists. In U. Sharma & S. Salend (Eds.), *The Oxford research encyclopedia of education.* Oxford University Press.

Jackson, L., Fitzpatrick, H., Alazemi, B., & Rude, H. (2018). Shifting gears: Re-framing the international discussion about inclusive education. *Journal of International Special Needs Education, 21*(2), 11–22.

Slee, R. (2018). *Inclusive education isn't dead, it just smelly funny.* Routledge.

UNESCO. (1994). *The Salamanca statement and framework for action on special needs education.* UNESCO.

Index